Practical Test Automation

Learn to Use Jasmine, RSpec, and Cucumber Effectively for Your TDD and BDD

Panos Matsinopoulos

Apress®

Practical Test Automation: Learn to Use Jasmine, RSpec, and Cucumber Effectively for Your TDD and BDD

Panos Matsinopoulos
KERATEA, Greece

ISBN-13 (pbk): 978-1-4842-6140-8   ISBN-13 (electronic): 978-1-4842-6141-5
https://doi.org/10.1007/978-1-4842-6141-5

Copyright © 2020 by Panos Matsinopoulos

Managing Director, Apress Media LLC: Welmoed Spahr
Acquisitions Editor: Louise Corrigan
Development Editor: James Markham
Coordinating Editor: Nancy Chen

Cover designed by eStudioCalamar

Cover image designed by Freepik (www.freepik.com)

Distributed to the book trade worldwide by Springer Science+Business Media New York, 1 New York Plaza, New York, NY 10004. Phone 1-800-SPRINGER, fax (201) 348-4505, e-mail orders-ny@springer-sbm.com, or visit www.springeronline.com. Apress Media, LLC is a California LLC and the sole member (owner) is Springer Science + Business Media Finance Inc (SSBM Finance Inc). SSBM Finance Inc is a **Delaware** corporation.

For information on translations, please e-mail booktranslations@springernature.com; for reprint, paperback, or audio rights, please e-mail bookpermissions@springernature.com.

Apress titles may be purchased in bulk for academic, corporate, or promotional use. eBook versions and licenses are also available for most titles. For more information, reference our Print and eBook Bulk Sales web page at http://www.apress.com/bulk-sales.

Any source code or other supplementary material referenced by the author in this book is available to readers on GitHub via the book's product page, located at www.apress.com/9781484261408. For more detailed information, please visit http://www.apress.com/source-code.

Printed on acid-free paper

Dedicated to my wife, Matina

Table of Contents

About the Author

Panos Matsinopoulos loves developing programs, both for web browsers and for mobile apps. He has been doing that for the last 25 years and has developed numerous applications. He also loves writing books, blogging, and teaching computer programming. He has organized a lot of programming classes for kids, adults, and elderly people. You can read more about him on his LinkedIn profile (`www.linkedin.com/in/panayotismatsinopoulos`) and find him on Twitter (`@pmatsino`).

About the Technical Reviewer

 **Alexander Chinedu Nnakwue** has a background in mechanical engineering from the University of Ibadan, Nigeria, and has been a front-end developer for over 3 years working on both web and mobile technologies. He also has experience as a technical author, writer, and reviewer. He enjoys programming for the Web, and occasionally, you can also find him playing soccer. He was born in Benin City and is currently based in Lagos, Nigeria.

Introduction

Part of developing an application is writing a set of automated tests. In fact, you should write them first, before the core code of your application. These tests function as a specification of the requirements of your application – what your application should be doing. They also function as a documentation of what your application is doing. In other words, they play a very important role, both before the actual implementation and after you deliver your application to your end users. And they have to be *automated*, that is, to be executed by a computer, not by a human.

Do you have the tools to write the automated tests, in such a way that they will cover both of these two needs, the specification of the requirements and the documentation of your application?

Absolutely yes!

And this book is all about it. It covers a series of such tools, both for the front-end developer and the back-end developer. And it follows a very practical approach. You develop a project, and you do it the right way: TDD and BDD, that is, Test-Driven and Behavior-Driven Development.

Moreover, although it is presenting its material using specific tools, the techniques that you learn can be applied to any other test automation tool that you might happen to work with.

Audience

This book is aimed at developers who know JavaScript and Ruby and want to improve their test-writing skills.

Contents of This Book

- Chapter 1, "Introduction to Jasmine": This chapter introduces you to Jasmine, a very popular JavaScript testing framework.

- Chapter 2, "Advanced Jasmine": This chapter continues your level-up on Jasmine by presenting its more advanced features.

- Chapter 3, "Using Minitest": In this chapter, you learn about minitest. This tool is the usual tool a Ruby developer writes their first automated tests with.

- Chapter 4, "Introduction to RSpec": In this chapter, you learn about RSpec, a very popular Ruby testing framework.

- Chapter 5, "Useful RSpec Tools": In this chapter, you continue to learn about the tools that RSpec is offering to you. RSpec is very feature rich.

- Chapter 6, "Introduction to Cucumber": In this chapter, you are introduced to BDD with Cucumber and Gherkin.

- Chapter 7, "Advanced Cucumber": In this chapter, you learn more advanced Cucumber techniques and develop a bigger project.

Conventions Used in This Book

This book has the following typographical conventions:

`Constant width`

It is used inside code snippets and listings and to indicate variables, functions, types, parameters, objects, and other programming, coding-related constructs.

`Constant width in Bold`

It is used inside code snippets and listings to indicate the code parts that you need to pay more attention to.

`$`

The symbol $ is used to denote an Operating System shell prompt, that is, where you should type a command that will be executed by your Operating System. For example, if you work with a Mac OS, you can open a terminal and type the command that follows this symbol.

Using Code Listings

All the code listings of this book are available for download at `https://github.com/Apress/practical-test-automation`.

CHAPTER 1

Introduction to Jasmine

In this chapter, you are going to learn Test-Driven Development (TDD) using Jasmine.

TDD is a very popular development methodology. You can find lots of articles online about it and pictures like these (Figure 1-1).

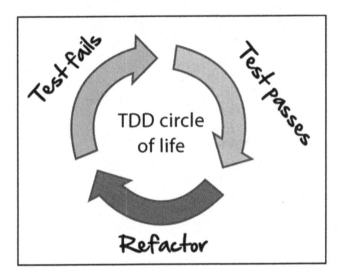

Figure 1-1. *TDD Flow*

On the other hand, Jasmine is a very popular testing framework for JavaScript code.

You are going to learn how to write your testing code and how to integrate it into a runner HTML page.

© Panos Matsinopoulos 2020
P. Matsinopoulos, *Practical Test Automation*, https://doi.org/10.1007/978-1-4842-6141-5_1

You will be able to see the test runner generating results as in Figure 1-2

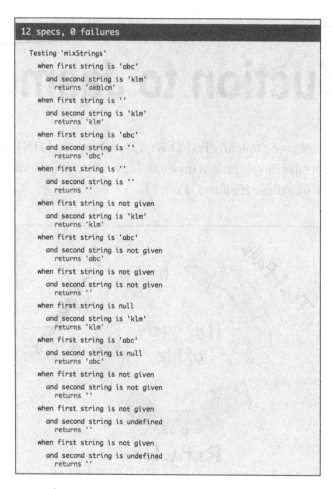

Figure 1-2. *Spec Runner Indicative Results*

and matching this information against the Jasmine code (Figure 1-3).

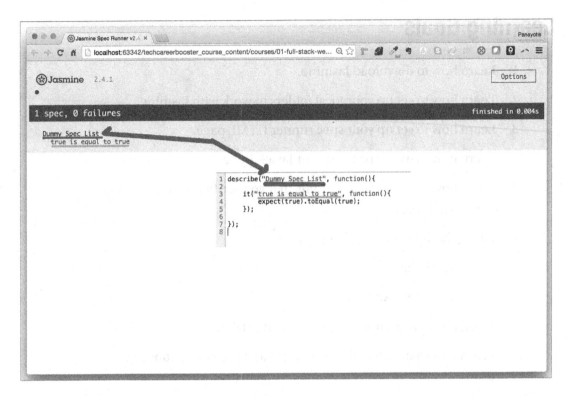

Figure 1-3. *Test Results and Dummy Code*

Finally, you will learn how to run Jasmine inside a JS Bin (Figure 1-4).

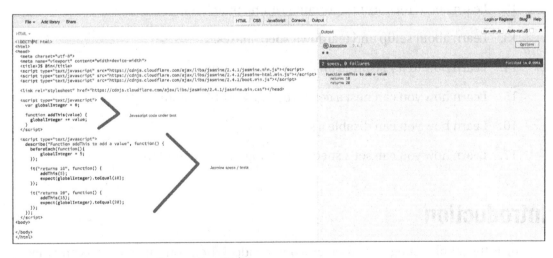

Figure 1-4. *Jasmine Through a JS Bin*

Learning Goals

1. Learn how to download Jasmine.

2. Learn how to set up your local folders to work with Jasmine.

3. Learn how to set up your spec runner HTML page.

4. Learn how to write specs for your JavaScript code.

5. Learn how to interpret the results that you see being output at the spec runner page.

6. Learn about the `describe` function.

7. Learn about the `it` function.

8. Learn about the `expect` function.

9. Learn about Test-Driven Development (TDD).

10. Learn how to transfer all your requirements to corresponding tests.

11. Learn how you can safely do refactorings of your code, assuming that you have specs running successfully and you have full test coverage of your code under test.

12. Learn about the most important Jasmine matchers.

13. Learn about setup and teardown spec phases.

14. Learn how to try Jasmine on the JS Bin platform.

15. Learn how you can nest a `describe` block within another.

16. Learn how you can disable a suite of specs.

17. Learn how you can set a spec as pending implementation.

Introduction

Testing is the art of writing code that tests other code. When you run your tests and they all pass, then you feel confident that the code under test is doing the work right.

You are going to have an introduction to testing, using the JavaScript testing library called Jasmine.

Download

The GitHub page `https://github.com/jasmine/jasmine/releases` has all the releases of Jasmine. You are going to download the latest one (Figure 1-5).

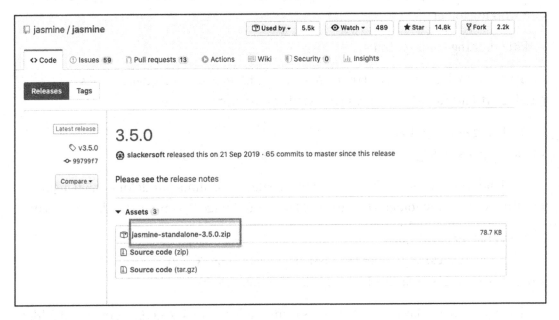

Figure 1-5. *Download the Latest Jasmine*

When you have the zip file downloaded, unzip it. This will create the folder `jasmine-standalone-3.5.0` (or whatever version is the latest one when you did the download). Inside that folder, there is a subfolder `lib/jasmine-3.5.0` which has the Jasmine code that you will need for your project.

A New JavaScript Project

You will now start a new JavaScript project. This will be a very simple JavaScript function that would take as input a string and return back an encrypted version of the string. The encryption will be very simple:

- All characters will be replaced with their next one. So "a" will be replaced by "b", "b" will be replaced by "c", and so on.

- If the input character is uppercase, then the output will be uppercase too.

- Also, only characters from the Latin alphabet will be allowed. Otherwise, an exception will be thrown.

Let's call that project String Encryption. Create a folder string-encryption in your working folder:

```
$ mkdir string-encryption
```

Then, cd to that folder. And then create the subfolder assets/javascripts/jasmine-standalone-3.5.0 inside the string-encryption folder:

```
$ cd string-encryption
$ mkdir -p assets/javascripts/jasmine-standalone-3.5.0
```

And then, create the subfolder assets/stylesheets/jasmine-standalone-3.5.0 inside the string-encryption folder. Do the same for assets/images/jasmine-standalone-3.5.0:

```
$ cd string-encryption
$ mkdir -p assets/stylesheets/jasmine-standalone-3.5.0
$ mkdir -p assets/images/jasmine-standalone-3.5.0
```

Then copy all the JavaScript *.js files from the lib/jasmine-3.5.0 download folder and put them inside the folder assets/javascripts/jasmine-standalone-3.5.0. Copy the CSS file lib/jasmine-3.5.0/jasmin.css to assets/stylesheets/jasmine-standalone-3.5.0. And, finally, copy the lib/jasmine-3.5.0/jasmine_favicon.png file inside assets/images/jasmine-standalone-3.5.0.

So you need to have something like Figure 1-6 in your working folder.

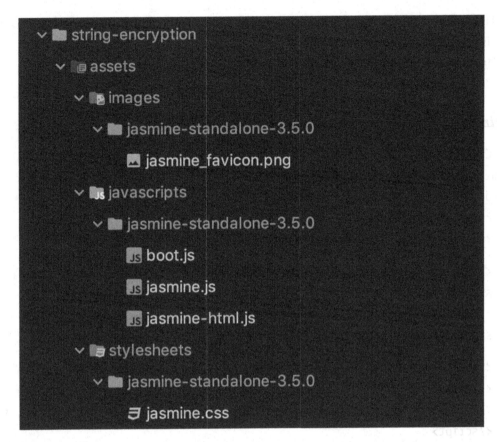

Figure 1-6. *Local folder setup for Jasmine*

Setting Up Jasmine

Basically, Jasmine will give you an environment to run your JavaScript tests. This is an HTML page that

- Will reference Jasmine

- Will reference your JavaScript files

- Will reference your JavaScript tests

- When loaded, will run your tests and display the results

This page is called a spec runner – although it could be called a test runner too. You need to understand that I, many times, call the tests specs instead, from the word specifications, because they specify the desired behavior of the code that I am developing.

The Jasmine convention for the name of the HTML page that will host and run your tests is SpecRunner.html.

Having said that, in the root folder of your project, create the HTML page SpecRunner.html with the following content (Listing 1-1).

Listing 1-1. Bare-Bones SpecRunner.html Page Content

```
<!DOCTYPE html>
<html lang="en">
<head>
    <meta charset="utf-8">
    <title>Jasmine Spec Runner v3.5.0</title>

    <link rel="shortcut icon" type="image/png" href="assets/images/jasmine-
    standalone-3.5.0/jasmine_favicon.png">
    <link rel="stylesheet" href="assets/stylesheets/jasmine-
    standalone-3.5.0/jasmine.css">

    <script src="assets/javascripts/jasmine-standalone-3.5.0/jasmine.js">
    </script>
    <script src="assets/javascripts/jasmine-standalone-3.5.0/jasmine-html.js">
    </script>
    <script src="assets/javascripts/jasmine-standalone-3.5.0/boot.js">
    </script>

    <!-- include source files here... -->
    <!-- ... -->

    <!-- include spec/test files here... -->
    <!-- ... -->
</head>
<body>

</body>
</html>
```

This is basically an empty body HTML page, and it works completely with JavaScript. In Figure 1-7, I point out the important parts of this HTML page.

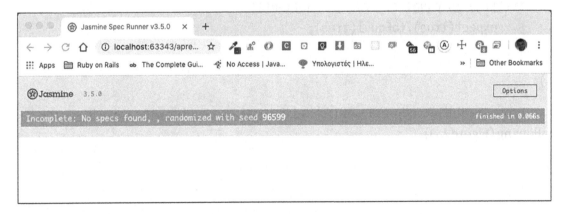

Figure 1-7. *Important Parts of the SpecRunner.html*

As you can see in the preceding picture (Figure 1-7), the SpecRunner.html source code initially references the Jasmine library files, and then it has two placeholders:

1. For the JavaScript code under test: In other words, you need to include the JavaScript source file that has the code that you want to run tests for.

2. For the JavaScript spec (a.k.a. test) files themselves.

If you open the SpecRunner.html page on your browser, you will see the following (Figure 1-8).

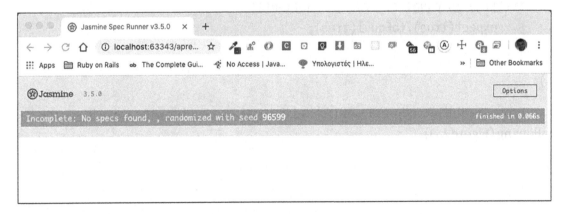

Figure 1-8. *SpecRunner Page Displayed – No Specs*

You can see the No specs found message telling you that the spec runner didn't find any specs to run. This is expected, of course, since you have not written any specs.

Write Your First Dummy Spec

You are going to write your first dummy spec, just to make sure that your spec runner can find specs and run them.

Let's change the content of your SpecRunner.html to refer to your spec list file.

So instead of

```
<!-- include spec/test files here... -->
<!-- ... -->
```

you have

```
<!-- include spec/test files here... -->
<script src="assets/javascripts/my-application-specs.js"></script>
```

And then, let's create the file assets/javascripts/my-application-specs.js with the following content (Listing 1-2).

Listing 1-2. Initial Content of the my-application-specs.js File

```
describe("Dummy Spec List", function(){

    it("true is equal to true", function(){
        expect(true).toEqual(true);
    });

});
```

If you save the preceding file and reload the page on your browser, you will see the following (Figure 1-9).

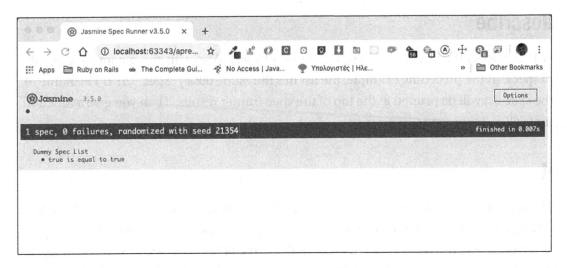

Figure 1-9. *Spec Runner Results – One Dummy Spec*

Great! You have successfully run one spec. This spec didn't test your application JavaScript code; it was only testing equality of true to itself. It was really a proof that the spec runner was successfully installed.

Until you start writing real tests, let's see the anatomy of this dummy test and compare it to the output we see on the SpecRunner (Figure 1-10).

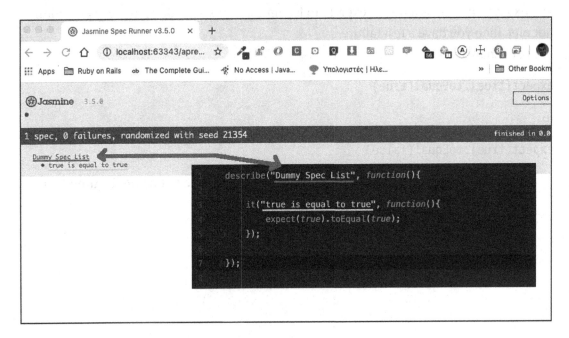

Figure 1-10. *Anatomy of the Dummy Spec*

describe

With the describe function, you start your list of specs. Also, you give a name to this list of specs. In the preceding example, the list has the name Dummy Spec List. The name of the spec list will be printed at the top of the spec runner results. Then you give a function that will call each one of your specs.

it

The specs themselves are called to the it function. A describe may be calling it many times. Each call is a different spec execution. In the example, you only have one.

The it function takes as first argument the name of the spec. This will be printed, nested, below the name of the list the spec belongs to. Then, the it function takes as argument a function which is the actual spec code. This will be executed, and if everything goes well, the spec run will be considered a pass. Otherwise, it will be considered a failure.

expect

The expect function is a way to express to Jasmine your expectations. If the expectation is not met, then you have a test failure.

Let's change the

```
expect(true).toEqual(true)
```

to

```
expect(true).toEqual(false)
```

Save and reload the page on your browser. You will see the following (Figure 1-11).

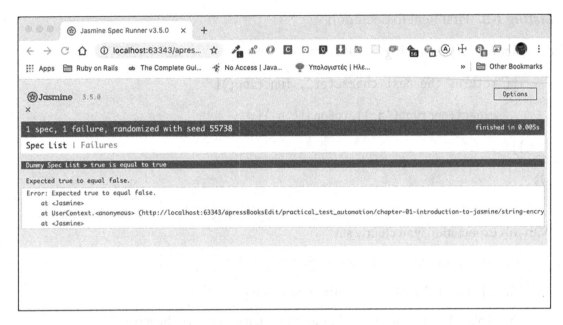

Figure 1-11. *Expectation Not Met – Test Failure*

Cool! That was expected, because true is never equal to false.

Start Your Application Implementation: Test-Driven Development (TDD)

Now, you are sure that your setup works ok. But you have not yet done any real work on your project. This is what you will start now.

You remember that you wanted to develop a JavaScript function that would encrypt a string. Shall you just try to write this function?

No! You will follow the Test-Driven Development approach. This means that you will first write what you expect this function to do and then you will try to make it work.

Let's write the following inside our assets/javascripts/my-application-specs.js (Listing 1-3).

Listing 1-3. First Real Expectation

```
describe("Encrypt String", function(){

    it("returns the next character", function(){

        expect(encrypt('a')).toEqual('b');

    });

});
```

It's a very simple spec. It says that if you call `encrypt('a')`, then it should return b. With this expectation, you clearly say

1. That your function name will be `encrypt`

2. That it will be taking one string parameter

3. That when called with `'a'` as argument, it will return the string `'b'`

If you save that and load the `SpecRunner.html` page on your browser, you will get the following (Figure 1-12).

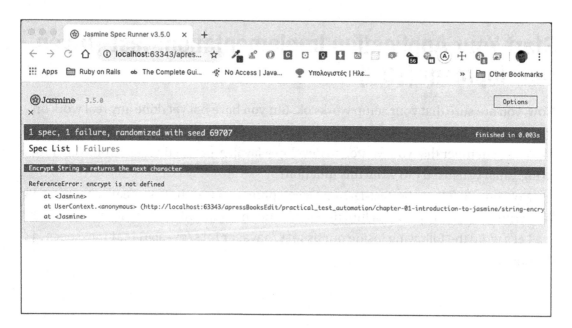

Figure 1-12. Encrypt Is Not Defined Error

That was expected. The encrypt function is not defined yet. You need to define this function in your project.

Remember that your SpecRunner.html has a placeholder for you to put JavaScript reference to your project JavaScript files:

```
<!-- include source files here... -->
<!-- ... -->
```

Let's create the file assets/javascripts/encrypt.js and put the following content inside:

```
function encrypt(inputString) {

}
```

And also, update the SpecRunner.html to reference your assets/javascripts/encrypt.js file:

```
<!-- include source files here... -->
<script src="assets/javascripts/encrypt.js"></script>
```

Now, everything is ready. The encrypt() function is defined, and your SpecRunner. html will locate it. Let's reload SpecRunner.html (Figure 1-13).

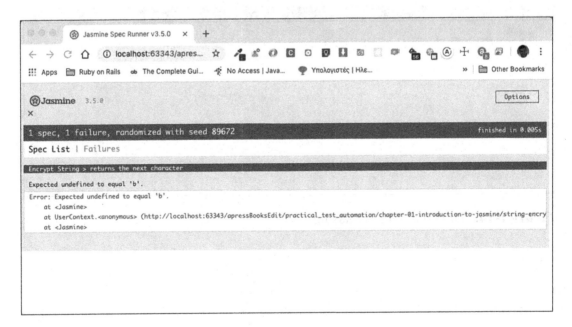

Figure 1-13. *New Error: Expected Undefined to Equal 'b'*

Ok. You got rid of the error `encrypt is not defined`. You have a new error though: `expected undefined to equal 'b'`. It is clear that the expectation that you have specified inside the spec is not met. The `encrypt('a')` returns `undefined,` and this is not equal to b.

That is reasonable. If you look at the current implementation of your `encrypt()` function, you will see that it is empty.

So let's try to write some proper implementation. Write the following inside the `assets/javascripts/encrypt.js` file:

```
function encrypt(inputString) {
    return 'b';
}
```

This function returns `'b'`. Does it satisfy the specification expectation? Let's load the `SpecRunner.html` page again (Figure 1-14).

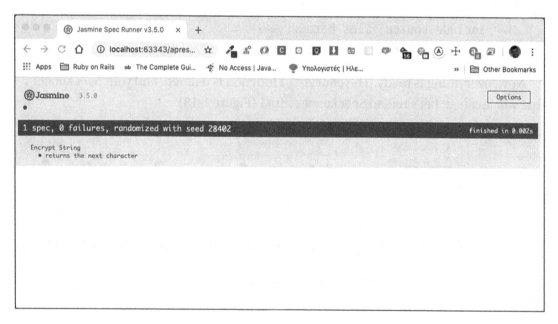

Figure 1-14. *The First Spec Is Passing*

Nice! The first spec that you wrote is passing successfully. Did you finish your function implementation? Is it correct? A Quality Assurance engineer reviews your spec code

```
describe("Encrypt String", function(){

    it("returns the next character", function(){

        expect(encrypt('a')).toEqual('b');

    });

});
```

and easily comes with the verdict. The spec does not make sure that your function works as expected. Let's review the function requirements:

- All characters should be replaced with their next one. So "a" should be replaced by "b", "b" should be replaced by "c", and so on.

- If the input character is uppercase, then the output will be uppercase too.

- If the input character is "z", then the output should be "a" – similarly for the "Z".

- Only characters from the Latin alphabet will be allowed. Otherwise, an exception will be thrown.

These requirements are not expressed inside your spec file. Hence, you cannot be sure that the function that you have implemented works as required.

Let's try to add some more expectations (Listing 1-4).

Listing 1-4. More Expectations

```
describe("Encrypt String", function(){

    it("returns the next character", function(){

        var expectations = {
            'a': 'b', 'b': 'c', 'c': 'd', 'd': 'e', 'e': 'f',
            'f': 'g', 'g': 'h', 'h': 'i', 'i': 'j', 'j': 'k',
            'k': 'l', 'l': 'm', 'm': 'n', 'n': 'o', 'o': 'p',
            'p': 'q', 'q': 'r', 'r': 's', 's': 't', 't': 'u',
```

```
            'u': 'v', 'v': 'w', 'w': 'x', 'x': 'y', 'y': 'z',
            'z': 'a',

            'A': 'B', 'B': 'C', 'C': 'D', 'D': 'E', 'E': 'F',
            'F': 'G', 'G': 'H', 'H': 'I', 'I': 'J', 'J': 'K',
            'K': 'L', 'L': 'M', 'M': 'N', 'N': 'O', 'O': 'P',
            'P': 'Q', 'Q': 'R', 'R': 'S', 'S': 'T', 'T': 'U',
            'U': 'V', 'V': 'W', 'W': 'X', 'X': 'Y', 'Y': 'Z',
            'Z': 'A'
        };

        for (var property in expectations) {
            if (expectations.hasOwnProperty(property)) {
                var charToEncrypt = property;
                var expectedEncryptedChar = expectations[property];

                expect(encrypt(charToEncrypt)).toEqual(expectedEncryptedChar);
            }
        }

    });

});
```

You have amended your spec to run the encrypt() method call and the corresponding expect(...) method call for each one of the characters of the Latin alphabet. Basically, using a loop (with the for JavaScript statement), you are telling that you

- `expect(encrypt('a')).toEqual('b');`

- `expect(encrypt('b')).toEqual('c');`

- `expect(encrypt('c')).toEqual('d');`

- `And so on`

Nice. Save all these and load the SpecRunner.html page again. What you will see is something like the following (Figure 1-15).

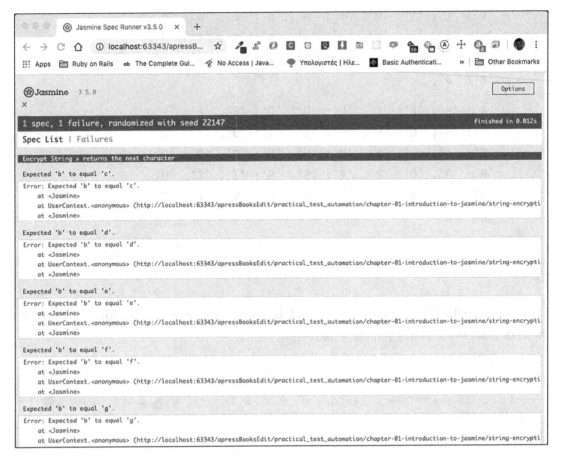

Figure 1-15. *Expectations Fail*

It seems that your function implementation is far behind from being ready. Almost all the expectations returned an error. Only the letter `'a'` has been successfully converted to `'b'`.

So you need to go back to the implementation of your function and revisit the code. You need to make it work so that all expectations are met.

Let's change the content of the file `assets/javascripts/encrypt.js` with the following (Listing 1-5).

Listing 1-5. Better Implementation of the encrypt Function

```javascript
function encrypt(inputString) {
    var mapping = {
        'a': 'b', 'b': 'c', 'c': 'd', 'd': 'e', 'e': 'f',
        'f': 'g', 'g': 'h', 'h': 'i', 'i': 'j', 'j': 'k',
```

```
      'k': 'l', 'l': 'm', 'm': 'n', 'n': 'o', 'o': 'p',
      'p': 'q', 'q': 'r', 'r': 's', 's': 't', 't': 'u',
      'u': 'v', 'v': 'w', 'w': 'x', 'x': 'y', 'y': 'z',
      'z': 'a',

      'A': 'B', 'B': 'C', 'C': 'D', 'D': 'E', 'E': 'F',
      'F': 'G', 'G': 'H', 'H': 'I', 'I': 'J', 'J': 'K',
      'K': 'L', 'L': 'M', 'M': 'N', 'N': 'O', 'O': 'P',
      'P': 'Q', 'Q': 'R', 'R': 'S', 'S': 'T', 'T': 'U',
      'U': 'V', 'V': 'W', 'W': 'X', 'X': 'Y', 'Y': 'Z',
      'Z': 'A'
    };
    return mapping[inputString];
}
```

If you save the preceding file and reload the page SpecRunner.html, you will see that the spec runs successfully (Figure 1-16).

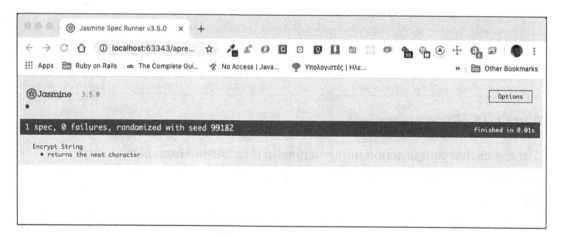

Figure 1-16. *Spec Runs Successfully*

Great!

More Specs

Your spec specifies the behavior of your function when given a string of one character. You need to add some examples to make sure that it works for multicharacter strings too.

Let's add one more expectation:

```
it("when input string is 'television' it returns 'ufmfwjtjpn'", function(){

    expect(encrypt('television')).toEqual('ufmfwjtjpo');

});
```

Note   The preceding expectation needs to be added after the existing `it` and before the closing `});` of the `describe`.

Save and then load the page `SpecRunner.html`. What you will see is the following (Figure 1-17).

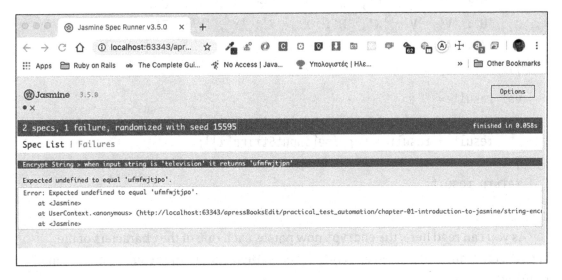

Figure 1-17. *Encrypting a Word Is Failing*

You have two specs and one failure. The encryption of a word has failed. You can see the message

```
Expected undefined to equal 'ufmfwjtjpo'
```

Hence, you now have to visit, again, the code of the encrypt() function and make it work for words too.

Let's change the implementation of encrypt() to be like the following (Listing 1-6).

Listing 1-6. Encrypting Words

```
function encrypt(inputString) {
    var mapping = {
        'a': 'b', 'b': 'c', 'c': 'd', 'd': 'e', 'e': 'f',
        'f': 'g', 'g': 'h', 'h': 'i', 'i': 'j', 'j': 'k',
        'k': 'l', 'l': 'm', 'm': 'n', 'n': 'o', 'o': 'p',
        'p': 'q', 'q': 'r', 'r': 's', 's': 't', 't': 'u',
        'u': 'v', 'v': 'w', 'w': 'x', 'x': 'y', 'y': 'z',
        'z': 'a',

        'A': 'B', 'B': 'C', 'C': 'D', 'D': 'E', 'E': 'F',
        'F': 'G', 'G': 'H', 'H': 'I', 'I': 'J', 'J': 'K',
        'K': 'L', 'L': 'M', 'M': 'N', 'N': 'O', 'O': 'P',
        'P': 'Q', 'Q': 'R', 'R': 'S', 'S': 'T', 'T': 'U',
        'U': 'V', 'V': 'W', 'W': 'X', 'X': 'Y', 'Y': 'Z',
        'Z': 'A'
    };

    var result = "";
    for (var i = 0; i < inputString.length; i++) {
        result = result + mapping[inputString[i]];
    }
    return result;
}
```

As you can read here, the encrypt now parses each one of the characters of the inputString, encrypts it, and appends the encrypted char to the result which is finally returned.

If you save this implementation and reload the SpecRunner.html on your browser, you will see the following (Figure 1-18).

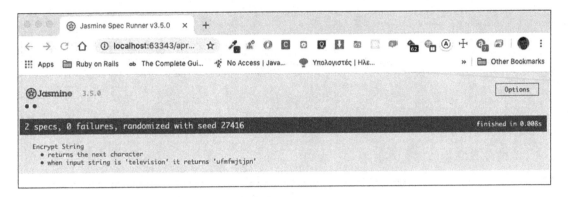

Figure 1-18. *Two Specs Successful – Words Being Converted*

Perfect! Now your encrypt() method works both for single characters and for words.

But you only have one spec of word encryption. Maybe, you would like to add some more specs to make you feel more confident. Actually, what would make you feel more confident would have been a spec like the following (Listing 1-7).

Listing 1-7. Spec for Encrypting Words with All Characters of the Latin Alphabet

```
it("can encrypt a word", function(){

    expect(encrypt('abcdefghijklmnopqrstuvwxyzABCDEFGHIJKLMNOPQRSTUVWXYZ')).
        toEqual('bcdefghijklmnopqrstuvwxyzaBCDEFGHIJKLMNOPQRSTUVWXYZA');

});
```

So, if you replace your last spec (that one with the 'television' word) with this, you would be more confident that the encrypt() function can convert words with the letters of the Latin alphabet.

Save this spec, load the SpecRunner.html on the browser, and you will see the following (Figure 1-19).

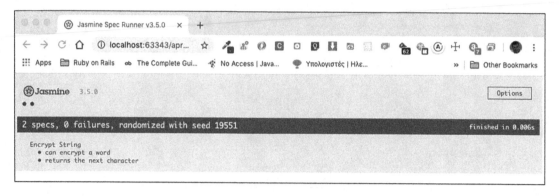

Figure 1-19. *Spec Results for Words with All Chars*

Nice! You are confident that your encrypt() function can encrypt both single-char strings and long words. But did you finish? Did you satisfy all the requirements? Let's revisit them:

1. All characters should be replaced with their next one. So "a" should be replaced by "b", "b" should be replaced by "c", and so on.

2. If the input character is uppercase, then the output will be uppercase too.

3. If the input character is "z", then the output should be "a" – similarly for the "Z".

4. Only characters from the Latin alphabet will be allowed. Otherwise, an exception will be thrown.

It's the last requirement that is not specified in any of the specs. Let's try to define the specification for that (Listing 1-8).

Listing 1-8. Spec for the Last Requirement

```
it("throws an exception if there is any character that does not belong to
the latin alphabet", function() {
    expect(function(){

        encrypt("This includes the blank character that does not belong to
        latin alphabet")

    }).toThrowError(ArgumentError, "non-latin alphabet character encountered");
});
```

The Jasmine pattern

```
expect(function() {

  ... call your function under test here ...

}).toThrowError(...);
```

is used to tell that an exception is expected to be thrown. Note that this will not work:

```
expect(

  ... call your function under test here ...

).toThrowError(...);
```

The function under test needs to be called from within an anonymous function. Hence, add the new spec inside your assets/javascripts/my-application-spec.js. This file then needs to be like the following (Listing 1-9).

Listing 1-9. Full Expectations Code

```
describe("Encrypt String", function(){

    it("returns the next character", function(){

        var expectations = {
            'a': 'b', 'b': 'c', 'c': 'd', 'd': 'e', 'e': 'f',
            'f': 'g', 'g': 'h', 'h': 'i', 'i': 'j', 'j': 'k',
            'k': 'l', 'l': 'm', 'm': 'n', 'n': 'o', 'o': 'p',
            'p': 'q', 'q': 'r', 'r': 's', 's': 't', 't': 'u',
            'u': 'v', 'v': 'w', 'w': 'x', 'x': 'y', 'y': 'z',
            'z': 'a',

            'A': 'B', 'B': 'C', 'C': 'D', 'D': 'E', 'E': 'F',
            'F': 'G', 'G': 'H', 'H': 'I', 'I': 'J', 'J': 'K',
            'K': 'L', 'L': 'M', 'M': 'N', 'N': 'O', 'O': 'P',
            'P': 'Q', 'Q': 'R', 'R': 'S', 'S': 'T', 'T': 'U',
            'U': 'V', 'V': 'W', 'W': 'X', 'X': 'Y', 'Y': 'Z',
            'Z': 'A'
        };
```

```
        for (var property in expectations) {
            if (expectations.hasOwnProperty(property)) {
                var charToEncrypt = property;
                var expectedEncryptedChar = expectations[property];

                expect(encrypt(charToEncrypt)).toEqual(expectedEncrypted
                Char);
            }
        }
    });

    it("can encrypt a word", function(){
        expect(encrypt('abcdefghijklmnopqrstuvwxyzABCDEFGHIJKLMNOPQR
        STUVWXYZ')).
        toEqual('bcdefghijklmnopqrstuvwxyzaBCDEFGHIJKLMNOPQRSTUVWXYZA');
    });

    it("throws an exception if there is any character that does not belong
    to the latin alphabet", function() {
        expect(function(){
            encrypt("This includes the blank character that does not belong
            to latin alphabet")
        }).toThrowError(ArgumentError, "non-latin alphabet character
        encountered");
    });
});
```

If you save and load the SpecRunner.html again, you will see the following (Figure 1-20).

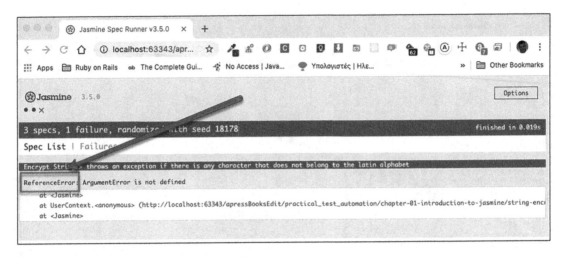

Figure 1-20. *ReferenceError Is Thrown*

The error that you see in the SpecRunner results is a runtime error and not an expectation error. It is a JavaScript error that is telling you that there is something wrong with the `ArgumentError` reference. This reference is not defined in your code, and that's why this error is raised.

Let's define this reference. It will be an object deriving from `Error`. In Listing 1-10, you can see the definition of `ArgumentError`.

Listing 1-10. `ArgumentError` Definition

```
function ArgumentError(message) {
    this.name = 'ArgumentError';
    this.message = message || 'Argument Error';
    this.stack = (new Error()).stack;
}
ArgumentError.prototype = Object.create(Error.prototype);
ArgumentError.prototype.constructor = ArgumentError;
```

Save this inside your `encrypt.js` file, above the definition of the `encrypt()` function, and then reload the `SpecRunner.html` page again. You will see Figure 1-21.

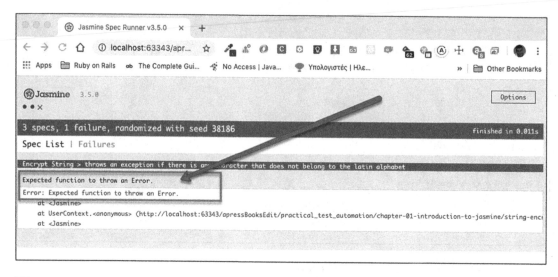

Figure 1-21. *Expectation Error*

The situation has improved. Now, you are getting a real expectation error, not a JavaScript runtime error. The expectation error is telling you that your function, the encrypt() function, should have thrown an error but it hasn't.

This is not coming with a surprise, because you have not changed, in any way, the encrypt() function to throw an error when it is given a non-Latin character.

Let's enhance encrypt() accordingly, so that it satisfies the expectation (Listing 1-11).

Listing 1-11. encrypt() Code That Is Throwing an Error

```
function encrypt(inputString) {
    var mapping = {
        'a': 'b', 'b': 'c', 'c': 'd', 'd': 'e', 'e': 'f',
        'f': 'g', 'g': 'h', 'h': 'i', 'i': 'j', 'j': 'k',
        'k': 'l', 'l': 'm', 'm': 'n', 'n': 'o', 'o': 'p',
        'p': 'q', 'q': 'r', 'r': 's', 's': 't', 't': 'u',
        'u': 'v', 'v': 'w', 'w': 'x', 'x': 'y', 'y': 'z',
        'z': 'a',

        'A': 'B', 'B': 'C', 'C': 'D', 'D': 'E', 'E': 'F',
        'F': 'G', 'G': 'H', 'H': 'I', 'I': 'J', 'J': 'K',
        'K': 'L', 'L': 'M', 'M': 'N', 'N': 'O', 'O': 'P',
        'P': 'Q', 'Q': 'R', 'R': 'S', 'S': 'T', 'T': 'U',
```

```
        'U': 'V', 'V': 'W', 'W': 'X', 'X': 'Y', 'Y': 'Z',
        'Z': 'A'
    };

    var result = "";
    for (var i = 0; i < inputString.length; i++) {
        var encryptedChar = mapping[inputString[i]];
        if (encryptedChar === undefined) {
            throw new ArgumentError("non-latin alphabet character
            encountered");
        }
        result = result + encryptedChar;
    }
    return result;
}
```

In this code, you are enhancing the `for` loop to check for the input character to be encrypted. If the input character is not mapped, this means that it is not part of the list of characters that the function can encrypt. In that case, it throws an `ArgumentError`.

Save the preceding code and reload the page `SpecRunner.html`. You will see the following (Figure 1-22).

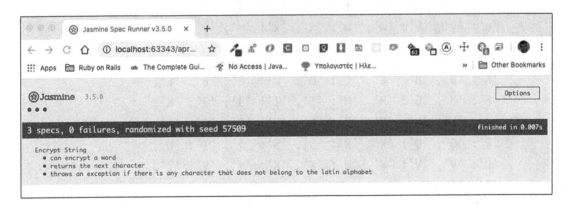

Figure 1-22. *All Specs Are Running Successfully*

Perfect! All specs are running successfully. You can enhance the spec that checks for invalid characters if you want, in order to cover for more examples with invalid characters. This is left as a small exercise to you.

Refactoring

You have finished the implementation of your encrypt() function. It is ready. It does what it is required to do, and all your specs are running successfully.

Now that you have done that, you can freely refactor the code of the encrypt() function to be easier to read and maintain (Listing 1-12).

Listing 1-12. Refactor the encrypt() Function

```
function ArgumentError(message) {
    this.name = 'ArgumentError';
    this.message = message || 'Argument Error';
    this.stack = (new Error()).stack;
}
ArgumentError.prototype = Object.create(Error.prototype);
ArgumentError.prototype.constructor = ArgumentError;

function encrypt(inputString) {
    var mapping = {
        'a': 'b', 'b': 'c', 'c': 'd', 'd': 'e', 'e': 'f',
        'f': 'g', 'g': 'h', 'h': 'i', 'i': 'j', 'j': 'k',
        'k': 'l', 'l': 'm', 'm': 'n', 'n': 'o', 'o': 'p',
        'p': 'q', 'q': 'r', 'r': 's', 's': 't', 't': 'u',
        'u': 'v', 'v': 'w', 'w': 'x', 'x': 'y', 'y': 'z',
        'z': 'a',

        'A': 'B', 'B': 'C', 'C': 'D', 'D': 'E', 'E': 'F',
        'F': 'G', 'G': 'H', 'H': 'I', 'I': 'J', 'J': 'K',
        'K': 'L', 'L': 'M', 'M': 'N', 'N': 'O', 'O': 'P',
        'P': 'Q', 'Q': 'R', 'R': 'S', 'S': 'T', 'T': 'U',
        'U': 'V', 'V': 'W', 'W': 'X', 'X': 'Y', 'Y': 'Z',
        'Z': 'A'
    };

    var encryptChar = function(inputChar) {
        var encryptedChar = mapping[inputChar];
```

```
    if (encryptedChar === undefined) {
        throw new ArgumentError("non-latin alphabet character
        encountered");
    }
    return encryptedChar;
};

return (
    inputString.
      split('').
      map(encryptChar).
      join('')
);
}
```

As you can see here, you defined a local function `encryptChar`, and you have
also got rid of the `for` loop. You are now using `split()`, `map()`, and `join()` JavaScript
functions instead.

If you save the preceding code and reload the `SpecRunner.html`, you will see that all
the specs are still running successfully. This makes you feel certain that your refactoring
changes didn't break the functionality of the `encrypt()` function.

TDD Flow

During your function development, you have followed a specific flow of development:

1. You have introduced the specs.

2. You saw the specs failing.

3. You have inserted the minimum amount of code to make the
    specs successful.

4. You have refactored the code.

This is the TDD (Test-Driven Development) flow of work. It is depicted on the
following diagram (Figure 1-23).

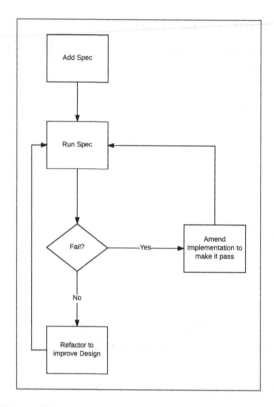

Figure 1-23. *TDD Flow of Development*

It is very important to understand this flow. TDD helps you develop a software module that is according to the requirements. Also, the end of the process is covered with tests, which means that further development or refactoring will never introduce any regression bugs without being noticed.

There is plenty of documentation on the Internet and lots of books about how to apply TDD properly.

Jasmine Matchers

Up until now, you have used two Jasmine-specific functions, the `toEqual()` and the `toThrowError()`. These are called Jasmine matchers.

There are plenty of Jasmine matchers that you can use. Read the following documentation so that you can see what each Jasmine matcher can do: `https://jasmine.github.io/api/3.5/matchers.html`.

Some indicative and commonly used matchers are as follows:

1. The toBe() matcher compares with ===.

2. The toMatch() matcher is for regular expressions.

3. The toBeDefined() matcher compares against undefined. It returns true if the actual expression is not undefined.

4. The toBeUndefined() matcher compares against undefined. It returns true if the actual expression is undefined.

5. The toBeNull() matcher compares against null. It returns true if the actual expression is null.

6. The toContain() matcher is for finding an item in an array.

7. The toBeLessThan() and toBeGreaterThan() matchers are for mathematical comparisons.

And you can always negate the matcher behavior by prefixing with a method call to not. For example, not.toMatch() returns true if the actual expression does not match the expected expression given.

Setup and Teardown

There are cases in which some specs in a suite (inside a describe block) might perform common things to set up their context and common things to tear it down.

If there are things that need to be executed before each spec (setup phase), you can put them once inside a beforeEach() block.

This is an example JavaScript code:

```
var globalInteger = 0;

function addThis(value) {
    globalInteger += value;
}
```

Then you can have a Jasmine test suite as follows (Listing 1-13).

Listing 1-13. Example with beforeEach

```
describe("Function addThis to add a value", function() {
    beforeEach(function(){
        globalInteger = 5;
    });

    it("returns 10", function() {
        addThis(5);
        expect(globalInteger).toEqual(10);
    });

    it("returns 20", function() {
        addThis(15);
        expect(globalInteger).toEqual(20);
    });
});
```

TRY THAT IN A JS BIN

You can try Jasmine in a JS Bin, without having any local page code for Jasmine and SpecRunner.html. How can you do that? You start a new JS Bin, and you make sure that you reference Jasmine libraries in the head section of your HTML part:

```
<script type="text/javascript" src="https://cdnjs.cloudflare.com/ajax/libs/
jasmine/3.5.0/jasmine.min.js"></script>
<script type="text/javascript" src="https://cdnjs.cloudflare.com/ajax/libs/
jasmine/3.5.0/jasmine-html.min.js"></script>
<script type="text/javascript" src="https://cdnjs.cloudflare.com/ajax/libs/
jasmine/3.5.0/boot.min.js"></script>
    <link rel="stylesheet" href="https://cdnjs.cloudflare.com/ajax/libs/
jasmine/3.5.0/jasmine.min.css"></head>
```

The preceding code is referencing the Jasmine library from the Cloudflare CDN network. Then you need to write the JavaScript code under test. That one, you write it inside the head section, using the `<script>` element. Then you need to write the Jasmine specs that test your JavaScript code. You use the `<script>` element too.

See Figure 1-24.

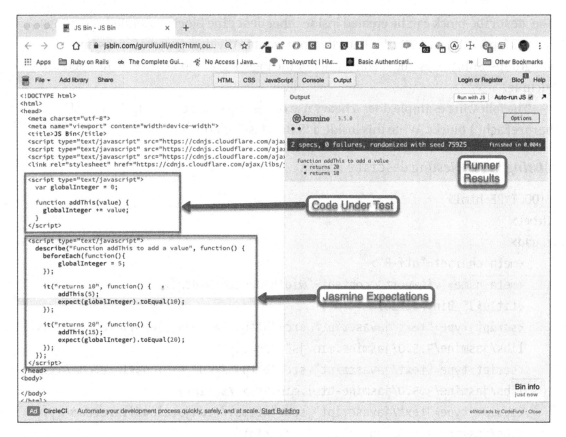

Figure 1-24. *Jasmine Through a JS Bin*

At the beginning of each spec and before the `it` is executed, the `beforeEach` block will be executed. This, in your preceding example, will set the global variable `globalInteger` to 5.

Like `beforeEach()`, one can use a teardown function by calling the `afterEach()` block. Whatever you put inside the `afterEach()` will be executed after each `it` block.

Another way you can share state between `beforeEach()`, `it()`, and `afterEach()` is by using the object `this`. The `this` object is accessible inside those blocks; and, not only that, at the end of an `it()`, it is reset to an empty object in order to avoid pollution of state and ripple unexpected effects from one `it()` call to the next. Keep reading in order to see an example usage of `this`.

Nesting **describe** Blocks

The describe block can be created inside other describe blocks essentially creating a tree of specs. You usually do that when you want to divide a group of specs into subgroups. Subgroups might convey better the logical cohesion between the specs they include.

The following example does a heavy use of nesting of describe blocks and of beforeEach() blocks. Write this inside a JS Bin (Listing 1-14).

Listing 1-14. Nesting describe Blocks

```
<!DOCTYPE html>
<html>
<head>
    <meta charset="utf-8">
    <meta name="viewport" content="width=device-width">
    <title>JS Bin</title>
    <script type="text/javascript" src="https://cdnjs.cloudflare.com/ajax/
    libs/jasmine/3.5.0/jasmine.min.js"></script>
    <script type="text/javascript" src="https://cdnjs.cloudflare.com/ajax/
    libs/jasmine/3.5.0/jasmine-html.min.js"></script>
    <script type="text/javascript" src="https://cdnjs.cloudflare.com/ajax/
    libs/jasmine/3.5.0/boot.min.js"></script>

    <link rel="stylesheet" href="https://cdnjs.cloudflare.com/ajax/libs/
    jasmine/3.5.0/jasmine.min.css"></head>

<script type="text/javascript">
    function maximumOfThree(a, b, c) {
        if (a > b ) {
            if (a > c) {
                return a;
            }
            else {
                return c;
            }
        }
```

```
        else if (b > c) {
            return b;
        }
        else {
            return c;
        }
    }
</script>

<script type="text/javascript">
    describe("Testing 'maximumOfThree'", function() {
        describe("when a is greater than b", function() {
            beforeEach(function() {
                this.a = 5;
                this.b = 4;
            });

            describe("when a is greater than c", function() {

                beforeEach(function() {
                    this.c = 3;
                });

                it("returns a", function() {
                    expect(maximumOfThree(this.a, this.b, this.c)).
                    toEqual(this.a);
                });
            });

            describe("when a is less than or equal to c", function(){
                beforeEach(function() {
                    this.c = 6;
                });
```

```
            it("returns c", function() {
                expect(maximumOfThree(this.a, this.b, this.c)).
                toEqual(this.c);
            });

        });

    });

    describe("when a is less than b", function() {
        beforeEach(function() {
            this.a = 5;
            this.b = 6;
        });

        describe("when b is greater than c", function() {
            beforeEach(function() {
                this.c = 5;
            });

            it("returns b", function() {
                expect(maximumOfThree(this.a, this.b, this.c)).
                toEqual(this.b);
            });
        });

        describe("when b is less than c", function() {
            beforeEach(function() {
                this.c = 7;
            });

            it("returns c", function() {
                expect(maximumOfThree(this.a, this.b, this.c)).
                toEqual(this.c);
            });
        });

    });

});
```

```
</script>
<body>

</body>
</html>
```

If you run it in a JS Bin, you will get the following (Figure 1-25).

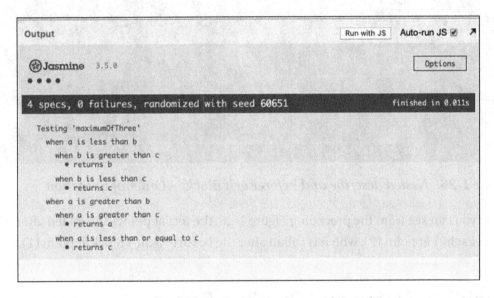

Figure 1-25. *Nested describe Blocks Generated Nested Results*

As you can see, the nested `describe` blocks generate nested results too. This is very convenient and makes the reader of the spec results feel confident about what is specified and what is not.

Note that in the preceding example, you used `beforeEach()` blocks to define the setup phase of each test. The `beforeEach()` blocks are called in the order they are defined – first the ones defined for the outer `describe` blocks and then the ones for the nested `describe` blocks.

```
<script type="text/javascript">
    describe("Testing 'maximumOfThree'", function() {
        describe("when a is greater than b", function() {
            beforeEach(function() {
                this.a = 5;
                this.b = 4;
            });

            describe("when a is greater than c", function() {

                beforeEach(function() {
                    this.c = 3;
                });

                it("returns a", function() {
                    expect(maximumOfThree(this.a, this.b, this.c)).toEqual(this.a);
                });
            });
        });
```

Figure 1-26. *Nested describe and beforeEach Blocks – Order of Execution*

As you can see from the preceding Figure 1-26, the test at point (3) is called after the beforeEach() at point (2), which is called after the beforeEach() block at point (1).

Disabling Suites and Pending Specs

There are times in which you want your group of specs, your test suite, to be disabled. Or you might want some of your specs to be considered as incomplete, pending completion.

In order to disable a suite of specs, use the function xdescribe() instead of describe(). Similarly, in order to mark a spec as pending, use the method xit(), instead of it().

Tasks and Quizzes

TASK DETAILS

1. You need to implement a JavaScript function using TDD methodology and the Jasmine specs.

2. Here are the requirements of the function:

   1. It should have the name `mixStrings`.

   2. It should take two string arguments.

   3. It should mix the arguments and return the mixed string. Mixing logic is the first char from the first string, then the first char from the second string, then the second char from the first string, then the second char from the second string, and so on. Examples are as follows:

      1. If the first string is `"foo"` and the second string is `"bar"`, the result string should be `"fboaor"`.

      2. If the first string is `"f"` and the second string is `"b"`, the result string should be `"fb"`.

   4. Special provision should be taken for the following edge cases:

      1. The first string is empty `""` or `null` or `undefined` and the second string non-empty. It should return the second string.

      2. The first string is non-empty and the second string is empty `""` or `null` or `undefined`. It should return the first string.

      3. When both strings are empty `""` or `null` or `undefined`, it should return an empty string `""`.

3. We give you some hints in order to help you:

   1. The following is an indicative spec runner result (Figure 1-27).

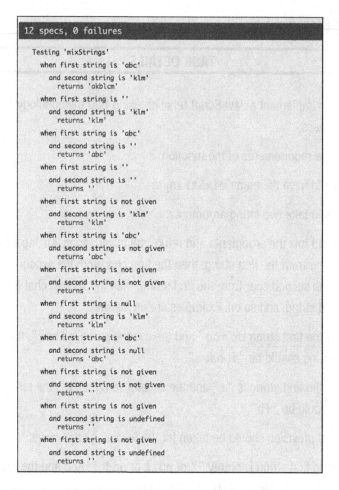

Figure 1-27. *Indicative Spec Runner Results*

2. Maybe you would like to use nested describe and beforeEach() blocks to set up the context of your tests.

3. Note that you may use expect() or fail() inside the beforeEach() blocks too, in order to make sure that you have set up the context of your tests correctly.

4. You may want to use the this object in order to share state between beforeEach() and it() blocks.

Key Takeaways

- How to install Jasmine

- How to set up the SpecRunner page

- How to write your expectations and then execute them in the runner

- How to follow the TDD flow of development

- How to use Jasmine in a JS Bin

In the following chapter, you will learn about stubbing and mocking and how you can use these very important techniques with Jasmine.

CHAPTER 2

Advanced Jasmine

This chapter introduces you to two very widely used areas of testing:

1. Stubbing

2. Mocking

You are going to learn these techniques using Jasmine (although you will come back when you will be doing tests using Ruby).

With stubbing, you are going to specify how a method should behave when another method returns specific values (Figure 2-1).

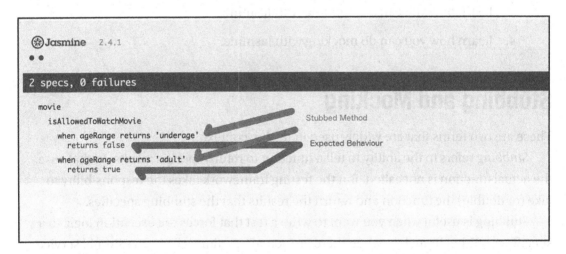

Figure 2-1. Stubbing Example

With mocking, you are going to specify which methods are expected to be called (Figure 2-2).

© Panos Matsinopoulos 2020
P. Matsinopoulos, *Practical Test Automation*, https://doi.org/10.1007/978-1-4842-6141-5_2

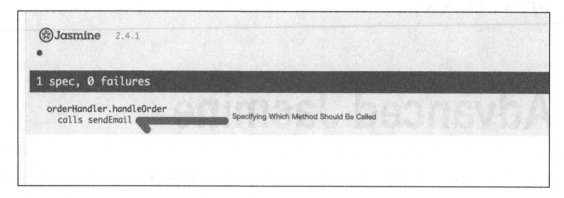

Figure 2-2. *Specifying Which Method Should Be Called*

Learning Goals

1. Learn about stubbing.

2. Learn about mocking.

3. Learn how you can do stubbing with Jasmine.

4. Learn how you can do mocking with Jasmine.

Stubbing and Mocking

These are two terms that are widely used in testing context.

Stubbing refers to the ability to tell a function to return specific results. In that case, the actual function is not called. But the testing framework takes the responsibility to fake (or double) the function and return the results that the stubbing specifies.

Stubbing is useful when you want to write a test that forces the execution logic to a specific condition branch or when there are actual function calls to an external service and you do not want these to take place in the test. Calling external services in tests might be delaying the execution of your test suite significantly. Also, calling external services, while testing, might render the tests flaky, their success depending on the availability of the external service.

Mocking is the ability to tell your test what are your expectations with regards to functions expected to be called. You use this technique when you want your test to verify that the unit under test is calling specific functions (the functions that are mocked); hence, your test being an implementation requirement, specifies how the implementation should be designed.

Stubbing with Jasmine

You are going to see a stubbing example using Jasmine. This will give you a better understanding of what stubbing is. Here is the SpecRunner.html file, integrated inside a JS Bin (Listing 2-1).

Listing 2-1. Stubbing, SpecRunner.html

```
<!DOCTYPE html>
<html lang="end">
<head>
  <meta charset="utf-8">
  <meta name="viewport" content="width=device-width">
  <title>JS Bin</title>
    <script type="text/javascript" src="https://cdnjs.cloudflare.com/ajax/
    libs/jasmine/3.5.0/jasmine.min.js"></script>
  <script type="text/javascript" src="https://cdnjs.cloudflare.com/ajax/
  libs/jasmine/3.5.0/jasmine-html.min.js"></script>
  <script type="text/javascript" src="https://cdnjs.cloudflare.com/ajax/
  libs/jasmine/3.5.0/boot.min.js"></script>

  <link rel="stylesheet" href="https://cdnjs.cloudflare.com/ajax/libs/
  jasmine/3.5.0/jasmine.min.css">

  <script type="text/javascript">
    var movie = {
      age: 5,
      ageRange: function(){
        console.log("ageRange called");
      },
```

```
      isAllowedToWatchMovie: function() {
        if (this.ageRange(this.age) === "underage") {
          return false;
        }
        else if (this.ageRange(this.age) === "adult") {
          return true;
        }
      }
    };
  </script>

  <script type="text/javascript">
    describe("movie", function() {
      describe("isAllowedToWatchMovie", function() {
        describe("when ageRange returns 'underage'", function() {
          beforeEach(function(){
            spyOn(movie, 'ageRange').and.returnValue('underage');
          });

          it("returns false", function() {
            expect(movie.isAllowedToWatchMovie()).toEqual(false);
          });
        });

        describe("when ageRange returns 'adult'", function() {
          beforeEach(function(){
            spyOn(movie, 'ageRange').and.returnValue('adult');
          });

          it("returns true", function() {
            expect(movie.isAllowedToWatchMovie()).toEqual(true);
          });
        });
      });
    });
  </script>
</head>
```

```
<body>

</body>
</html>
```

If you run this in a JS Bin, you will see the following result (Figure 2-3).

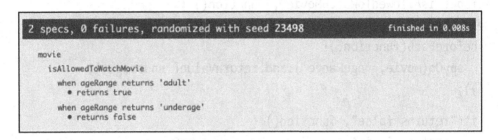

Figure 2-3. *Spec Results for the Stubbing Example*

As you can see from the spec results, you are developing a movie object, and you are specifying the behavior of the isAllowedToWatchMovie function. The specs say that the isAllowedToWatchMovie implementation should rely on another function, the ageRange function. If the ageRange result is "underage", then isAllowedToWatchMovie should return false. If the ageRange result is "adult", then isAllowedToWatchMovie should return true.

These two statements do the stubbing:

```
spyOn(movie, 'ageRange').and.returnValue('underage');
...
spyOn(movie, 'ageRange').and.returnValue('adult');
```

This forces the calls to ageRange to return specific values.

These specs specify what isAllowedToWatchMovie should behave like assuming that the other part of the implementation (the ageRange method) does its job correctly. Under this assumption, the isAllowedToWatchMovie method is ready, because the specs are green. But does the ageRange method do its job correctly? There is no spec that verifies that. If you look at the ageRange method implementation, you will see that it only logs something to the console. It does not actually return "underage" nor "adult". So why do the specs of isAllowedToWatchMovie don't fail? They do not fail because when you stub a method, the actual implementation is never called. The Jasmine framework will track the call to the method but will prevent the actual implementation of the method to be called.

This leaves you with the task to implement specs for the ageRange method. Let's enhance your suite of specs. It should be like Listing 2-2.

Listing 2-2. Implement Specs for the ageRange Method

```
describe("movie", function() {
  describe("isAllowedToWatchMovie", function() {
    describe("when ageRange returns 'underage'", function() {
      beforeEach(function(){
        spyOn(movie, 'ageRange').and.returnValue('underage');
      });

      it("returns false", function() {
        expect(movie.isAllowedToWatchMovie()).toEqual(false);
      });
    });

    describe("when ageRange returns 'adult'", function() {
      beforeEach(function(){
        spyOn(movie, 'ageRange').and.returnValue('adult');
      });

      it("returns true", function() {
        expect(movie.isAllowedToWatchMovie()).toEqual(true);
      });
    });
  });

  describe("ageRange", function() {
    describe("when age less than 18", function() {
      beforeEach(function(){
        movie.age = 17;
      });

      it("returns 'underage'", function() {
        expect(movie.ageRange()).toEqual('underage');
      });
    });
```

```
describe("when age greater than 18", function() {
  beforeEach(function(){
      movie.age = 25;
  });

  it("returns 'adult'", function() {
    expect(movie.ageRange()).toEqual('adult');
  });
 });
 });
});
```

You can see the new specs for the ageRange method inside the corresponding describe block. If you run the spec runner in a JS Bin, you will see the following (Figure 2-4).

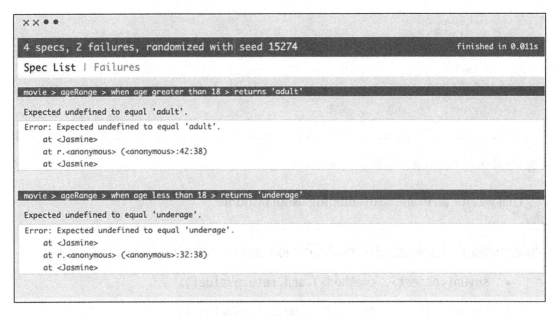

Figure 2-4. *ageRange Specs Added but They Fail*

As you can see, the isAllowedToWatchMovie specs still succeed, but the ageRange specs do not. You need to tune the implementation of ageRange in order to satisfy the specs.

Here is an implementation of ageRange that does that (Listing 2-3).

Listing 2-3. ageRange Implementation Satisfying Specs

```
ageRange: function(){
  if (this.age < 18) {
    return "underage";
  }
  else {
    return 'adult';
  }
},
```

If you run the specs in a JS Bin again, you will get the following (Figure 2-5).

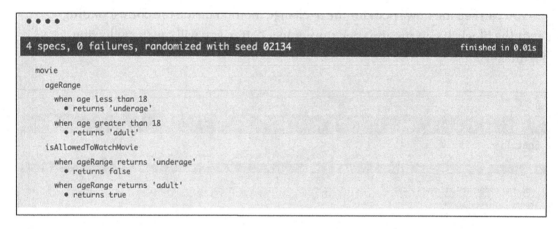

Figure 2-5. *Running All Specs – Success*

That was it – an example of stubbing using Jasmine.

Information   These are the most common ways to use stubbing with Jasmine:

- spyOn(<object>, <method>).and.returnValue()

- spyOn(<object>, <method>).and.returnValues()

- spyOn(<object>, <method>).and.callFake(function() {})

- spyOn(<object>, <method>).and.throwError

You can read more about them in the Jasmine documentation.

Mocking with Jasmine

With mocking, you try to test that a piece of code satisfies some implementation requirements, that it calls a function or a method. So, while with stubbing you drive the test execution logic to specific paths, with mocking you test that specific paths are taken.

The basic mocking technique with Jasmine is the following:

1. You set a spy on the method you want to mock.

2. You call `.and.callThrough()` to make sure that the method is actually called.

3. You then call a mocking expectation method like

   – `.toHaveBeenCalled()`

   – `.toHaveBeenCalledTimes()`

   – And so on

Let's see the following example (Figure 2-6).

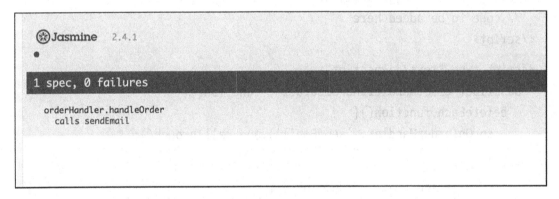

Figure 2-6. *Spec Result for a Mocking Example*

You want to achieve the preceding example. As you can see, you want to specify the behavior of the method `handleOrder` of the object with the name `orderHandler`. What you specify is that this method should be calling the method `sendEmail`.

This is a mocking example. Let's write that using Jasmine (Listing 2-4).

Listing 2-4. Mocking Using Jasmine

```html
<!DOCTYPE html>
<html lang="end">
<head>
  <meta charset="utf-8">
  <meta name="viewport" content="width=device-width">
  <title>JS Bin</title>
  <script type="text/javascript" src="https://cdnjs.cloudflare.com/ajax/
  libs/jasmine/3.5.0/jasmine.min.js"></script>
  <script type="text/javascript" src="https://cdnjs.cloudflare.com/ajax/
  libs/jasmine/3.5.0/jasmine-html.min.js"></script>
  <script type="text/javascript" src="https://cdnjs.cloudflare.com/ajax/
  libs/jasmine/3.5.0/boot.min.js"></script>

  <link rel="stylesheet" href="https://cdnjs.cloudflare.com/ajax/libs/
  jasmine/3.5.0/jasmine.min.css">

  <script type="text/javascript">
    // code to be added here
  </script>

  <script type="text/javascript">
    describe("orderHandler.handleOrder", function(){
      beforeEach(function(){
        spyOn(orderHandler, 'sendEmail').and.callThrough();
      });

      it("calls sendEmail", function() {
        orderHandler.handleOrder();

        expect(orderHandler.sendEmail).toHaveBeenCalled();
      });
    });
  </script>
</head>
<body>

</body>
</html>
```

In the beforeEach() block, you are setting your spy functionality on the method sendEmail of the object orderHandler. Also, you are calling .and.callThrough(). If you do not do that, you are stubbing, not mocking. The .and.callThrough() will actually do the call to the sendEmail() method.

Then, inside the it block, you call the method that you are testing – orderHandler. handleOrder() – and then you are checking that your expectation has been met: expect(orderHandler.sendEmail).toHaveBeenCalled().

If you run the spec runner inside a JS Bin, you will get the following (Figure 2-7).

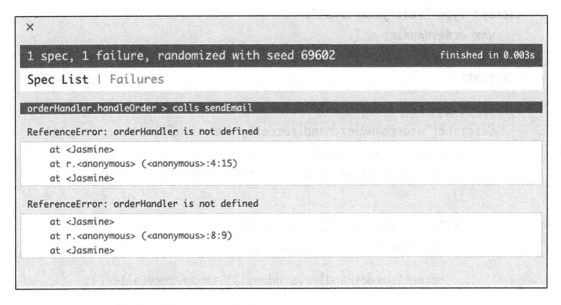

Figure 2-7. *orderHandler Is Not Defined*

The specs fail because the orderHandler is not defined. You are going to define the orderHandler object (Listing 2-5).

Listing 2-5. orderHandler Is Now Defined

```
<!DOCTYPE html>
<html lang="end">
<head>
    <meta charset="utf-8">
    <meta name="viewport" content="width=device-width">
    <title>JS Bin</title>
```

```
<script type="text/javascript" src="https://cdnjs.cloudflare.com/ajax/
libs/jasmine/3.5.0/jasmine.min.js"></script>
<script type="text/javascript" src="https://cdnjs.cloudflare.com/ajax/
libs/jasmine/3.5.0/jasmine-html.min.js"></script>
<script type="text/javascript" src="https://cdnjs.cloudflare.com/ajax/
libs/jasmine/3.5.0/boot.min.js"></script>

<link rel="stylesheet" href="https://cdnjs.cloudflare.com/ajax/libs/
jasmine/3.5.0/jasmine.min.css">
<script type="text/javascript">
    var orderHandler = {
    };
</script>

<script type="text/javascript">
    describe("orderHandler.handleOrder", function(){
        beforeEach(function(){
            spyOn(orderHandler, 'sendEmail').and.callThrough();
        });

        it("calls sendEmail", function() {
            orderHandler.handleOrder();

            expect(orderHandler.sendEmail).toHaveBeenCalled();
        });
    });
</script>
</head>
<body>

</body>
</html>
```

If you run the specs, you get the error that the sendEmail() method does not exist
(Figure 2-8).

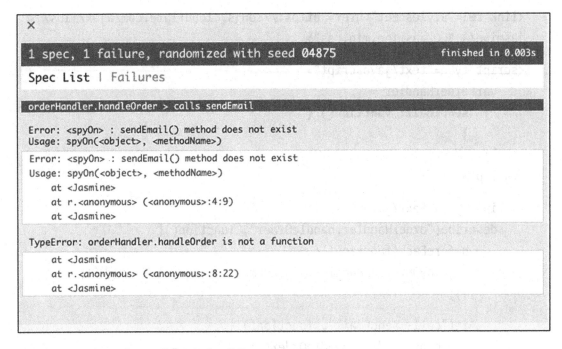

Figure 2-8. *sendEmail() Method Does Not Exist*

Then you proceed to define the sendEmail method inside the orderHandler object (Listing 2-6).

Listing 2-6. Define the sendEmail() Method

```html
<!DOCTYPE html>
<html lang="end">
<head>
    <meta charset="utf-8">
    <meta name="viewport" content="width=device-width">
    <title>JS Bin</title>
    <script type="text/javascript" src="https://cdnjs.cloudflare.com/ajax/
    libs/jasmine/3.5.0/jasmine.min.js"></script>
    <script type="text/javascript" src="https://cdnjs.cloudflare.com/ajax/
    libs/jasmine/3.5.0/jasmine-html.min.js"></script>
    <script type="text/javascript" src="https://cdnjs.cloudflare.com/ajax/
    libs/jasmine/3.5.0/boot.min.js"></script>
```

```
<link rel="stylesheet" href="https://cdnjs.cloudflare.com/ajax/libs/
jasmine/3.5.0/jasmine.min.css">

<script type="text/javascript">
    var orderHandler = {
        sendEmail: function() {
        }
    };
</script>

<script type="text/javascript">
    describe("orderHandler.handleOrder", function(){
        beforeEach(function(){
            spyOn(orderHandler, 'sendEmail').and.callThrough();
        });

        it("calls sendEmail", function() {
            orderHandler.handleOrder();

            expect(orderHandler.sendEmail).toHaveBeenCalled();
        });
    });
</script>
</head>
<body>

</body>
</html>
```

Now it is complaining that handleOrder is not a function (Figure 2-9).

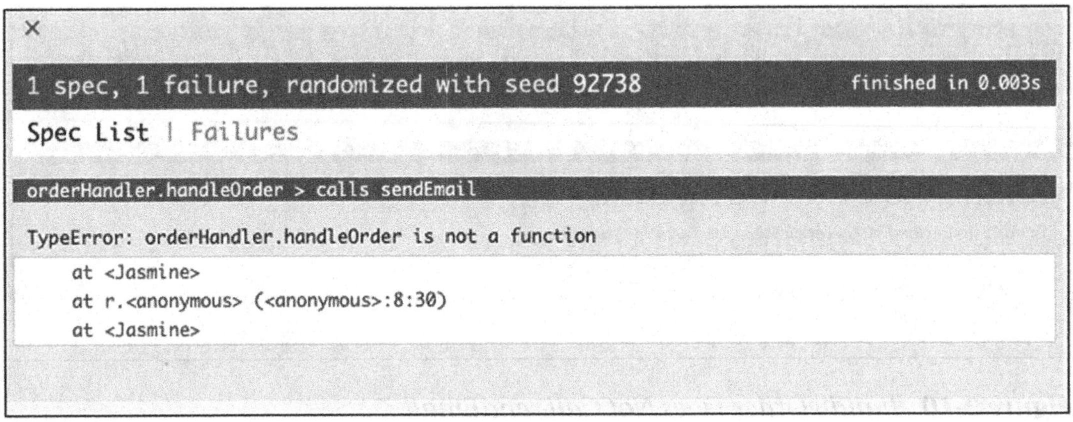

Figure 2-9. *handleOrder Is Not a Function*

Let's define the handleOrder function. Here is its empty definition inside the orderHandler object:

```
<script type="text/javascript">
    var orderHandler = {
      sendEmail: function() {

      },
      handleOrder: function() {

      }
    };
</script>
```

Now, the specs fail because the expectation is not met. The handleOrder() method does not call the sendEmail() method (Figure 2-10).

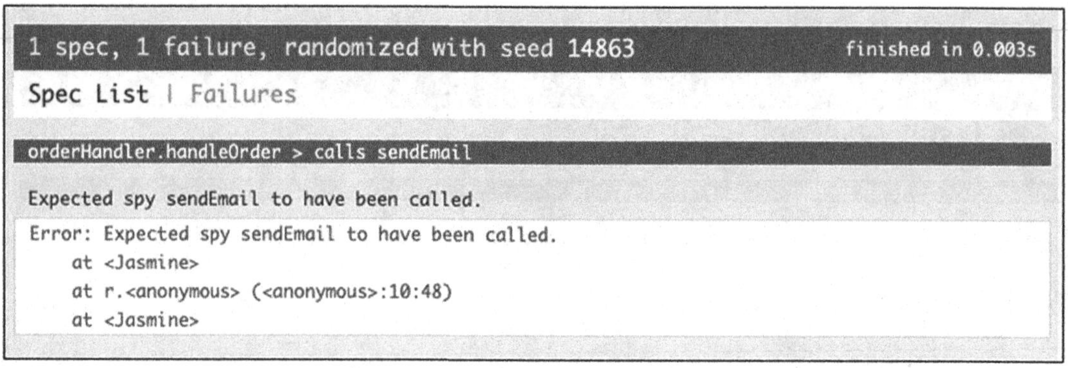

```
1 spec, 1 failure, randomized with seed 14863          finished in 0.003s

Spec List | Failures

orderHandler.handleOrder > calls sendEmail

Expected spy sendEmail to have been called.

Error: Expected spy sendEmail to have been called.
    at <Jasmine>
    at r.<anonymous> (<anonymous>:10:48)
    at <Jasmine>
```

Figure 2-10. *handleOrder Does Not Call sendEmail*

Hence, in order to satisfy this spec, what remains to be done is to have handleOrder() call the sendEmail() method. Here is the addition of this call inside the handleOrder() method implementation:

```
<script type="text/javascript">
    var orderHandler = {
      sendEmail: function() {

      },
      handleOrder: function() {

          this.sendEmail();

      }
    };
</script>
```

That's it! If you run the specs, they will succeed.

Information   There are many other Jasmine methods that are related to mocking. Here is a short list of them:

- toHaveBeenCalled()

- toHaveBeenCalledTimes()

- toHaveBeenCalledWith()

- .calls.any()

- `.calls.count()`
- `.calls.argsFor()`
- `.calls.allArgs()`
- `.calls.all()`
- `.calls.mostRecent()`
- `.calls.first()`
- `.calls.reset()`

Stubbing and Mocking As Testing Tools

Stubbing and mocking are very interesting tools in your testing toolbox. They need some advanced expertise to be mastered. They need also to be applied carefully. They both belong to the white-box testing methods, because the testing code tests against the actual implementation code, that is, the implementation code is visible, inside a white transparent box, and the tester/test can see it. White-box testing tools are vulnerable to change whenever the implementation they are testing changes. Hence, you should use them only when absolutely necessary.

Task Details

1. With mocking, you need to implement a spec runner in a JS Bin that would work like the following (Figure 2-11).

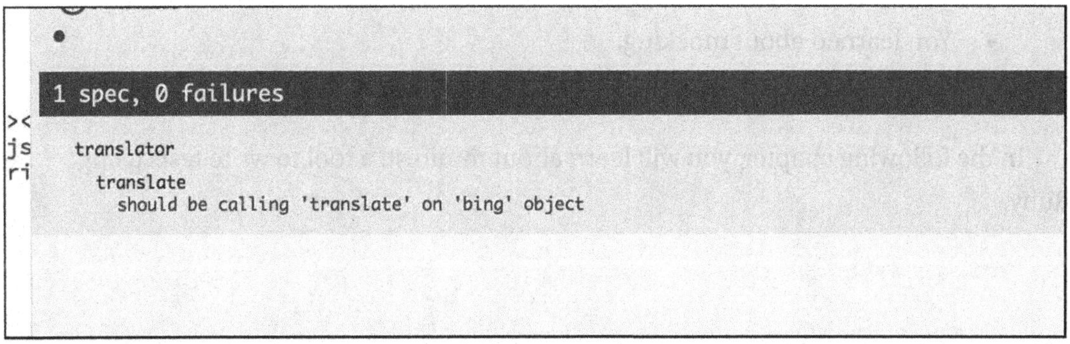

```
1 spec, 0 failures

    translator
        translate
            should be calling 'translate' on 'bing' object
```

Figure 2-11. *Task 1 – Mocking*

2. As you can derive from the preceding picture

- Your specs are mocking on the method `translate` of the object `translator`. The `translate` method takes a string argument.

- Your mock says that the `translate` method of the `translator` object would be calling the `translate` method on another object, the `bing` object.

- Note that the `bing.translate` method takes a string argument and returns another random string. But what it returns is irrelevant to this task.

- You will need to make sure that mocking is verifying that the `bing.translate` method is called with the correct argument. See `.toHaveBeenCalledWith()` in the Jasmine documentation.

3. Here are some hints to help you implement this task:

1. You will need a `bing` object with a `translate` method that takes as input a string argument.

2. You will need the `translator` object with another method `translate`. This takes a string argument too.

3. Since you are doing mocking, you will definitely need the help of `.and.callThrough()`.

Key Takeaways

- You learned about stubbing.

- You learned about mocking.

- You learned how to use these tools with Jasmine.

In the following chapter, you will learn about minitest, a tool to write tests using Ruby.

CHAPTER 3

Using Minitest

In this chapter, I am introducing you to the world of Test-Driven Development (TDD) using a popular tool called minitest (Figure 3-1). You have already studied TDD in the JavaScript world, in the two previous chapters. However, from now on, you will be living in the Ruby ecosystem. This chapter will be your foundation to better understanding the next tools that you will deal with, in the following chapters.

Figure 3-1. *Minitest*

Learning Goals

1. Learn about minitest API.

2. Learn about Test-Driven Development.

3. Learn how to write a test class in minitest.

4. Learn how to write test cases in minitest.

5. Learn how to run a single test file.

© Panos Matsinopoulos 2020
P. Matsinopoulos, *Practical Test Automation*, https://doi.org/10.1007/978-1-4842-6141-5_3

6. Learn how to run a single test.

7. Learn how to identify the errors from the failures.

8. Learn about the refactoring process.

9. Learn about the random order of test execution.

10. Learn how to have many files inside your test suite.

11. Learn how to integrate rake.

12. Learn how to load all the files of your application before starting a test.

13. Learn how to integrate minitest with RubyMine.

Introduction

You start your trip to test automation with one very popular family of test libraries, the `minitest`. The minitest is coming as a gem that you can include in your project.

Let's start with an example.

First Unit Test

Let's start a new project in RubyMine.

RubyMine   I use RubyMine to write my Ruby projects. It is the most advanced IDE to write your Ruby and Ruby on Rails projects. Try it out; it will boost your productivity to the sky.

Let's call it `string_combiner`. Make sure it is using any Ruby 2.x. Create the necessary file `.ruby-version` at the root folder of your project.

Tip   I use rbenv to install and manage the different versions of Ruby my Ruby projects use.

Also, add the `Gemfile` with the following content (Listing 3-1).

Listing 3-1. Gemfile

```
# File: Gemfile
#
source 'https://rubygems.org'

gem 'minitest'
```

Make sure that you have a bundler gem installed and run `bundle`. This will install the minitest gem:

```
$ bundle
Fetching gem metadata from https://rubygems.org/............
Resolving dependencies...
Installing minitest 5.14.0
Using bundler 2.1.4
Bundle complete! 1 Gemfile dependency, 2 gems now installed.
Use `bundle info [gemname]` to see where a bundled gem is installed.
$
```

TDD: Test-Driven Development

Having the test library installed, you will now follow the TDD approach to develop a class that will combine two strings into one. TDD means to first write the test and then implement the code that satisfies the test requirements.

Let's create the `test` folder that will contain our tests:

```
$ mkdir test
```

Verify That You Can Run the Test Suite

Inside the `test` folder, let's create the first test file. Let's name it `test_string_combiner.rb` and have the following content (Listing 3-2).

Listing 3-2. test_string_combiner.rb Initial Content

```ruby
# File: test_string_combiner.rb
#
require 'minitest/autorun'

class TestStringCombiner < Minitest::Test
  def test_foo
    assert_equal true, false
  end
end
```

Things that you need to pay attention to are as follows:

1. Your test file needs to require a minitest/autorun file.

2. There is a class that contains your tests. This class needs to derive from Minitest::Test.

3. The test class is usually named with the prefix Test, and the class under test follows. So now that you want to write a test for the class StringCombiner, you name your test class TestStringCombiner.

4. The tests themselves are public methods whose names start with the prefix test_.

In the preceding example, you call the minitest method assert_equal, which takes at least two arguments that need to be equal; otherwise, it will raise an error, and the test will fail.

Let's run the test suite for this file (run it from the root folder of your project):

```
$ bundle exec ruby test/test_string_combiner.rb
Run options: --seed 21807

# Running:

F

Finished in 0.001140s, 877.5602 runs/s, 877.5602 assertions/s.

  1) Failure:
TestStringCombiner#test_foo [test/test_string_combiner.rb:7]:
```

```
Expected: true
  Actual: false
```

```
1 runs, 1 assertions, 1 failures, 0 errors, 0 skips
```

The test run was executed without any problem, but your test suite has one test that failed. You can see

1. The test that failed

2. The line on which the test failed: [test/test_string_combiner.rb:7]

3. What value was expected

4. What value was returned

And now let's correct the assertion because it was incorrectly written on purpose. The file test/test_string_combiner.rb needs to be like Listing 3-3.

Listing 3-3. Update test_string_combiner.rb

```
# File: test_string_combiner.rb
#
require 'minitest/autorun'

class TestStringCombiner < Minitest::Test
  def test_foo
    assert_equal true, true
  end
end
```

And if you run it again, you will see that all tests succeed:

```
$ bundle exec ruby test/test_string_combiner.rb
Run options: --seed 53692
```

```
# Running:
```

.

```
Finished in 0.000928s, 1077.5549 runs/s, 1077.5549 assertions/s.

1 runs, 1 assertions, 0 failures, 0 errors, 0 skips
$
```

Perfect!

Test Real Requirements

Now that you know that the test suite runs without problem, let's try to write some real requirements in the form of tests for the StringCombiner class. The following is the new version of the file test_string_combiner.rb (Listing 3-4).

Listing 3-4. Real Requirements

```ruby
# File: test_string_combiner.rb
#
require 'minitest/autorun'

class TestStringCombiner < Minitest::Test
  def test_combines_two_strings
    string1 = 'foo'
    string2 = 'bar'
    string_combiner = StringCombiner.new(string1, string2)

    # fire
    assert_equal 'fboaor', string_combiner.combine
  end
end
```

You can see that

1. It has a method, test_combines_two_strings, that demonstrates how the StringCombiner object should work.

2. It first prepares the test data (lines 7-9).

3. It then fires the test method under test.

Red Light

If you run this, it will fail:

```
$ bundle exec ruby test/test_string_combiner.rb
Run options: --seed 51206

# Running:

E

Finished in 0.001031s, 970.0986 runs/s, 0.0000 assertions/s.

  1) Error:
TestStringCombiner#test_combines_two_strings:
NameError: uninitialized constant TestStringCombiner::StringCombiner
    test/test_string_combiner.rb:9:in `test_combines_two_strings'

1 runs, 0 assertions, 0 failures, 1 errors, 0 skips
$
```

The error `NameError: uninitialized constant TestStringCombiner::String Combiner` is very clear. On line 9, you have `StringCombiner`. It is a constant, and Ruby tries to resolve it within the TestStringCombiner class. But it does not exist. This should be your production code that is under test.

Let's create it. Inside the root folder of your project, create the file `string_combiner.rb` and define that class (Listing 3-5).

Listing 3-5. string_combiner.rb First Version

```
# File: string_combiner.rb
#
class StringCombiner
end
```

Then try to run the test again. You will get the same error. So, although you have created the class `StringCombiner`, the test cannot find it. But this is normal. The `string_combiner.rb` file needs to be required so that the constant is found.

Update the test_string_combiner.rb file to require the file. Add the line require_
relative '../string_combiner' below the existing require command, and try to run
the test again:

```
$ bundle exec ruby test/test_string_combiner.rb
Run options: --seed 40013

# Running:

E

Finished in 0.000982s, 1018.4668 runs/s, 0.0000 assertions/s.

  1) Error:
TestStringCombiner#test_combines_two_strings:
ArgumentError: wrong number of arguments (2 for 0)
    test/test_string_combiner.rb:10:in `initialize'
    test/test_string_combiner.rb:10:in `new'
    test/test_string_combiner.rb:10:in `test_combines_two_strings'

1 runs, 0 assertions, 0 failures, 1 errors, 0 skips
$
```

Things are getting better. You just got rid of the error that had to do with the
name StringCombiner. Now, the error is again on line 10 where you initialize the
StringCombiner by using two arguments instead of zero.

Since you are in TDD mode and the test is telling you that the StringCombiner class
needs to be initialized using two arguments, you are going to do that. The following is the
new version of the string_combiner.rb file (Listing 3-6).

Listing 3-6. New Version of string_combiner.rb

```
# File: string_combiner.rb
#
class StringCombiner
  def initialize(string1, string2)
  end
end
```

You have added the correct initializer. Now, let's try to run the test again:

```
$ bundle exec ruby test/test_string_combiner.rb
Run options: --seed 34366

# Running:

E

Finished in 0.000933s, 1071.7689 runs/s, 0.0000 assertions/s.

  1) Error:
TestStringCombiner#test_combines_two_strings:
NoMethodError: undefined method `combine' for #<StringCombiner:0x007fca49ac
ac40>
    test/test_string_combiner.rb:13:in `test_combines_two_strings'

1 runs, 0 assertions, 0 failures, 1 errors, 0 skips
$
```

A new error this time is telling you that the method combine is not something that the object of class StringCombiner responds to.

Cool! That was expected! Remember…you are doing TDD.

Let's add the method. The following is the new version of the file string_combiner.rb (Listing 3-7).

Listing 3-7. Updated string_combiner.rb

```
# File: string_combiner.rb
#
class StringCombiner
  def initialize(string1, string2)
  end

  def combine
  end
end
```

Let's now run the test again:

```
$ bundle exec ruby test/test_string_combiner.rb
Run options: --seed 9827

# Running:

F

Finished in 0.001069s, 935.4047 runs/s, 935.4047 assertions/s.

  1) Failure:
TestStringCombiner#test_combines_two_strings [test/test_string_combiner.
rb:13]:
Expected: "fboaor"
  Actual: nil

1 runs, 1 assertions, 1 failures, 0 errors, 0 skips
$
```

Now, you don't have errors. You have a failing test. It is clearly mentioning that the assertion failed on line 13. The result of the call to `string_combiner.combine` was `nil`, when it should have been `fboaor`.

So you need to change the implementation of the `combine` method to carry out the correct work. Let's do that. The following is the new version of the `string_combiner.rb` file (Listing 3-8).

Listing 3-8. First combine Method Implementation

```
# File: string_combiner.rb
#
class StringCombiner
  def initialize(string1, string2)
  end

  def combine
    'fboaor'
  end
end
```

If you run this, you will see that your test is now green, that is, it is running successfully:

```
$ bundle exec ruby test/test_string_combiner.rb
Run options: --seed 23160

# Running:

.

Finished in 0.000996s, 1004.3761 runs/s, 1004.3761 assertions/s.

1 runs, 1 assertions, 0 failures, 0 errors, 0 skips
$
```

Bingo! Your project is ready. Let's ship it to the QA (Quality Assurance) team to approve it.

Without any doubt, this implementation will not pass any QA check. The test that you have written is quite poor and does not make anyone confident that the implementation would work for any combination of strings.

Make the Test Better

You can put one more test in the test suite that will prove that your code is not well implemented.

Let's do that. See the following version of test/test_string_combiner.rb (Listing 3-9).

Listing 3-9. Add One More Test

```
# File: test_string_combiner.rb
#
require 'minitest/autorun'
require_relative '../string_combiner'

class TestStringCombiner < Minitest::Test
  def test_combines_two_strings
    string1 = 'foo'
    string2 = 'bar'
```

```ruby
    string_combiner = StringCombiner.new(string1, string2)

    # fire
    assert_equal 'fboaor', string_combiner.combine
  end

  def test_combines_two_string_case_2
    string1 = 'john'
    string2 = 'woo'
    string_combiner = StringCombiner.new(string1, string2)

    # fire
    assert_equal 'jwoohon', string_combiner.combine
  end
end
```

If you run your tests again, you will see that the new test will fail:

```
$ bundle exec ruby test/test_string_combiner.rb
Run options: --seed 29200

# Running:

F.

Finished in 0.000979s, 2042.4837 runs/s, 2042.4837 assertions/s.

  1) Failure:
TestStringCombiner#test_combines_two_string_case_2 [test/test_string_
combiner.rb:22]:
Expected: "jwoohon"
  Actual: "fboaor"

2 runs, 2 assertions, 1 failures, 0 errors, 0 skips
$
```

It is obvious that, first, you have to improve the test strategy for this particular problem. Let's see a version of test/test_string_combiner.rb that has more test cases (Listing 3-10).

Listing 3-10. More Test Cases

```ruby
# File: test_string_combiner.rb
#
require 'minitest/autorun'
require_relative '../string_combiner'

class TestStringCombiner < Minitest::Test
  def test_combines_two_strings_with_equal_length
    string1 = 'foo'
    string2 = 'bar'
    string_combiner = StringCombiner.new(string1, string2)

    # fire
    assert_equal 'fboaor', string_combiner.combine
  end

  def test_combines_two_strings_first_string_longer_than_second
    string1 = 'jonathan'
    string2 = 'woo'
    string_combiner = StringCombiner.new(string1, string2)

    # fire
    assert_equal 'jwoonoathan', string_combiner.combine
  end

  def test_combines_two_strings_first_string_shorter_than_second
    string1 = 'maria'
    string2 = 'jonathan'
    string_combiner = StringCombiner.new(string1, string2)

    # fire
    assert_equal 'mjaorniaathan', string_combiner.combine
  end

  def test_combines_two_strings_first_is_blank
    string1 = ''
    string2 = 'maria'
    string_combiner = StringCombiner.new(string1, string2)
```

```ruby
    # fire
    assert_equal 'maria', string_combiner.combine
  end

  def test_combines_two_strings_second_is_blank
    string1 = 'john'
    string2 = ''
    string_combiner = StringCombiner.new(string1, string2)

    # fire
    assert_equal 'john', string_combiner.combine
  end

  def test_combines_two_strings_first_is_nil
    string1 = nil
    string2 = 'maria'
    string_combiner = StringCombiner.new(string1, string2)

    # fire
    assert_equal 'maria', string_combiner.combine
  end

  def test_combines_two_strings_second_is_nill
    string1 = 'john'
    string2 = nil
    string_combiner = StringCombiner.new(string1, string2)

    # fire
    assert_equal 'john', string_combiner.combine
  end

  def test_combines_two_strings_both_are_nil
    string1 = nil
    string2 = nil
    string_combiner = StringCombiner.new(string1, string2)

    # fire
    assert_equal nil, string_combiner.combine
  end
```

```ruby
def test_combines_two_strings_general_case
  string1 = ('a'..'z').to_a.sample(rand(100)).join
  string2 = ('a'..'z').to_a.sample(rand(100)).join
  string_combiner = StringCombiner.new(string1, string2)

  # fire
  expected_result = ''
  # first take the chars from the first string and interpolate the chars
  of the second.
  string1.split('').each_with_index do |char, index|
    expected_result = "#{expected_result}#{char}#{string2[index]}"
  end
  # if the second string is longer than the first, then we have some
  second string chars that we have to amend.
  # Note that given a string "x", the "x[-5..-1]", for example, takes the
  last 5 chars of the string.
  if string2.length > string1.length
    expected_result = "#{expected_result}#{string2[-(string2.length -
    string1.length)..-1]}"
  end

  assert_equal expected_result, string_combiner.combine
  end
end
```

The preceding test set includes examples of all the case types that you need to cover: the first string longer than the second, the other way around, nil strings, blank strings, and so on. It also has a very general case, with random strings with length up to 99 characters.

It really seems a much better test coverage than the original one.

Let's run the tests again:

```
Run options: --seed 4718

# Running:

FFFUse assert_nil if expecting nil from test/test_string_combiner.rb:77:in
`test_combines_two_strings_both_are_nil'. This will fail in MT6.
```

.FFFFF

Finished in 0.010968s, 820.5367 runs/s, 820.5367 assertions/s.

  1) Failure:
TestStringCombiner#test_combines_two_strings_with_equal_length [test/test_
string_combiner.rb:13]:
Expected: "fboaor"
  Actual: nil

  2) Failure:
TestStringCombiner#test_combines_two_strings_second_is_blank [test/test_
string_combiner.rb:50]:
Expected: "john"
  Actual: nil

  3) Failure:
TestStringCombiner#test_combines_two_strings_general_case [test/test_
string_combiner.rb:97]:
--- expected
+++ actual
@@ -1 +1 @@
-"pnkmfieerdvsuogljjtwoayzxtlqakbumgvbxfychrp"
+nil

  4) Failure:
TestStringCombiner#test_combines_two_strings_first_string_longer_than_
second [test/test_string_combiner.rb:22]:
Expected: "jwoonoathan"
  Actual: nil

  5) Failure:
TestStringCombiner#test_combines_two_strings_second_is_nill [test/test_
string_combiner.rb:68]:
Expected: "john"
  Actual: nil

```
  6) Failure:
TestStringCombiner#test_combines_two_strings_first_string_shorter_than_
second [test/test_string_combiner.rb:31]:
Expected: "mjaorniaathan"
  Actual: nil

  7) Failure:
TestStringCombiner#test_combines_two_strings_first_is_nil [test/test_
string_combiner.rb:59]:
Expected: "maria"
  Actual: nil

  8) Failure:
TestStringCombiner#test_combines_two_strings_first_is_blank [test/test_
string_combiner.rb:40]:
Expected: "maria"
  Actual: nil

9 runs, 9 assertions, 8 failures, 0 errors, 0 skips
```

As you can see, only one test succeeded – the first one. This is expected. You didn't change anything in the implementation of the StringCombiner in any way.

Make Them Green

Having written all the test cases that you want to cover, you can then proceed into the implementation of StringCombiner that will make your test cases go green. Here is the version of the string_combiner.rb file that does that (Listing 3-11).

Listing 3-11. Version That Satisfies Tests

```
# File: string_combiner.rb
#
class StringCombiner
  def initialize(string1, string2)
    @string1, @string2 = string1, string2
  end
```

```
def combine
  result = ''
  # first take the chars from the first string and interpolate the chars
  of the second.
  string1.split('').each_with_index do |char, index|
    result = "#{result}#{char}#{string2[index]}"
  end
  if string2.length > string1.length
    result = "#{result}#{string2[-(string2.length - string1.
    length)..-1]}"
  end
  result
  end

  private

  attr_reader :string1, :string2
end
```

The new version of StringCombiner

(1)   Stores the initialization strings into instance variables

(2)   Has an implementation of the #combine method that combines
      the two strings, hopefully giving correct results. Tests will prove
      that.

Let's run the tests again:

```
$ bundle exec ruby test/test_string_combiner.rb
Run options: --seed 21146

# Running:

E.E...E..

Finished in 0.001433s, 6279.8292 runs/s, 4186.5528 assertions/s.

  1) Error:
TestStringCombiner#test_combines_two_strings_first_is_nil:
NoMethodError: undefined method `split' for nil:NilClass
```

```
/Users/...string_combiner.rb:11:in `combine'
test/test_string_combiner.rb:59:in `test_combines_two_strings_first_is_nil'
```

2) Error:
TestStringCombiner#test_combines_two_strings_second_is_nill:
NoMethodError: undefined method `[]' for nil:NilClass
```
    /Users/...string_combiner.rb:12:in `block in combine'
    /Users/...string_combiner.rb:11:in `each'
    /Users/...string_combiner.rb:11:in `each_with_index'
    /Users/...string_combiner.rb:11:in `combine'
    test/test_string_combiner.rb:68:in `test_combines_two_strings_second_
    is_nill'
```

3) Error:
TestStringCombiner#test_combines_two_strings_both_are_nil:
NoMethodError: undefined method `split' for nil:NilClass
```
    /Users/...string_combiner.rb:11:in `combine'
    test/test_string_combiner.rb:77:in `test_combines_two_strings_both_are_nil'
```

9 runs, 6 assertions, 0 failures, 3 errors, 0 skips
$

As you can read on the last line of the output, you had six successful tests and three errors. Note that these are not failures. These are errors. Error is when the test fails with a runtime error, but not with an assertion error. Failure is when the test runs successfully, but its assertion fails.

Let's see the first error:

1) Error:
TestStringCombiner#test_combines_two_strings_first_is_nil:
NoMethodError: undefined method `split' for nil:NilClass
```
    /Users/...string_combiner.rb:11:in `combine'
    test/test_string_combiner.rb:59:in `test_combines_two_strings_first_is_nil'
```

You are trying to call a split method on something that is nil. This happens on line 11 of the string_combiner.rb file:

```
string1.split('')
```

Also, the test that is failing is the test_combines_two_strings_first_is_nil.

I guess that it is easy for you to figure out why the test is failing. It is because the first string is nil and calling the split on it raises the NoMethodError. Hence, our string_combiner.rb needs to cater for nil value for string inputs.

Let's improve the StringCombiner#combine implementation with a line return string2 if string1.nil? at the top of its body:

```
def combine
  return string2 if string1.nil?

  ...
```

This tells the combine method to return the second string, if the first string is nil.

Let's run the tests again:

```
$ bundle exec ruby test/test_string_combiner.rb
Run options: --seed 28772

# Running:

.EUse assert_nil if expecting nil from test/test_string_combiner.rb:77:in
`test_combines_two_strings_both_are_nil'. This will fail in MT6.
.......

Finished in 0.001320s, 6820.0108 runs/s, 6062.2318 assertions/s.

  1) Error:
TestStringCombiner#test_combines_two_strings_second_is_nill:
NoMethodError: undefined method `[]' for nil:NilClass
    /Users/...string_combiner.rb:14:in `block in combine'
    /Users/...string_combiner.rb:13:in `each'
    /Users/...string_combiner.rb:13:in `each_with_index'
    /Users/...string_combiner.rb:13:in `combine'
    test/test_string_combiner.rb:68:in `test_combines_two_strings_second_
    is_nill'

9 runs, 8 assertions, 0 failures, 1 errors, 0 skips
$
```

Better. You now have only one error and eight tests that are green. Let's see how you can fix the error left. The error is again NoMethodError. You are trying to call [ ], that is, the array or hash access operator on something that is nil. The line that is failing is line 14:

```
result = "#{result}#{char}#{string2[index]}"
```

Reading the error message and the line at error carefully, it seems that string2 is nil when this line of code is being executed. The test that is failing is TestStringCombiner#test_combines_two_strings_second_is_nill: which confirms that string2 is indeed nil.

Let's enhance our #combine method to cater for that too:

```
def combine
  return string2 if string1.nil?
  return string1 if string2.nil?

  ...
```

Now, we are returning string1 (which is not nil) if string2 is nil.

Let's run the tests again:

```
$ bundle exec ruby test/test_string_combiner.rb
Run options: --seed 36495

# Running:

DEPRECATED: Use assert_nil if expecting nil from test/test_string_combiner.
rb:77. This will fail in Minitest 6.
.........

Finished in 0.001316s, 6841.4168 runs/s, 6841.4168 assertions/s.

9 runs, 9 assertions, 0 failures, 0 errors, 0 skips
$
```

Bingo! All of your nine tests have run successfully. With the existing test coverage, you are pretty confident that your implementation satisfies the functional requirements exactly as they are specified inside the test suite.

assert_nil

You may have noticed the warning that you are getting when you run your tests:

```
DEPRECATED: Use assert_nil if expecting nil from test/test_string_combiner.
rb:77. This will fail in Minitest 6.
```

It is telling you that you should be using the method assert_nil whenever you want to compare a value against nil. Also, it is telling you which test you have to correct. This is the test test_combines_two_strings_both_are_nil. Line 77 of test/test_string_combiner.rb is

```
assert_equal nil, string_combiner.combine
```

Let's do that. The new version should have

```
assert_nil string_combiner.combine
```

on line 77.

And let's run the tests again:

```
$ bundle exec ruby test/test_string_combiner.rb
Run options: --seed 60984

# Running:

.........

Finished in 0.001388s, 6484.2853 runs/s, 6484.2853 assertions/s.

9 runs, 9 assertions, 0 failures, 0 errors, 0 skips
$
```

Perfect! No warning anymore. Remember that assert_nil is there for you to assert that something is nil.

Refactor

Now that you have your test suite green, you can proceed with refactoring, the process that you use to make your implementation code cleaner or generally change your implementation code without changing its functionality. The functionality offered will be the same and specified precisely by your test suite. You will make changes to the implementation of the StringCombiner#combine method; but, for any change that you make, you will make sure that it continues to offer the same functionality and all the tests are running green.

The new, refactored implementation of the method #combine is shown in Listing 3-12.

Listing 3-12. New Refactored Implementation

```ruby
def combine
  return string2 if string1.nil?
  return string1 if string2.nil?

  # First interpolate the second string into the first.
  result = string1.
      split('').
        each_with_index.
        reduce('') {|result, (item, index)| result = "#{result}#{item}
        #{string2[index]}"}

  # If we have characters left, then append them to the result
  if string2.length > string1.length
    result = "#{result}#{string2[-(string2.length - string1.length)..-1]}"
  end

  result
end
```

This implementation uses the #reduce() method instead of iterating with #each. Otherwise, it is not different from the previous.

But as I said, the fact that you have good test coverage makes you very confident to proceed with changes in your code. You can now run the tests again and check whether you have broken anything:

```
$ bundle exec ruby test/test_string_combiner.rb
Run options: --seed 46505
```

```
# Running:

Finished in 0.001317s, 6831.1403 runs/s, 6831.1403 assertions/s.

9 runs, 9 assertions, 0 failures, 0 errors, 0 skips
$
```

As you can see, everything is still green, passing.

Running a Single Test

Sometimes you may want to run a single test from your test suite. How can you do that?

You use the option --name followed by the method name that corresponds to the test that you want to run. For example, let's suppose that you want to run the test on line 25, which is the method with the name test_combines_two_strings_first_string_ shorter_than_second. This is how you can run this particular test only:

```
$ bundle exec ruby test/test_string_combiner.rb --name test_combines_two_
strings_first_string_shorter_than_second
Run options: --name test_combines_two_strings_first_string_shorter_than_
second --seed 18437

# Running:

.

Finished in 0.000915s, 1093.0144 runs/s, 1093.0144 assertions/s.

1 runs, 1 assertions, 0 failures, 0 errors, 0 skips
$
```

As you can see from the output, the runner executed only one test, the one that you have specified on the command line with the option –name.

seed

You may have noticed the lines Run options: --seed XXXXX that are printed at the start of each test suite run. This is a feature that minitest offers that picks up your tests and runs them in random order. So, every time you run your tests, they are not executed in the same order. This is actually very good. Your tests should be independent to each other. Each test should be isolated and should succeed no matter what was the test that ran before it.

If your tests have execution interdependencies and a test might fail if a specific test runs before it, either exactly before or not, but succeeds when run alone, then, this random order of execution of the whole test suite will finally reveal this interdependence problem, maybe not on the first or second run, but at a run in the multiple runs of your test suite.

When your test suite has a failing test that is not failing if this test runs alone, then you can use the seed number that the test suite prints at the start of the execution and run the tests in the same (failing) order again and again until you find out the reason why your test is failing.

This is how you can start the test/test_string_combiner.rb using the seed 46505, for example, a seed from a previous run:

```
$ bundle exec ruby test/test_string_combiner.rb --seed 46505
Run options: --seed 46505

# Running:

.........

Finished in 0.001095s, 8218.8553 runs/s, 8218.8553 assertions/s.

9 runs, 9 assertions, 0 failures, 0 errors, 0 skips
$
```

You can see that giving the --seed 46505, you have asked minitest to run the test suite with the execution order that corresponds to that number.

Multiple Files

Usually, you don't put all of your tests inside a single file. You break the unit tests into one file per class tested. Let's see an example of that. Let's suppose that you want another class in your project called Customer. You will put its functional requirements inside the file test/test_customer.rb. The file and its functional requirements are shown in Listing 3-13.

Remember, you are doing TDD, Test-Driven Development. So you first write the requirements in the form of tests, and then you write the implementation that satisfies these requirements.

Listing 3-13. Tests for the Customer class

```ruby
# File: test/test_customer.rb
#
require 'minitest/autorun'

class TestCustomer < Minitest::Test
  def test_has_public_first_name
    customer = Customer.new('John', 'Papas')

    assert_equal 'John', customer.first_name
  end

  def test_has_public_last_name
    customer = Customer.new('John', 'Papas')

    assert_equal 'Papas', customer.last_name
  end

  def test_has_public_name_combining_first_and_last_name
    customer = Customer.new('John', 'Papas')

    assert_equal 'John Papas', customer.name
  end
end
```

You now understand how easy it is to write the basic functional requirements, the unit tests for your class Customer. You have written three tests that have to do with the first name, last name, and full name of the customer. That's a good start, and let's run the tests for the particular file:

```
$ bundle exec ruby test/test_customer.rb
Run options: --seed 17242

# Running:

EEE
```

Finished in 0.000952s, 3149.9006 runs/s, 0.0000 assertions/s.

```
  1) Error:
TestCustomer#test_has_public_name_combining_first_and_last_name:
NameError: uninitialized constant TestCustomer::Customer
    test/test_customer.rb:19:in `test_has_public_name_combining_first_and_
    last_name'

  2) Error:
TestCustomer#test_has_public_last_name:
NameError: uninitialized constant TestCustomer::Customer
    test/test_customer.rb:13:in `test_has_public_last_name'

  3) Error:
TestCustomer#test_has_public_first_name:
NameError: uninitialized constant TestCustomer::Customer
    test/test_customer.rb:7:in `test_has_public_first_name'

3 runs, 0 assertions, 0 failures, 3 errors, 0 skips
$
```

You can see that you have three errors. This is because the Customer class has not been defined. Let's define it and require it from the test file. Also, you will implement the class so that all tests are going green. Here is the customer.rb file (Listing 3-14).

Listing 3-14. customer.rb Content

```
# File: customer.rb
#
class Customer
  def initialize(first_name, last_name)
    @first_name, @last_name = first_name, last_name
  end

  def name
    "#{first_name} #{last_name}"
  end

  attr_reader :first_name, :last_name
end
```

Then make sure that your test/test_customer.rb file has the require_relative '../customer' line at the top:

```
# File: test/test_customer.rb
#
require 'minitest/autorun'
require_relative '../customer'
...
```

Run the tests again:

```
$ bundle exec ruby test/test_customer.rb
Run options: --seed 63265

# Running:

...

Finished in 0.001003s, 2991.5966 runs/s, 2991.5966 assertions/s.

3 runs, 3 assertions, 0 failures, 0 errors, 0 skips
$
```

Perfect! The tests that have to do with the Customer class are running green. What about the StringCombiner tests? Are they still green? Generally, after having finished with a set of unit tests, you usually want to run the whole test suite. How can you do that when you have multiple test files?

I guess that the first thing that might come to your mind is to create a single test/test_runner.rb file that would load all the test files that your suite has (Listing 3-15).

Listing 3-15. test_runner.rb Loads All Test Files

```
# File: test/test_runner.rb
#
load 'test/test_customer.rb'
load 'test/test_string_combiner.rb'
```

As you can see in the preceding code, the `test/test_runner.rb` file will load all the test files. So you only have to invoke that file with your ruby call:

```
$ bundle exec ruby test/test_runner.rb
Run options: --seed 64322

# Running:

............

Finished in 0.001574s, 7625.4675 runs/s, 7625.4675 assertions/s.

12 runs, 12 assertions, 0 failures, 0 errors, 0 skips
$
```

Perfect. 12 runs, 12 assertions – 9 from the `test/test_string_combiner.rb` file and 3 from the `test/test_customer.rb` file.

However, this has the minor caveat that you have to update this file every time you add a new test file. Can you avoid that?

Yes. Look at the following version of the `test/test_runner.rb` file (Listing 3-16).

Listing 3-16. New Version of the test/test_runner.rb File

```
# File: test/test_runner.rb
#
Dir.glob("test/**/test_*.rb").each do |file|
  load file unless file == 'test/test_runner.rb'
end
```

This one loads all the files inside the folder `test` and its subfolders. The files need to have filenames that start with the prefix `test_`. Also, it excludes, from loading, the `test/test_runner.rb` itself.

If you run this, you will see all the tests being run successfully again:

```
$ bundle exec ruby test/test_runner.rb
Run options: --seed 40052

# Running:

............
```

```
Finished in 0.001574s, 7625.4675 runs/s, 7625.4675 assertions/s.

12 runs, 12 assertions, 0 failures, 0 errors, 0 skips
$
```

Using rake

Alternatively, instead of having the test_runner.rb file, you can use rake and write a custom task that would do the job for you.

First, add the gem 'rake' inside your Gemfile (Listing 3-17).

Listing 3-17. Gemfile with rake

```
# File: Gemfile
#
source 'https://rubygems.org'

gem 'minitest'
gem 'rake'
```

and execute bundle to install rake:

```
$ bundle
Fetching gem metadata from https://rubygems.org/
Resolving dependencies...
Using rake 13.0.1
Using bundler 2.1.4
Using minitest 5.14.0
Bundle complete! 2 Gemfile dependencies, 3 gems now installed.
Use `bundle info [gemname]` to see where a bundled gem is installed.
$
```

Then, remove the file test/test_runner.rb, because you will not need it. And create the Rakefile with the following content (Listing 3-18).

Listing 3-18. Rakefile

```
# File: Rakefile
#

desc "Run all the test in your test folder"
task :test do
  Dir.glob("test/**/test_*.rb").each do |file|
    load file
  end
end

task default: :test
```

Now, run `bundle exec rake` on your project folder:

```
$ bundle exec rake
Run options: --seed 14731

# Running:

...........

Finished in 0.002176s, 5514.1560 runs/s, 5514.1560 assertions/s.

12 runs, 12 assertions, 0 failures, 0 errors, 0 skips
$
```

Perfect! `bundle exec rake` will load the whole test suite and run it.

Require All Files of Your Project

You can see that on each one of the test files, we are requiring the project file that the test is about to test. For example, the test file `test/test_string_combiner.rb` is requiring the file `string_combiner.rb` with the command `require_relative 'string_combiner'`. Or the file `test/test_customer.rb` will require the file `customer.rb` with the command `require_relative 'customer'`.

However, I believe that this is not a good practice, because when a test starts, the Ruby memory has not loaded all the files that comprise your application. So the context of loaded constants and classes is not the same as it will, probably, be at your production

93

environment. In your production environment, usually, you want all the classes loaded at boot-up of your application, before it starts doing the actual work.

Hence, in order to have your test suite match your production environment as much as possible, you might want to load all your project files before any test runs.

Let's try one technique that you can do that:

(1)   Let's require all the project files using an all.rb file like the following (Listing 3-19).

Listing 3-19. all.rb

```
# File: all.rb
#
require_relative 'customer'
require_relative 'string_combiner'
```

(2)   Then you create the file test/test_helper.rb that will require the all.rb and whatever other file your test files need (Listing 3-20).

Listing 3-20. test/test_helper.rb File

```
# File: test/test_helper.rb
#
require 'minitest/autorun'
require_relative '../all'
```

(3)   Update the Rakefile so that, first, it requires the test/test_ helper.rb file and then it excludes the test/test_helper.rb file from being loaded as a test file (Listing 3-21).

Listing 3-21. Rakefile requiring test_helper

```
# File: Rakefile
#

desc "Run all the test in your test folder"
task :test do
  require_relative 'test/test_helper'

  Dir.glob("test/**/test_*.rb").each do |file|
```

```
      load file unless file == 'test/test_helper.rb'
    end
  end

task default: :test
```

(4)   Then make sure you remove the require and require_relative statements from your test files.

(5)   Run the tests. You are ready!

```
$ bundle exec rake
Run options: --seed 39148

# Running:

............

Finished in 0.002229s, 5383.7975 runs/s, 5383.7975 assertions/s.

12 runs, 12 assertions, 0 failures, 0 errors, 0 skips
$
```

Now that you have done those changes, there is a problem in case you want to run a single test.

Try this command:

```
$ bundle exec ruby test/test_string_combiner.rb --name test_combines_two_
strings_first_string_shorter_than_second
```

You will get this error here:

```
Traceback (most recent call last):
test/test_string_combiner.rb:3:in `<main>': uninitialized constant Minitest
(NameError)
```

This is now due to the fact that you have removed the file requirements from the test files. Hence, the test/test_helper.rb is not required. How can we remedy this? You need to call ruby command with the option -I and the option -r. Here is how:

```
$ bundle exec ruby -I. -r test/test_helper test/test_string_combiner.rb
--name test_combines_two_strings_first_string_shorter_than_second
```

If you do that, then the tests will run successfully:

```
Run options: --name test_combines_two_strings_first_string_shorter_than_
second --seed 27061

# Running:

.

Finished in 0.000853s, 1172.3330 runs/s, 1172.3330 assertions/s.

1 runs, 1 assertions, 0 failures, 0 errors, 0 skips
```

The -I. tells ruby that there is one more path, the current path (. corresponds to the current path), to be added to the load path (i.e., to the $LOAD_PATH variable); and the -r <file> tells ruby which file to require before running the script that is given as the next argument.

RubyMine Integration

It's good to know how to run tests from the command line, but since you are using RubyMine, I will show you how RubyMine can easily integrate with minitest.

Let's create a RubyMine project for the string combiner project, like the following (Figure 3-2).

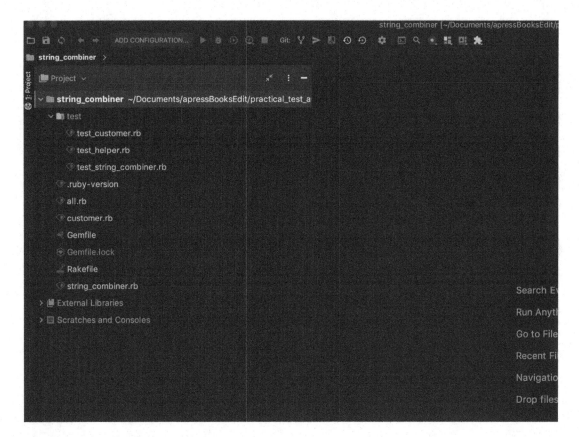

Figure 3-2. *RubyMine Project for String Combiner*

Then, right-click the project name and select Run ➤ All tests in string_combiner
(Figure 3-3).

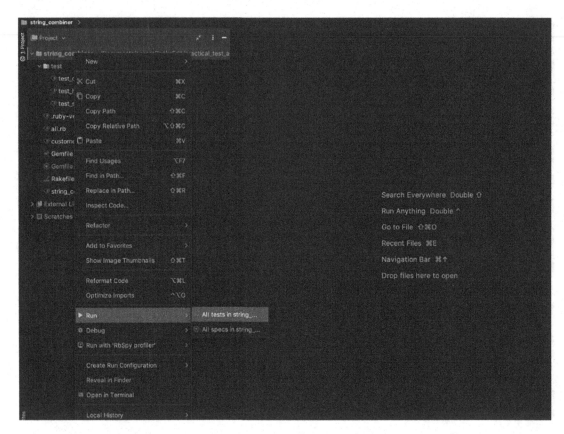

Figure 3-3. *Right-Click and Select Run ➤ All tests in string_combiner*

When you do that, you will probably have errors that would tell you that RubyMine was not able to run your tests, something like the following (Figure 3-4).

Figure 3-4. *RubyMine Cannot Run the Tests*

In order to make this succeed, you need to follow the next steps:

(1)   While having your project in RubyMine, select "Run ➤ Edit
      Configurations…" (Figure 3-5).

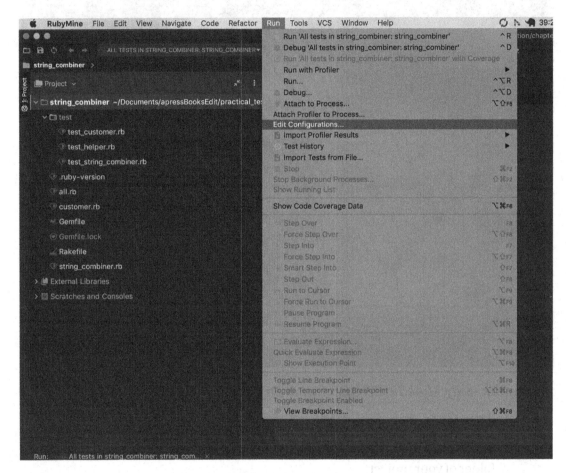

Figure 3-5. *Edit Project Run Configurations*

(2)   Then select "Templates" and "Test::Unit/Shoulda/Minitest"; make
      sure that the "Configuration" tab is selected and the Mode is "All
      tests in folder." You will have to fill in the "Working directory" and
      some extra "Ruby arguments" (Figure 3-6).

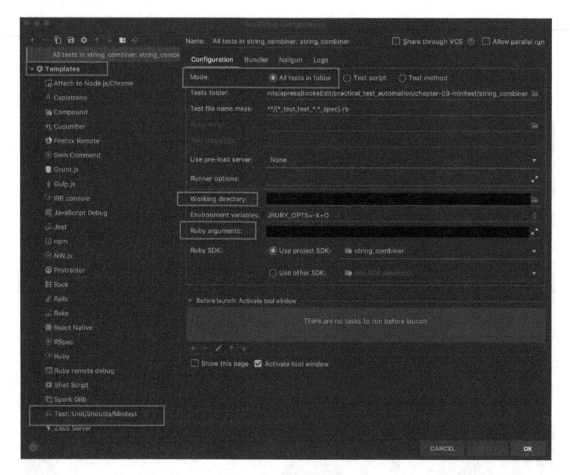

Figure 3-6. *RubyMine Test Configuration Defaults*

(3)   The "Working directory" needs to be filled in with the full path to
your "test" folder. Click the folder button and navigate to the "test"
folder of your project.

The Ruby arguments that you need to add are `-I. -r
'test_helper'`.

Hence, you need to have something like the following (Figure 3-7).

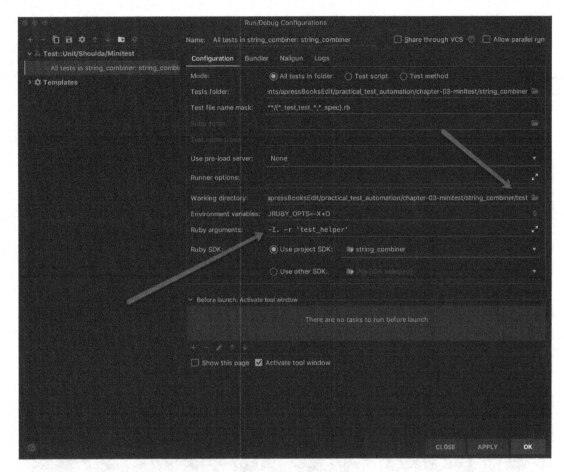

Figure 3-7. *Working Directory and Ruby Arguments*

(4)   Then you click OK, and you are ready to repeat your try to run your tests.

Right-click the project name and select Run ➤ All tests in string_combiner. Your tests should succeed (Figure 3-8).

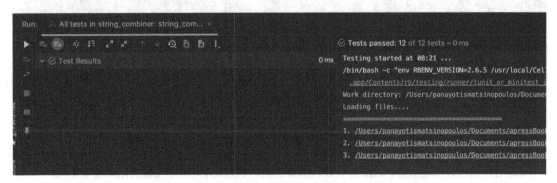

Figure 3-8. *RubyMine Ran Tests Successfully*

You can also run an individual file. Pick up one of the files that contain tests, and right-click. Then select "Run ➤ 'Run test...'."

Moreover, you can also run an individual test. In order to do that, you need to open the file with the tests in your editor area. Then you need to right-click inside the method body that corresponds to the test that you want to run, like the following (Figure 3-9).

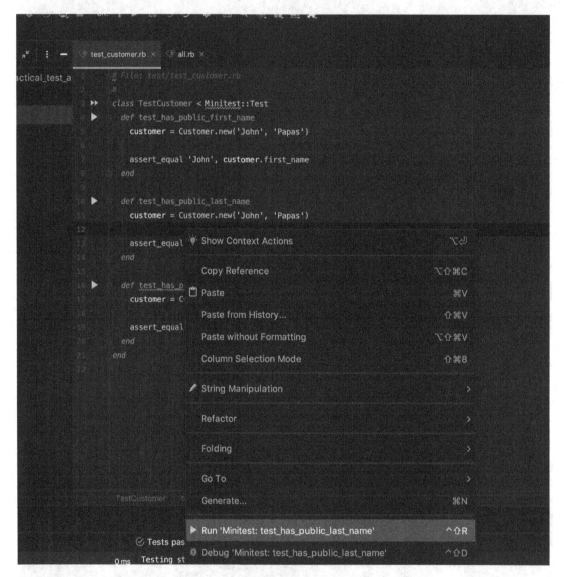

Figure 3-9. *Selecting to Run an Individual Test*

On the preceding screenshot, you can see that I have right-clicked inside the file `test/test_customer.rb`, in the body of the method `test_has_public_last_name`. And

I am about to select to run the individual test. If I do that, RubyMine will execute the particular test and will print the result at the bottom tab.

But how does RubyMine report back to you a test that is failing? Let's see that.

You will first change a test method implementation to make it fail. Go to file `test/test_customer.rb` and change the method implementation of the test `test_has_public_last_name` to be as follows:

```
def test_has_public_last_name
  customer = Customer.new('John', 'Papas')

  assert_equal 'Papas', customer.last_name.downcase
end
```

In other words, the original line

```
assert_equal 'Papas', customer.last_name
```

was changed to

```
assert_equal 'Papas', customer.last_name.downcase
```

Now, right-click your project and select to run all tests. When you do that, you will have the test `test_has_public_last_name` failing (Figure 3-10).

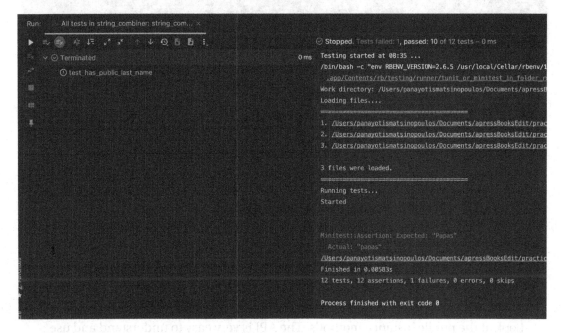

Figure 3-10. *RubyMine: One Test Has Failed*

RubyMine is displaying the line at which the failing test failed. You can click this line in order to quickly jump to the failing line of test code in the editor (Figure 3-11).

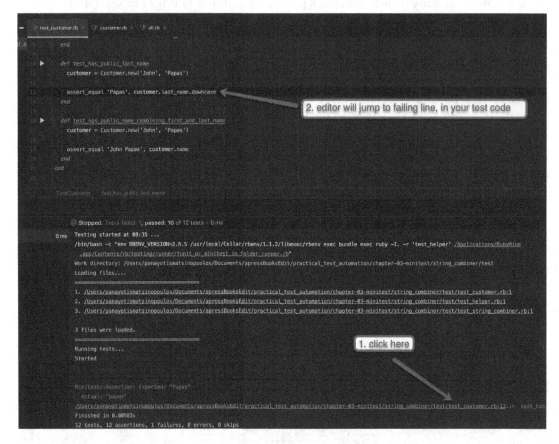

Figure 3-11. *Click to Jump to the Failing Test Line*

That was our first encounter with the RubyMine integration of minitest. Experiment with the keyboard shortcut and options if you want to improve your skills.

Minitest: Other Assert Commands

You have learned about the assert_equal and assert_nil commands that minitest offers to carry out assertions. These are very powerful, but minitest is not limited only to these two assertion commands.

All the minitest assertion methods can be found here: Minitest::Assertions.

Look at the public instance methods. The API is very easy to understand and use.

Task Details

WRITE TESTS USING MINITEST

You will need to write `minitest` tests for the following class (Listing 3-22).

Listing 3-22. Class to Write Tests For

```ruby
# File: sum_of_three.rb
#
class SumOfThree

  attr_accessor :array_of_integers

  def initialize(array_of_integers)
    @array_of_integers = array_of_integers
  end

  # Tries to find 3 integers that sum up to 0.
  # In other words given an array a, we want to find
  # the 3 integers that satisfy the equation:
  #
  #    a[i] + a[j] + a[k] == 0
  #
  # where i != j && i != k && j !=k
  #
  # The algorithm first sorts the input array, and then follows a clever
  algorithm that does not have to
  # use any search for pairs.
  #
  # This is the pseudo-algorithm
  #
  #   sort(array_of_integers);
  #
  #   for i = 0 to n - 3 do
  #     a = S[i];
  #     j = i+1;
  #     k = size_of_array - 1;
  #     while (j < k) do
```

```
#       b = S[j];
#       c = S[k];
#       if (a + b + c == 0) then
#         return a, b, c; # This is the happy case and we stop
#       else if (a + b + c > 0) then
#         k = k - 1; # In this case, the b + c is big enough and we need to
#         make it smaller. We know for sure that c is quite big
#                        # because it has been set as the value of the element
#                          that is on the far right, a.k.a. the biggest one.
#                        # So, let us try to use the previous element, which is
#                          smaller than c. Hence we will make the (b+c) factor
#                        # smaller and the (a + b + c) moving closer to 0.
#       else
#         j = j + 1; # In this case, the b + c is small enough so that the
#         (a + b + c) < 0. We need to increase b + c but
#                        # not so much to go over 0. We need to increase it a
#                          little bit. That's why we decide to pick up the
#                        # next biggest element, which is j + 1.
#       end
#     end
#   end
#
def find_three
  array_of_integers.sort!
  i = 0
  size_of_array = array_of_integers.size
  while i <= size_of_array - 3
    a = array_of_integers[i]
    j = i + 1
    k = size_of_array - 1

    while j < k
      b = array_of_integers[j]
      c = array_of_integers[k]
      sum = a + b + c
      if sum.zero?
        return [a, b, c]
```

```
        elsif sum.positive?
          k -= 1
        else
          j += 1
        end
      end

      i += 1
    end
    []
  end
end
```

As you can read from the comments, this class is initialized with an array of integers. Then one can call the instance method #find_three that returns back a subset of these integers. The subset is of size 3, that is, it contains three of the integers in the original array. The property of these three integers returned is that they sum up to 0:

1. Create a RubyMine project for that.

2. Write your tests using minitest.

3. Make sure that you use a test_helper.rb file.

4. Make sure that you use a Gemfile to install all the necessary gems.

5. Make sure that you can run your tests from the command line using the bundle exec rake command.

6. Write enough tests to make sure that your class works as expected.

7. Make sure that you cover the edge cases like empty array, array with less than three integers, and so on.

Key Takeaways

- Minitest API

- TDD with minitest

- Writing minitest test classes

- Running the whole test suite or an individual filename

- Refactoring your tests to improve implementation

- Using rake

- Integrating minitest with RubyMine

In the following chapter, you will be introduced to RSpec.

CHAPTER 4

Introduction to RSpec

RSpec advertises as being the tool that makes TDD (Test-Driven Development) and BDD (Behavior-Driven Development) fun. This is an introduction to RSpec (Figure 4-1) that will give you enough knowledge to write your first Ruby application and cover it with RSpec specifications – or, actually, since you are doing TDD, to first write the specifications and then implement the application. It is the foundation for the next chapters that deal with more advanced concepts of RSpec and testing in general.

Figure 4-1. *Introduction to RSpec*

Learning Goals

1. Learn about installing RSpec.

2. Learn about getting the version of RSpec installed.

3. Learn how to initialize your project to use RSpec.

© Panos Matsinopoulos 2020
P. Matsinopoulos, *Practical Test Automation*, https://doi.org/10.1007/978-1-4842-6141-5_4

4. Learn how the RSpec configuration is set up.

5. Learn about the structure of the files/folders related to RSpec.

6. Learn about the conversational pattern of RSpec.

7. Learn about the example groups.

8. Learn about the examples.

9. Learn about the Ruby blocks that are sent to `describe` and `it` methods.

10. Learn how to execute the RSpec suite.

11. Learn about the expectations.

12. Learn about the documentation formatter.

13. Learn how to follow the TDD workflow to develop your application.

14. Learn about the different phases of a test.

15. Learn about the exception that is raised when RSpec expectation fails.

16. Learn about hooks.

17. Learn about helper methods.

18. Learn about `let`.

19. Learn about memoization, when it is useful, and when it is tricky.

20. Learn how to use contexts.

21. Learn how to run a dry run of your specs.

22. Learn how to run specs in a specific file.

23. Learn how to run a specific example from a specific file.

24. Learn how RubyMine integrates with RSpec.

Introduction

You will first install RSpec. RSpec is coming in the form of four gems:

1. `rspec-support`

2. `rspec-core`

3. `rspec-expectations`

4. `rspec-mocks`

There is also the gem `rspec` that, when installed, installs all the other gems. And this is the gem that you are going to install here.

New Project

Let's create a new project, named `coffee_shop`. It needs to be a Ruby project with Ruby 2.x installed. Start that project in RubyMine. Moreover, make sure that you have the rbenv integration with the `.ruby-version` file specified having the version of the Ruby you are using. For example, my `.ruby-version` file, in the root folder of my project, has the content `2.6.5` (Figure 4-2).

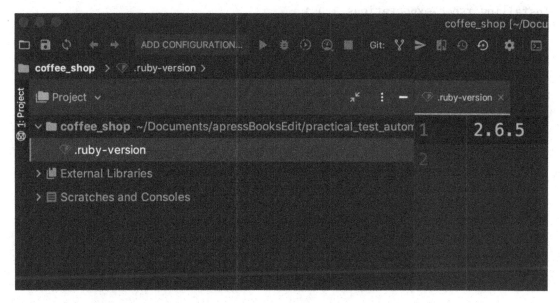

Figure 4-2. RubyMine coffee_shop Project with the .ruby-version File

Then create the file Gemfile with the following content (Listing 4-1).

Listing 4-1. Gemfile

```
# File: Gemfile
#
source 'https://rubygems.org'

gem 'rspec'
gem 'rake'
```

The preceding Gemfile specifies project dependencies on the rspec and rake gems. Let's do bundle to install them:

```
$ bundle
Fetching gem metadata from https://rubygems.org/..........
Resolving dependencies...
Using rake 13.0.1
Installing diff-lcs 1.3
Installing rspec-support 3.9.2
Using bundler 2.1.4
Installing rspec-core 3.9.1
Installing rspec-expectations 3.9.1
Installing rspec-mocks 3.9.1
Installing rspec 3.9.0
Bundle complete! 2 Gemfile dependencies, 8 gems now installed.
Use `bundle info [gemname]` to see where a bundled gem is installed.
$
```

Here is a screenshot of your project in RubyMine (Figure 4-3).

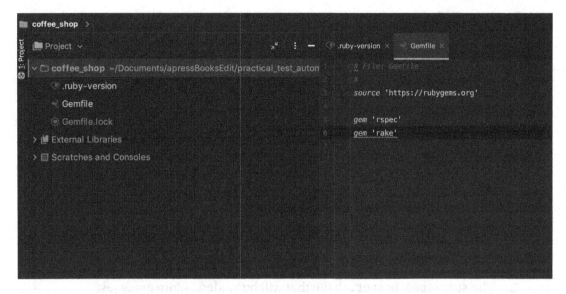

Figure 4-3. *Project in RubyMine*

rspec Version

Now that you have RSpec installed, you can invoke the main binary that is shipped with RSpec, the rspec, and get the version of RSpec installed as a confirmation that you have a proper installation. Run the following command:

```
$ bundle exec rspec --version
RSpec 3.9
  - rspec-core 3.9.1
  - rspec-expectations 3.9.1
  - rspec-mocks 3.9.1
  - rspec-support 3.9.2
$
```

You can see that the version of RSpec at the time of writing is 3.9. You may have a later version installed on your machine. But any version 3.x will do.

Initialize RSpec

Having installed the rspec gem, the next step that you have to do is to initialize your project in order to be ready to use RSpec. Run the following command:

```
$ bundle exec rspec --init
  create   .rspec
  create   spec/spec_helper.rb
$
```

The rspec --init command created two files:

1. The .rspec file that contains default running options for the command-line test runner

2. The spec/spec_helper.rb file that will be loaded before every test run session, thanks to the --require spec_helper line that exists inside the .rspec file

RSpec Configuration

The spec/spec_helper.rb file initially contains a call to the RSpec.configure method that is used to configure the RSpec behavior. RSpec comes with some sensible defaults, and if you read the comments in the spec/spec_helper.rb file, you can switch on/off anything that you feel like doing so.

My recommendation, to start with, is to switch on the random execution of the tests (as you had with minitest). Hence, please, make sure that

```
config.order = :random
Kernel.srand config.seed
```

are not commented out.

And another recommendation is to disable monkey patching. Make sure that the following line is not commented out:

```
config.disable_monkey_patching!
```

Ruby Comments   Please, remember that the lines between =begin and =end
are considered comments and not actual Ruby statements.

Here, I give you the contents of the spec/spec_helper.rb file as it has to be, after
having applied the changes that I have recommended in the preceding text (Listing 4-2).

Listing 4-2.   spec/spec_helper.rb with RSpec Recommended Configuration

```
# This file was generated by the `rspec --init` command. Conventionally, all
# specs live under a `spec` directory, which RSpec adds to the `$LOAD_PATH`.
# The generated `.rspec` file contains `--require spec_helper` which will cause
# this file to always be loaded, without a need to explicitly require it
  in any
# files.
#
# Given that it is always loaded, you are encouraged to keep this file as
# light-weight as possible. Requiring heavyweight dependencies from this file
# will add to the boot time of your test suite on EVERY test run, even for an
# individual file that may not need all of that loaded. Instead, consider
  making
# a separate helper file that requires the additional dependencies and performs
# the additional setup, and require it from the spec files that actually need
# it.
#
# See http://rubydoc.info/gems/rspec-core/RSpec/Core/Configuration
RSpec.configure do |config|
  # rspec-expectations config goes here. You can use an alternate
  # assertion/expectation library such as wrong or the stdlib/minitest
  # assertions if you prefer.
  config.expect_with :rspec do |expectations|
    # This option will default to `true` in RSpec 4. It makes the
      `description`
    # and `failure_message` of custom matchers include text for helper methods
    # defined using `chain`, e.g.:
    #    be_bigger_than(2).and_smaller_than(4).description
```

```
#      # => "be bigger than 2 and smaller than 4"
# ...rather than:
#      # => "be bigger than 2"
expectations.include_chain_clauses_in_custom_matcher_descriptions = true
end

# rspec-mocks config goes here. You can use an alternate test double
# library (such as bogus or mocha) by changing the `mock_with` option here.
config.mock_with :rspec do |mocks|
  # Prevents you from mocking or stubbing a method that does not exist on
  # a real object. This is generally recommended, and will default to
  # `true` in RSpec 4.
  mocks.verify_partial_doubles = true
end

# This option will default to `:apply_to_host_groups` in RSpec 4 (and will
# have no way to turn it off -- the option exists only for backwards
# compatibility in RSpec 3). It causes shared context metadata to be
# inherited by the metadata hash of host groups and examples, rather than
# triggering implicit auto-inclusion in groups with matching metadata.
config.shared_context_metadata_behavior = :apply_to_host_groups

# The settings below are suggested to provide a good initial experience
# with RSpec, but feel free to customize to your heart's content.

# This allows you to limit a spec run to individual examples or groups
# you care about by tagging them with `:focus` metadata. When nothing
# is tagged with `:focus`, all examples get run. RSpec also provides
# aliases for `it`, `describe`, and `context` that include `:focus`
# metadata: `fit`, `fdescribe` and `fcontext`, respectively.
# config.filter_run_when_matching :focus

# Allows RSpec to persist some state between runs in order to support
# the `--only-failures` and `--next-failure` CLI options. We recommend
# you configure your source control system to ignore this file.
# config.example_status_persistence_file_path = "spec/examples.txt"

# Limits the available syntax to the non-monkey patched syntax that is
# recommended. For more details, see:
```

```
#    - http://rspec.info/blog/2012/06/rspecs-new-expectation-syntax/
#    - http://www.teaisaweso.me/blog/2013/05/27/rspecs-new-message-
       expectation-syntax/
#    - http://rspec.info/blog/2014/05/notable-changes-in-rspec-3/#zero-
       monkey-patching-mode
config.disable_monkey_patching!

# This setting enables warnings. It's recommended, but in some cases may
# be too noisy due to issues in dependencies.
# config.warnings = true

# Many RSpec users commonly either run the entire suite or an individual
# file, and it's useful to allow more verbose output when running an
# individual spec file.
#if config.files_to_run.one?
#  # Use the documentation formatter for detailed output,
#  # unless a formatter has already been configured
#  # (e.g. via a command-line flag).
#  config.default_formatter = "doc"
#end

# Print the 10 slowest examples and example groups at the
# end of the spec run, to help surface which specs are running
# particularly slow.
# config.profile_examples = 10

# Run specs in random order to surface order dependencies. If you find an
# order dependency and want to debug it, you can fix the order by providing
# the seed, which is printed after each run.
#    --seed 1234
config.order = :random

# Seed global randomization in this process using the `--seed` CLI option.
# Setting this allows you to use `--seed` to deterministically reproduce
# test failures related to randomization by passing the same `--seed` value
# as the one that triggered the failure.
Kernel.srand config.seed
end
```

Inside the **spec** Folder

When you worked with `minitest`, your tests lived inside the folder `test`. RSpec assumes that all your tests are going to live inside the folder `spec`, or any of its subfolders. Also, the files that are going to be considered test files are the ones that will have a filename ending in `_spec.rb`. Hence, the file `spec/spec_helper.rb` is not considered a file with tests, whereas, if we had the file with the name `spec/customer_spec.rb`, this would have been considered a file with tests.

Describing

Let's assume that you want to model the ideal sandwich, just to start with something more fun.

RSpec is using the words `describe` and `it` to express concepts of your model in a conversational format.

This could have been the start of a dialog, a conversation, about the ideal sandwich:

- Describe an ideal sandwich.

- First, `it` is delicious.

See this dialog in Figure 4-4.

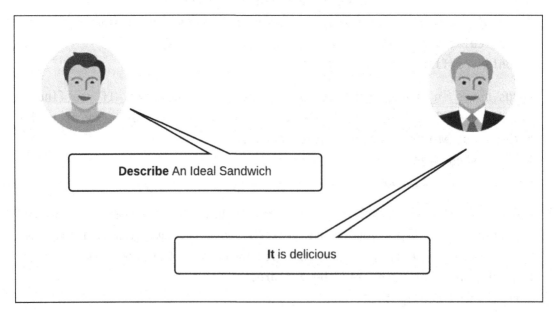

Figure 4-4. `describe it` *Conversation*

Let's create the file `spec/sandwich_spec.rb` with the following content (Listing 4-3).

Listing 4-3. spec/sandwich_spec.rb

```
# File: spec/sandwich_spec.rb
#
RSpec.describe 'An ideal sandwich' do
  it 'is delicious' do
    expect(true).to eq(false)
  end
end
```

This is a *spec* file. I use the word *spec* or *specification* rather than *test* when I am in the context of RSpec.

In fact, when you are in the RSpec context, you say that the *spec* file contains/defines *example groups*. Each example group is defined using the `RSpec.describe` call.

The first argument to the `RSpec.describe` call is the documentation (or description or name) string for the particular example group. The do ... end block that is sent to `RSpec.describe` defines the body of the example group. The body usually defines one or more examples. Each example is defined with the call to method `it`. An example group may have many calls to `it`, and each one is going to be a different example in the example group. The first argument to `it` is the documentation (or description or name) string for the particular example. The block do ... end that is sent to `it` is the actual implementation of the example (Figure 4-5).

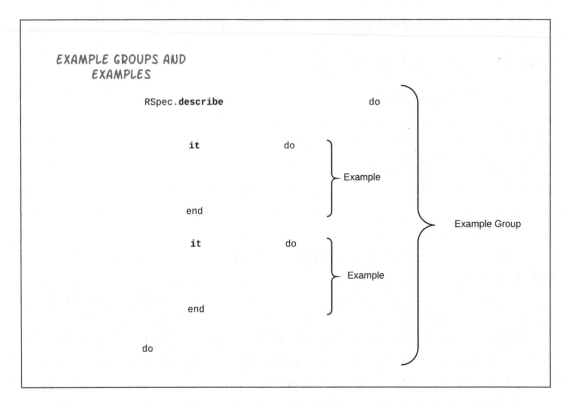

Figure 4-5. *Example Groups and Examples*

Sanity Check

Now that you have the basics explained and the first spec file in place, let's execute the RSpec runner:

```
$ bundle exec rspec

Randomized with seed 63375
F
Randomized with seed 6735
F

Failures:

  1) An ideal sandwich is delicious
     Failure/Error: expect(true).to eq(false)
```

```
    expected: false
         got: true

    (compared using ==)

    Diff:
    @@ -1,2 +1,2 @@
    -false
    +true

  # ./spec/sandwich_spec.rb:5:in `block (2 levels) in <top (required)>'
Finished in 0.05128 seconds (files took 0.25256 seconds to load)
1 example, 1 failure

Failed examples:

rspec ./spec/sandwich_spec.rb:4 # An ideal sandwich is delicious

Randomized with seed 6735

$
```

The suite has run successfully, that is, without any errors. But you have one failure. Do you see the output line 1 example, 1 failure? The RSpec runner (bundle exec rspec) identified the single example defined in your suite and executed it. However, this failed with the failure

```
1) An ideal sandwich is delicious
    Failure/Error: expect(true).to eq(false)

      expected: false
           got: true

      (compared using ==)

      Diff:
      @@ -1,2 +1,2 @@
      -false
      +true

  # ./spec/sandwich_spec.rb:5:in `block (2 levels) in <top (required)>'
```

It is clearly mentioning that spec/sandwich_spec.rb failed at line 5: expect(true).
to eq(false). This seems to be quite easy to explain (Figure 4-6).

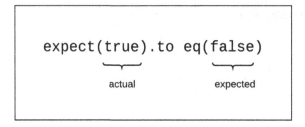

Figure 4-6. *Expected vs. Actual*

The example line that exercises the expectation of the specification, expect(true).
to eq(false), is mentioning that the value true, which is the *actual* value, needs to be
equal to the value false, which is the *expected* value. And since true is not equal to
false, the specification fails when evaluated by the RSpec runner.

Easy to explain and easy to fix. The following is the new version of the spec/
sandwich_spec.rb file (Listing 4-4).

Listing 4-4. New Version of the spec/sandwich_spec.rb File

```
# File: spec/sandwich_spec.rb
#
RSpec.describe 'An ideal sandwich' do
  it 'is delicious' do
    expect(true).to eq(true)
  end
end
```

If you save and run the RSpec runner again, you will get this:

```
$ bundle exec rspec

Randomized with seed 4291

.

Finished in 0.00097 seconds (files took 0.11265 seconds to load)
1 example, 0 failures

Randomized with seed 4291

$
```

Nice! This is reporting 1 `example, 0 failures`. You can see the green . implying one example has been successfully evaluated.

Documentation Formatter

The RSpec runner comes with a very useful results formatter. It prints out the specs (each `describe` and `it` documentation string) in a nested/tree-like format which finally works as a very good documentation of your project specifications.

Let's try that with the current specs that you have:

```
$ bundle exec rspec --format doc

Randomized with seed 6501

An ideal sandwich
  is delicious

Finished in 0.00081 seconds (files took 0.07047 seconds to load)
1 example, 0 failures

Randomized with seed 6501

$
```

Do you see the

```
An ideal sandwich
  is delicious
```

part of the output? These are the `describe` and `it` documentation/name strings in your spec file. You can also see that the example that ran successfully is displayed with green color.

You can set the runner to always have this output, by default, if you set the appropriate configuration line inside the `.rspec` file in the root folder of your project. Just add this line `--format doc`:

```
--require spec_helper
--format doc
```

And then try to run again your specs by simply giving `bundle exec rspec`. You will see that the output is using the documentation formatter.

123

Let's Write a Real Specification

Now that you have set the scene to be able to run your specs, let's write your first real specification for the sandwich model. Remember that you are doing TDD/BDD. So you first write the specs and then the implementation in the core code that satisfies the specs.

The following is the new version of the file spec/sandwich_spec.rb (Listing 4-5).

Listing 4-5. First Real Specification

```
# File: spec/sandwich_spec.rb
#
RSpec.describe 'An ideal sandwich' do
  it 'is delicious' do
    sandwich = Sandwich.new('delicious', [])

    taste = sandwich.taste
    expect(taste).to eq('delicious')
  end
end
```

Usually, the tests are logically divided into four phases:

1. The *setup* phase.

2. The *fire* phase.

3. The *assertion* phase.

4. The *teardown* phase.

You may find these phases called with other names too:

1. Setup

2. Exercise

3. Verify

4. Teardown

However, usually, you find only three phases, as you have in the preceding example. See Figure 4-7.

```
sandwich = Sandwich.new('delicious', [])    } Setup

taste = sandwich.taste                       } Fire

expect(taste).to eq('delicious')             } Assertion
```

Figure 4-7. *Three Phases of Test Code*

Keep this in your mind whenever you design a test. You need to make sure you understand where is the *setup* code, where is the *fire* code, and where is the *assertion* code. If this is not clear from your code, then you need to make it be. Tests need to be simple and easy to identify those phases.

However, identification of those phases is not very straightforward, at all times. For example, you might mix the *fire* and the *assertion* together in order to avoid using temporary variables. See the new version of the spec/sandwich_spec.rb file (Listing 4-6).

Listing 4-6. Mixed Fire and Assertion Phase

```
# File: spec/sandwich_spec.rb
#
RSpec.describe 'An ideal sandwich' do
  it 'is delicious' do
    sandwich = Sandwich.new('delicious', [])

    expect(sandwich.taste).to eq('delicious')
  end
end
```

You can now see that the *fire* phase has been mixed with the *assertion* phase. But, even so, the test is still clear and the reader can understand that the part inside the expect(....) parentheses is the *fire* part (Figure 4-8).

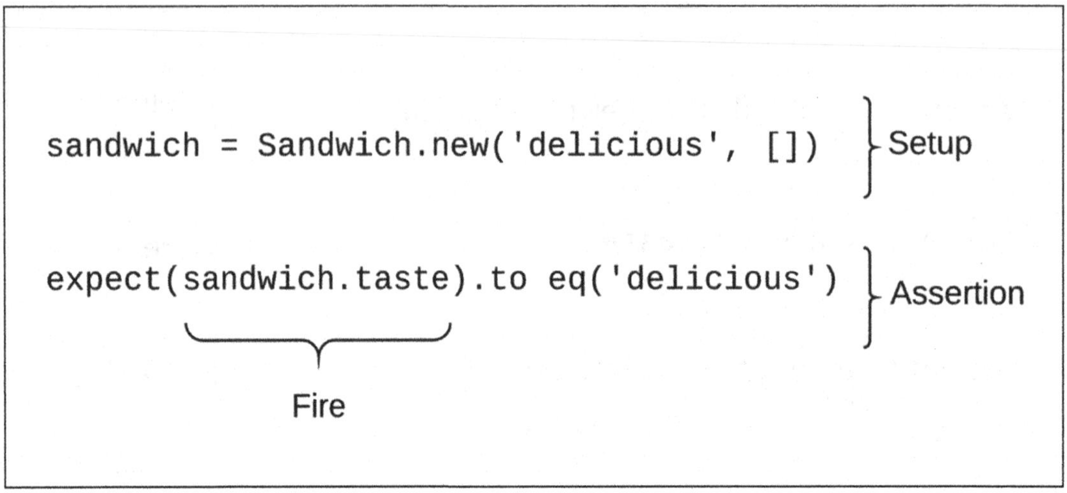

```
sandwich = Sandwich.new('delicious', [])      } Setup

expect(sandwich.taste).to eq('delicious')     } Assertion
          _____/
                   Fire
```

Figure 4-8. *Fire Phase Mixed with Assertion Phase*

Before you give a go to run the preceding spec, let's also tell something about the expect method. The expect method call takes as argument the *actual* value. Then you can call an *expectation target*. In your case, this is `.to`. The expectation target then takes as an argument an RSpec matcher. In your example, this is the eq() method call. I will talk about all these in more detail later on. But, until then, you can read the expect(<actual>).to eq(<expected>) as *we expect the value <actual> to be equal to the value <expected>*. If the expectation fails, then expect raises the exception RSpec to ols::Expectations::ExpectationNotMetError and terminates the example execution considering that as failed (Figure 4-9).

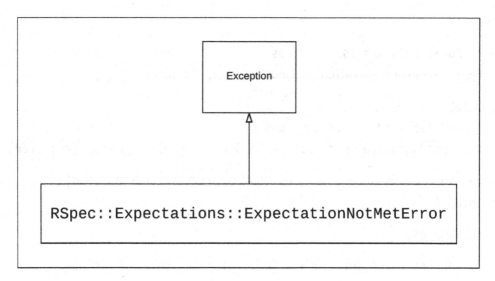

Figure 4-9. *RSpec Expectation Not Met Error*

Sidenote   Since the RSpec tools::Expectations::ExpectationNotMe tError superclass is Exception, this means that a rescue without specifying this particular class will not rescue these types of exceptions. Remember that the default for rescue is StandardError.

Run and Watch That Fail and Then Fix It

I will keep on saying that you are doing TDD (Test-Driven Development). So you first need to see your tests failing. Let's run rspec to see that:

```
$ bundle exec rspec

Randomized with seed 43204

An ideal sandwich
  is delicious (FAILED - 1)
```

```
Failures:

  1) An ideal sandwich is delicious
     Failure/Error: sandwich = Sandwich.new('delicious', [])

     NameError:
       uninitialized constant Sandwich
     # ./spec/sandwich_spec.rb:5:in `block (2 levels) in <top (required)>'

Finished in 0.00236 seconds (files took 0.21178 seconds to load)
1 example, 1 failure

Failed examples:

rspec ./spec/sandwich_spec.rb:4 # An ideal sandwich is delicious

Randomized with seed 43204

$
```

The failure that you get is `uninitialized constant Sandwich`. Fair enough. Let's create this class. In the root folder of your project, create the file `sandwich.rb` and put the following content inside (Listing 4-7).

Listing 4-7. sandwich.rb First Version

```
# File: sandwich.rb
#
class Sandwich
end
```

Also, you create the file `all.rb` that will require all the necessary files of your application (Listing 4-8).

Listing 4-8. all.rb Requires All Files

```
# File: all.rb
#
require_relative 'sandwich'
```

Then, you tell the spec/spec_helper.rb to load your application before exercising any example. Add the following line at the bottom of your spec/spec_helper.rb file:

```
require_relative '../all'
```

Then run the bundle exec rspec command again:

```
$ bundle exec rspec

Randomized with seed 64232

An ideal sandwich
  is delicious (FAILED - 1)

Failures:

  1) An ideal sandwich is delicious
     Failure/Error: sandwich = Sandwich.new('delicious', [])

     ArgumentError:
       wrong number of arguments (given 2, expected 0)
     # ./spec/sandwich_spec.rb:5:in `initialize'
     # ./spec/sandwich_spec.rb:5:in `new'
     # ./spec/sandwich_spec.rb:5:in `block (2 levels) in <top (required)>'

Finished in 0.00257 seconds (files took 0.19019 seconds to load)
1 example, 1 failure

Failed examples:

rspec ./spec/sandwich_spec.rb:4 # An ideal sandwich is delicious

Randomized with seed 64232

$
```

You've got rid of the uninitialized constant error. Now you have an ArgumentError. This has to do with the call to sandwich = Sandwich.new('delicious', []). This is expected. Your Sandwich class does not have an initializer that could take two arguments. Let's correct that (Listing 4-9).

Listing 4-9. sandwich.rb File with the Correct Initializer

```ruby
# File: sandwich.rb
#
class Sandwich
  def initialize(taste, toppings)
    @taste = taste
    @toppings = toppings
  end
end
```

Now, you run the spec again:

```
$ bundle exec rspec

Randomized with seed 12272

An ideal sandwich
  is delicious (FAILED - 1)

Failures:

  1) An ideal sandwich is delicious
     Failure/Error: expect(sandwich.taste).to eq('delicious')

     NoMethodError:
       undefined method `taste' for #<Sandwich:0x00007fc39518e358
       @taste="delicious", @toppings=[]>
     # ./spec/sandwich_spec.rb:7:in `block (2 levels) in <top (required)>'

Finished in 0.00223 seconds (files took 0.17754 seconds to load)
1 example, 1 failure

Failed examples:

rspec ./spec/sandwich_spec.rb:4 # An ideal sandwich is delicious

Randomized with seed 12272

$
```

The runner is complaining that your Sandwich instance does not have a method taste. Let's add that (Listing 4-10).

Listing 4-10. taste Method Added

```
# File: sandwich.rb
#
class Sandwich
  def initialize(taste, toppings)
    @taste = taste
    @toppings = toppings
  end

  def taste
  end
end
```

And let's run again:

```
$ bundle exec rspec

Randomized with seed 65088

An ideal sandwich
  is delicious (FAILED - 1)

Failures:

  1) An ideal sandwich is delicious
     Failure/Error: expect(sandwich.taste).to eq('delicious')

       expected: "delicious"
            got: nil

       (compared using ==)
     # ./spec/sandwich_spec.rb:7:in `block (2 levels) in <top (required)>'

Finished in 0.0376 seconds (files took 0.1894 seconds to load)
1 example, 1 failure
```

Failed examples:

```
rspec ./spec/sandwich_spec.rb:4 # An ideal sandwich is delicious
```

Randomized with seed 65088

`$`

Now you have an expectation failure. The spec on line 7 expected the actual to be "delicious", but it is nil. Line 7 of the spec is

```
expect(sandwich.taste).to eq('delicious')
```

In other words, the sandwich.taste should return "delicious", but it does not. Let's fix that (Listing 4-11).

Listing 4-11. Fix taste Method Implementation

```
# File: sandwich.rb
#
class Sandwich
  def initialize(taste, toppings)
    @taste = taste
    @toppings = toppings
  end

  def taste
    @taste
  end
end
```

Let's run the tests again:

```
$ bundle exec rspec
```

Randomized with seed 28975

```
An ideal sandwich
  is delicious
```

```
Finished in 0.00108 seconds (files took 0.11061 seconds to load)
1 example, 0 failures

Randomized with seed 28975

$
```

Bingo! You just finished, once more, a round of a TDD workflow:

1. Write the spec.

2. Run it to see it failing.

3. Fix it.

However, there is one more phase in the TDD workflow: the refactoring phase. Let's do a small improvement on our Sandwich class (Listing 4-12).

Listing 4-12. Refactoring the Sandwich Class

```
# File: sandwich.rb
#
class Sandwich
  attr_reader :taste

  def initialize(taste, toppings)
    @taste = taste
    @toppings = toppings
  end
end
```

After the refactoring phase, you then run the specs again to make sure that you have not broken anything:

```
$ bundle exec rspec

Randomized with seed 31688

An ideal sandwich
  is delicious
```

```
Finished in 0.00328 seconds (files took 0.1915 seconds to load)
1 example, 0 failures

Randomized with seed 31688

$
```

Sharing Setup Code

You will now add one more example as part of your Sandwich specification (Listing 4-13).

Listing 4-13. More Specs in Sandwich

```
# File: spec/sandwich_spec.rb
#
RSpec.describe 'An ideal sandwich' do
  it 'is delicious' do
    sandwich = Sandwich.new('delicious', [])

    expect(sandwich.taste).to eq('delicious')
  end

  it 'lets me add toppings' do
    sandwich = Sandwich.new('delicious', [])

    sandwich.toppings << 'cheese'

    expect(sandwich.toppings).not_to be_empty
  end
end
```

You can see that between lines 10 and 16. The *actual* is sandwich.toppings, and the expectation is that it should not be empty.

Let's run the specs:

```
$ bundle exec rspec

Randomized with seed 27729

An ideal sandwich
  is delicious
```

```
  lets me add toppings (FAILED - 1)

Failures:

  1) An ideal sandwich lets me add toppings
     Failure/Error: sandwich.toppings << 'cheese'

     NoMethodError:
       undefined method `toppings' for #<Sandwich:0x00007fc83583b300
       @taste="delicious", @toppings=[]>
     # ./spec/sandwich_spec.rb:13:in `block (2 levels) in <top (required)>'

Finished in 0.00383 seconds (files took 0.21256 seconds to load)
2 examples, 1 failure

Failed examples:

rspec ./spec/sandwich_spec.rb:10 # An ideal sandwich lets me add toppings

Randomized with seed 27729

$
```

The first example was successful. The second failed. Following the TDD approach, you fill in the necessary bits of code inside the Sandwich class to make this second example succeed too (Listing 4-14).

Listing 4-14. Fill In Necessary Bits of Code to Make All Suite Green

```
# File: sandwich.rb
#
class Sandwich
  attr_reader :taste, :toppings

  def initialize(taste, toppings)
    @taste = taste
    @toppings = toppings
  end
end
```

If you run the specs again, you will see them succeed:

```
$ bundle exec rspec

Randomized with seed 45205

An ideal sandwich
  lets me add toppings
  is delicious

Finished in 0.01153 seconds (files took 0.2327 seconds to load)
2 examples, 0 failures

Randomized with seed 45205

$
```

However, there is a repetition in the example file (Figure 4-10).

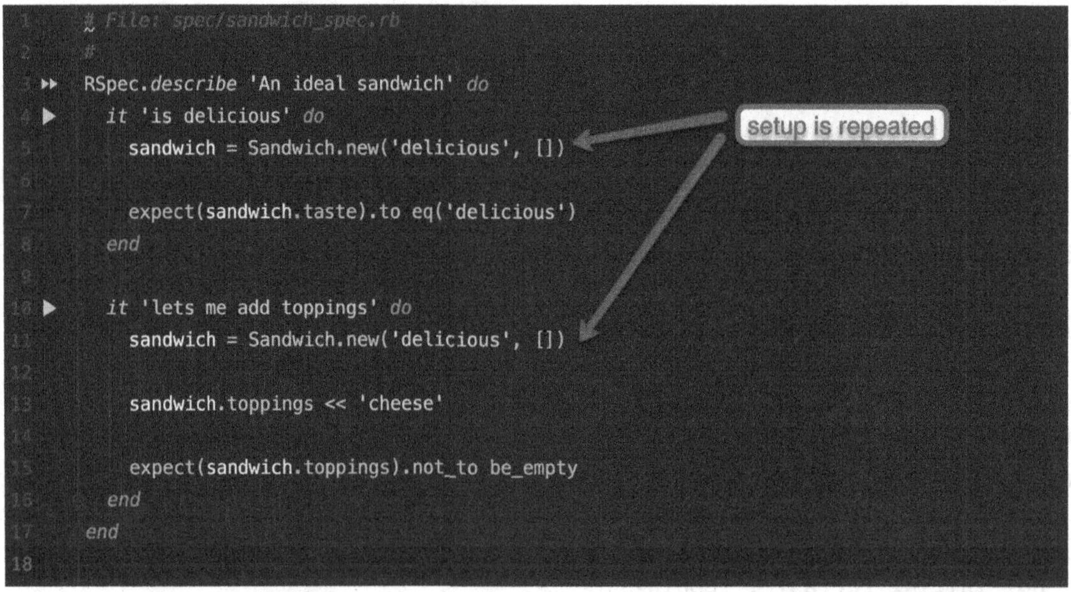

Figure 4-10. *Setup Is Repeated*

You can see that the setup code is repeated at the beginning of your two examples. If you had many more, that repetition would increase the cost of changing and maintaining the setup phase of these examples. Can you DRY (Do not Repeat Yourself) the example group code?

Yes, you can. RSpec offers various ways you can do this.

before Hook

One way you can put your common setup code into one place is to use the before hook. The before hook hosts a piece of code that will be executed before the execution of every example.

Let's do that for the spec/sandwich_spec.rb file (Listing 4-15).

Listing 4-15. Use of the before Block

```
# File: spec/sandwich_spec.rb
#
RSpec.describe 'An ideal sandwich' do
  before do
    @sandwich = Sandwich.new('delicious', [])
  end

  it 'is delicious' do
    expect(@sandwich.taste).to eq('delicious')
  end

  it 'lets me add toppings' do
    @sandwich.toppings << 'cheese'

    expect(@sandwich.toppings).not_to be_empty
  end
end
```

Inside the body of the block that is attached to the RSpec.describe call, you use the method before with a block attached. This is the way you define code that you want to be executed every time an example starts. Hence

1. Before the example is delicious, the runner will instantiate the variable @sandwich with the value Sandwich.new('delicious', []).

2. Then it will execute the is delicious code.

3. Then it will clear all the memory that is related to the example that finished before starting the next example.

4. Before the example `lets me add toppings`, it will execute the code inside the `before` block. It will instantiate a new `@sandwich` instance.

5. Then it will execute the code for the example `lets me add toppings`.

And so on.

The technique used here, with the `before` hook, eliminates the need to have the setup code written multiple times. However, you need to turn your local `sandwich` variables to references to the instance variable `@sandwich` (Figure 4-11).

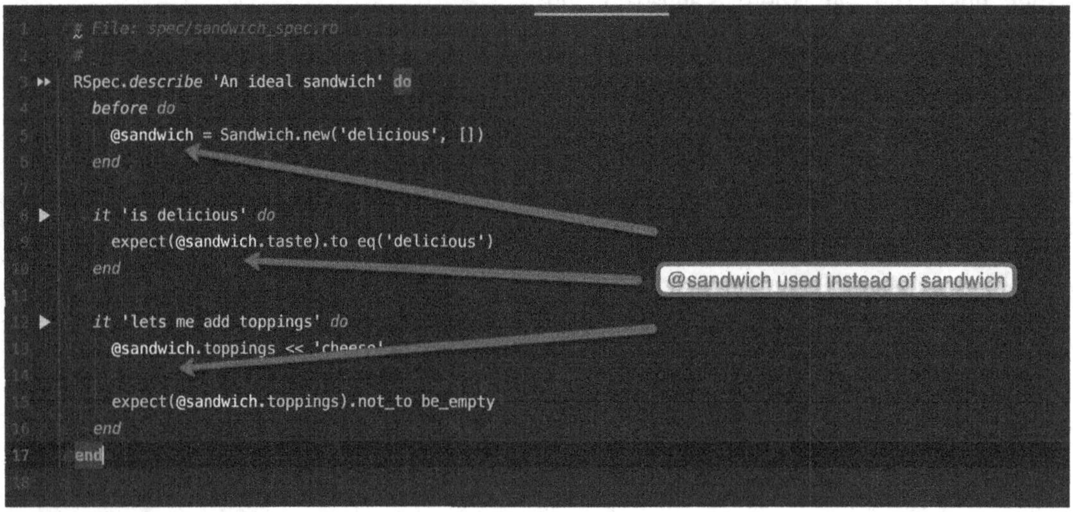

Figure 4-11. *@sandwich Used Instead of sandwich*

The `before` hooks are great if you want to prepare the common setup of your examples. They are also very useful if this has to do with things that need to take place in a world outside of your application, for example, to clean up the database that your application might be accessing. You might want every example to run on a clean database.

However, when it comes to instantiating variables, the `before` hook is not very handy. The maintenance of the instance variable is error prone and involves lots of find/and/replace actions with your editor.

Helper Methods

Another technique that you can use are helper methods. The helper methods are methods defined inside the RSpec.describe do ... end block, that is, at the example group level. They can then be used by the do ... end blocks of your it method calls, that is, at the example level.

The following is the version of spec/sandwich_spec.rb that uses this technique (Listing 4-16).

Listing 4-16. Using Helper Methods

```
# File: spec/sandwich_spec.rb
#
RSpec.describe 'An ideal sandwich' do
  def sandwich
    @sandwich ||= Sandwich.new('delicious', [])
  end

  it 'is delicious' do
    expect(sandwich.taste).to eq('delicious')
  end

  it 'lets me add toppings' do
    sandwich.toppings << 'cheese'

    expect(sandwich.toppings).not_to be_empty
  end
end
```

You can now see that you went back using non-instance variables. The sandwich is now a call to a method that is defined inside the RSpec.describe do ... end block. Note how the method definition is using memoization. Only the first time that it is called it actually calls Sandwich.new('delicious', []). Every other call to the sandwich method returns the value of the instance variable @sandwich and does not instantiate a new Sandwich. For example, for the spec lets me add toppings, only line 13 instantiates a Sandwich. Line 15, which calls sandwich again, uses the value stored in @sandwich.

Save the preceding code and run the specs again. You will see that they will be green.

The preceding technique is useful, and you will find it in many specifications in many projects. However, the memoization is a little bit tricky when the actual value is falsey. If the actual value is falsey, then memoization like this does not really work.

The following irb Ruby code demonstrates the problem with memoization and falsey values:

```
$ irb
irb(main):001:0> def do_something
irb(main):002:1>   puts 'I am doing something'
irb(main):003:1>   false
irb(main):004:1> end
=> :do_something
irb(main):005:0> foo ||= do_something
I am doing something
=> false
irb(main):006:0> foo ||= do_something
I am doing something
=> false
irb(main):007:0>
```

As you can see, the second call to foo ||= do_something calls the method do_something and does not only evaluate the foo variable. On the other hand, if do_something returns true, the second call to foo ||= do_something will not evaluate the do_something and will return the value of foo. See how this latter case works in the following:

```
irb(main):007:0> def do_something
irb(main):008:1>   puts 'I am doing something'
irb(main):009:1>   true
irb(main):010:1> end
=> :do_something
irb(main):011:0> foo ||= do_something
I am doing something
=> true
irb(main):012:0> foo ||= do_something
=> true
```

Let's see another technique that is very popular with RSpec and allows for sharing of code.

Share with `let`

Instead of defining helper methods, you can call the method `let` that evaluates a block of Ruby code only once, at the first time you use the name of the `let`. Here is the new version of `spec/sandwich_spec.rb` that is using `let` (Listing 4-17).

Listing 4-17. Using let

```
# File: spec/sandwich_spec.rb
#
RSpec.describe 'An ideal sandwich' do
  let(:sandwich) do
    Sandwich.new('delicious', [])
  end

  it 'is delicious' do
    expect(sandwich.taste).to eq('delicious')
  end

  it 'lets me add toppings' do
    sandwich.toppings << 'cheese'

    expect(sandwich.toppings).not_to be_empty
  end
end
```

The preceding `let` binds the block of code `Sandwich.new('delicious', [])` to the name `sandwich`. Then you can use the `sandwich` name in your examples. The `sandwich` will be evaluated only once, and subsequent calls will use the first-time evaluated value.

If you save and run your tests, you will see that everything is green again.

Context

RSpec uses one more method of grouping examples, tests. This is called `context`, and it is no different from `RSpec.describe`. Actually, it is an alias to `RSpec.describe`. The point is that with `context`, you make the grouping of the examples more intuitive since you group examples according to the *context* the examples assume they live in.

Let's see that with an example. Write the file spec/coffee_spec.rb as follows (Listing 4-18).

Listing 4-18. Using Context

```ruby
# File: spec/coffee_spec.rb
#
RSpec.describe 'A coffee' do
  let(:coffee) { Coffee.new }

  it 'costs 1 euro' do
    expect(coffee.price).to eq(1)
  end

  context 'with milk' do
    before { coffee.add_milk }

    it 'costs 1.2 euro' do
      expect(coffee.price).to eq(1.2)
    end
  end
end
```

Before I explain what is going on in this spec file, let's run it **without actually evaluating the examples**. You will do what is called a **dry run** in order to see the output of the example definitions:

```
$ bundle exec rspec --dry-run

Randomized with seed 32424

A coffee
  costs 1 euro
  with milk
    costs 1.2 euro

An ideal sandwich
  is delicious
  lets me add toppings
```

```
Finished in 0.00288 seconds (files took 0.19913 seconds to load)
4 examples, 0 failures

Randomized with seed 32424

$
```

This is a nice formatted output of your specs without any evaluation. But it is displaying how you have structured your specs. See how the with milk context is creating a new indentation for the examples that it is grouping (Figure 4-12).

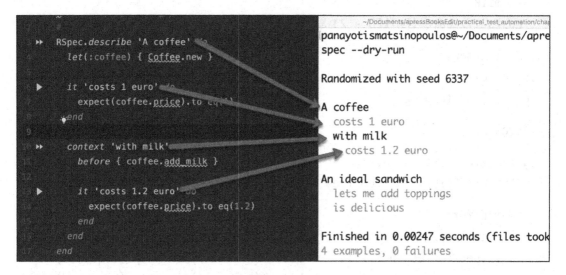

Figure 4-12. *context Creates a New Indentation*

You can see how the context created a new block of indented documentation for the grouped examples.

Something else that you need to be aware of is that context can create before hooks as the describe does. And the before hooks are evaluated only for the examples that belong to the particular context.

Running Specific Examples

Now let's try to run the suite of specs with a normal (not dry) run:

```
$ bundle exec rspec

Randomized with seed 64299

A coffee
  costs 1 euro (FAILED - 1)
  with milk
    costs 1.2 euro (FAILED - 2)

An ideal sandwich
  is delicious
  lets me add toppings

Failures:

  1) A coffee costs 1 euro
     Failure/Error: let(:coffee) { Coffee.new }

     NameError:
       uninitialized constant Coffee
     # ./spec/coffee_spec.rb:4:in `block (2 levels) in <top (required)>'
     # ./spec/coffee_spec.rb:7:in `block (2 levels) in <top (required)>'

  2) A coffee with milk costs 1.2 euro
     Failure/Error: let(:coffee) { Coffee.new }

     NameError:
       uninitialized constant Coffee
     # ./spec/coffee_spec.rb:4:in `block (2 levels) in <top (required)>'
     # ./spec/coffee_spec.rb:11:in `block (3 levels) in <top (required)>'

Finished in 0.00612 seconds (files took 0.21116 seconds to load)
4 examples, 2 failures
```

Failed examples:

```
rspec ./spec/coffee_spec.rb:6 # A coffee costs 1 euro
rspec ./spec/coffee_spec.rb:13 # A coffee with milk costs 1.2 euro
```

Randomized with seed 64299

```
$
```

You can see that you have two failures, both coming from the spec/coffee_spec.rb file.

You may have hundreds of spec files and only one failing. How can you run the rspec runner for that particular file only? Easy stuff: just give the filename as argument to RSpec tools:

```
$ bundle exec rspec spec/coffee_spec.rb
```

Randomized with seed 47485

```
A coffee
  costs 1 euro (FAILED - 1)
  with milk
    costs 1.2 euro (FAILED - 2)
```

Failures:

```
  1) A coffee costs 1 euro
     Failure/Error: let(:coffee) { Coffee.new }

     NameError:
       uninitialized constant Coffee
     # ./spec/coffee_spec.rb:4:in `block (2 levels) in <top (required)>'
     # ./spec/coffee_spec.rb:7:in `block (2 levels) in <top (required)>'

  2) A coffee with milk costs 1.2 euro
     Failure/Error: let(:coffee) { Coffee.new }

     NameError:
       uninitialized constant Coffee
     # ./spec/coffee_spec.rb:4:in `block (2 levels) in <top (required)>'
     # ./spec/coffee_spec.rb:11:in `block (3 levels) in <top (required)>'
```

```
Finished in 0.00302 seconds (files took 0.18583 seconds to load)
2 examples, 2 failures
```

```
Failed examples:
```

```
rspec ./spec/coffee_spec.rb:6 # A coffee costs 1 euro
rspec ./spec/coffee_spec.rb:13 # A coffee with milk costs 1.2 euro
```

```
Randomized with seed 47485
```

```
$
```

As you can see, you just run only the examples inside the file spec/coffee_spec.rb. Let's try to fix the first of the examples that is failing.

Create the file coffee.rb and add the class definition for Coffee, like the following (Listing 4-19).

Listing 4-19. First Version of the coffee.rb File

```
# File: coffee.rb
#
class Coffee
  def price
    1
  end
end
```

Make sure that the file all.rb requires the coffee.rb file too (Listing 4-20).

Listing 4-20. all.rb Requires coffee.rb

```
# File: all.rb
#
require_relative 'sandwich'
require_relative 'coffee'
```

Now, let's run the specs for the particular file again:

```
$ bundle exec rspec spec/coffee_spec.rb
```

```
Randomized with seed 36624
```

```
A coffee
  costs 1 euro
  with milk
    costs 1.2 euro (FAILED - 1)

Failures:

  1) A coffee with milk costs 1.2 euro
     Failure/Error: before { coffee.add_milk }

     NoMethodError:
       undefined method `add_milk' for #<Coffee:0x00007fd9691b0f18>
     # ./spec/coffee_spec.rb:11:in `block (3 levels) in <top (required)>'

Finished in 0.0039 seconds (files took 0.20848 seconds to load)
2 examples, 1 failure

Failed examples:

rspec ./spec/coffee_spec.rb:13 # A coffee with milk costs 1.2 euro

Randomized with seed 36624

$
```

Nice! Only one failure, for the example A coffee with milk costs 1.2 euro.

Imagine that your spec/coffee_spec.rb file contains many more examples, but you only want to run the particular one that failed. How can you do that? You will do that by specifying both the filename and the line number corresponding to the failing example. Actually, the last rspec run gives you the command ready to copy and paste into your terminal (Figure 4-13).

```
Failures:

  1) A coffee with milk costs 1.2 euro
     Failure/Error: before { coffee.add_milk }

     NoMethodError:
       undefined method `add_milk' for #<Coffee:0x00007fd9691b0f18>
     # ./spec/coffee_spec.rb:11:in `block (3 levels) in <top (required)>'

Finished in 0.0039 seconds (files took 0.20848 seconds to load)
2 examples, 1 failure                    ⎡ command to run on your terminal (copy & paste) ⎤

Failed examples:

rspec ./spec/coffee_spec.rb:13 # A coffee with milk costs 1.2 euro

Randomized with seed 36624
```

Figure 4-13. *rspec Gives You the Command to Run a Specific Example*

Let's do that. Run the command for the specific failing example:

```
$ bundle exec rspec spec/coffee_spec.rb:13
Run options: include {:locations=>{"./spec/coffee_spec.rb"=>[13]}}

Randomized with seed 54173

A coffee
  with milk
    costs 1.2 euro (FAILED - 1)

Failures:

  1) A coffee with milk costs 1.2 euro
     Failure/Error: before { coffee.add_milk }

     NoMethodError:
       undefined method `add_milk' for #<Coffee:0x00007fc4968af3b0>
     # ./spec/coffee_spec.rb:11:in `block (3 levels) in <top (required)>'

Finished in 0.00136 seconds (files took 0.18474 seconds to load)
1 example, 1 failure
```

Failed examples:

rspec ./spec/coffee_spec.rb:13 # A coffee with milk costs 1.2 euro

Randomized with seed 54173

$

In order to finish with this example, let's fix the code for the Coffee class to make this example go green. The following is the new version of the coffee.rb file (Listing 4-21).

Listing 4-21. New Version of coffee.rb

```ruby
# File: coffee.rb
#
class Coffee
  INGREDIENT_PRICES = {
      'milk' => 0.2
  }

  def initialize
    @ingredients = []
  end

  def price
    1 + sum_of_ingredients_price
  end

  def add_milk
    @ingredients << 'milk'
  end

  private

  def sum_of_ingredients_price
    @ingredients.reduce(0) do |result, ingredient|
      result += result + INGREDIENT_PRICES[ingredient]
    end
  end
end
```

If you now run the command for the example that was failing before, you will see that it is green:

```
$ bundle exec rspec spec/coffee_spec.rb:13
Run options: include {:locations=>{"./spec/coffee_spec.rb"=>[13]}}

Randomized with seed 39570

A coffee
  with milk
    costs 1.2 euro

Finished in 0.00213 seconds (files took 0.1954 seconds to load)
1 example, 0 failures

Randomized with seed 39570

$
```

Having fixed one file with specs, you now go ahead and run the whole suite again:

```
$ bundle exec rspec

Randomized with seed 15573

A coffee
  costs 1 euro
  with milk
    costs 1.2 euro

An ideal sandwich
  is delicious
  lets me add toppings

Finished in 0.00668 seconds (files took 0.1776 seconds to load)
4 examples, 0 failures

Randomized with seed 15573

$
```

Everything is green. If you want, be happy to refactor the implementation. If refactoring breaks any of the application specifications, you will know that by running the whole test suite again.

RubyMine Integration

Before you continue with more advanced topics on Rspec, let's make sure that you can run your RSpec suite from within RubyMine.

Right-click your project name, in the RubyMine project explorer, and then select to run all specs in your project, as in the following screenshot (Figure 4-14).

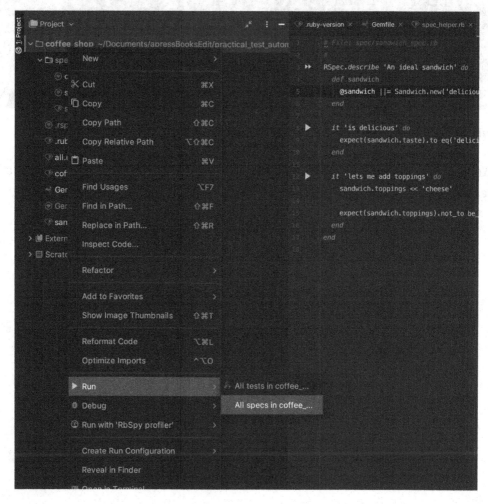

Figure 4-14. *RubyMine – Run All Specs*

When you do that, RubyMine will execute all the specs in your project (Figure 4-15).

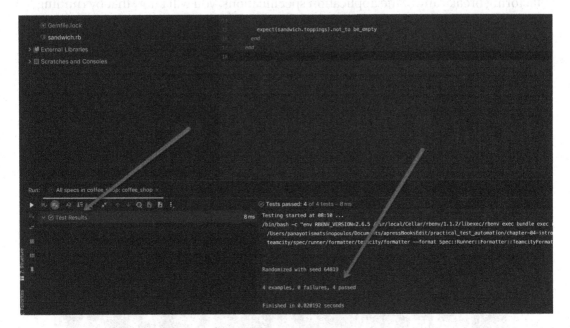

Figure 4-15. *RubyMine – Run All Specs Results*

You can even run an individual file. Just right-click and select to run the particular file, as in Figure 4-16 for the `sandwich_spec.rb`.

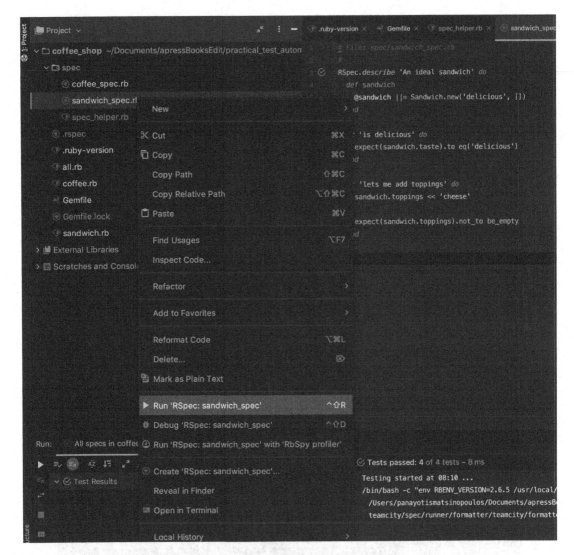

Figure 4-16. RubyMine – Run a Specific Spec File

The result will appear again at the bottom tab of RubyMine.

And, finally, you can run an individual example or example group. In the following screenshot, I show how I right-click inside the example lets me add toppings and then I select to run the particular example (Figure 4-17).

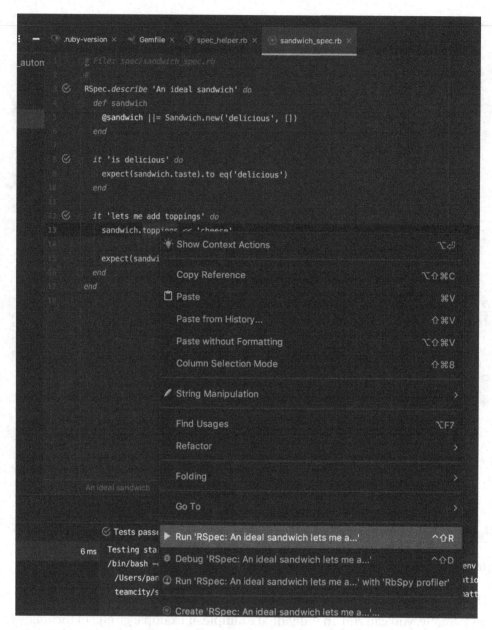

Figure 4-17. *RubyMine – Run a Specific Example*

Note that every time you run your specs through RubyMine, it creates a run configuration, and you can re-execute it with the click of a button (Figure 4-18).

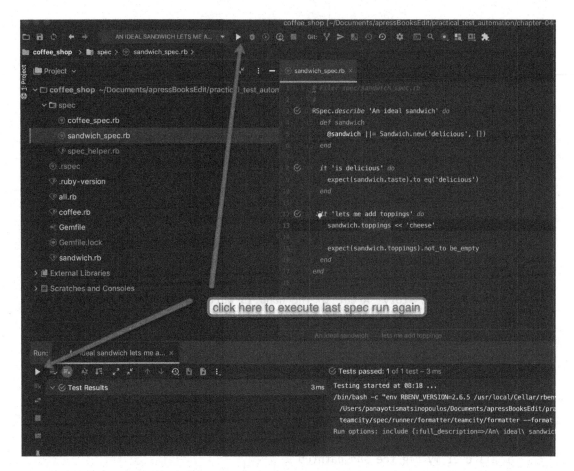

Figure 4-18. *How to Run the Last Spec Again*

Before I close these notes about the integration with RubyMine, I would like to make you aware of the keyboard shortcuts that can be used to execute the whole suite or a specific example. For example, on my Mac, when the cursor is inside an example, then I can press the keyboard combination `Ctrl+Shift+R,` and it will run the `rspec` for the particular example (or `context/describe` if my cursor is in a `context/describe`).

Task Details

WRITE TESTS USING RSPEC

You are requested to implement a class that will satisfy the following requirements:

```
A Mad Libs Story Teller
  when it gets the story template 'A ((an animal)) in the ((a body part)) is
  worth ((a number)) in the ((a place))'
    then its third question to ask is 'Give me a number'
    then its fourth question to ask is 'Give me a place'
    then its first question to ask is 'Give me an animal'
    then its second question to ask is 'Give me a body part'
    and words for placeholders 'cat', 'hand', 'twelve' and 'London'
      produces the story 'A cat in the hand is worth twelve in the London'
  when it gets the story template 'I had a ((an adjective)) sandwich for
  lunch today. It dripped all over my ((a body part)) and ((a noun))'
    then its second question to ask is 'Give me a body part'
    then its third question to ask is 'Give me a noun'
    then its first question to ask is 'Give me an adjective'
    and words for placeholders 'smelly', 'big toe' and 'bathtub'
      produces the story 'I had a smelly sandwich for lunch today. It dripped
      all over my big toe and bathtub'

Finished in 0.00213 seconds (files took 0.07707 seconds to load)
9 examples, 0 failures
```

This is the screenshot of the output of the RSpec documentation that might be easier for you to read (Figure 4-19).

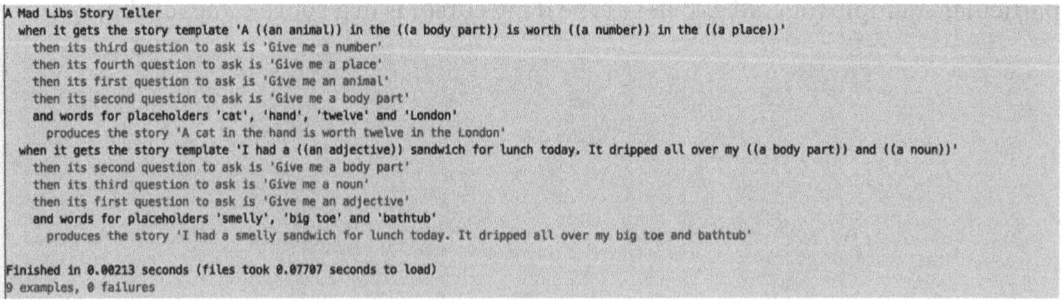

Figure 4-19. *Task – RSpec Formatted Documentation*

This exercise is based on the following business requirements:

There is a game called Mad Libs. This is based on a story template. For example, "I ((a verb)) to eat ((a food))." This story template has two placeholders: the "((a verb))" and the "((a food))." The game is played with one person holding the story template hidden from the others. But this person asks them questions based on the placeholder content. For this example, the first question is "Give me a verb." And the second question is "Give me a food." The other person answers, and the person who holds the story template compiles the story based on these answers. Hence, if the person who answers gives the answers "run" and "pizza," then the story that is compiled is "I run to eat pizza."

What you have to implement is not the whole interaction of the game, just the class that has the business rules the game relies on.

In fact, you need to implement that behavior that is documented by the RSpec documentation output that you see in the preceding figure. You have to implement both the class that satisfies these requirements and the RSpec specs that describe them.

Key Takeaways

- How to install and initialize RSpec

- How to configure RSpec

- How to write specs in a specific folder and naming convention

- How to output results in a documentation format

- How to share the setup code between specs

- How to write specs inside a context

RSpec is very powerful. In the next chapter, you are going to learn what extra tools it offers.

CHAPTER 5

Useful RSpec Tools

RSpec is a very feature-rich library. In this chapter, you learn about the most frequently used features (Figure 5-1), and you try to apply them to a real Ruby application. Also, you will be requested to develop a Ruby class and test cover it with RSpec.

Figure 5-1. *Useful RSpec Tools*

Learning Goals

1. Learn about RSpec *before* and *after* hooks.

2. Learn about the `subject` reference.

3. Learn about named `subjects`.

© Panos Matsinopoulos 2020
P. Matsinopoulos, *Practical Test Automation*, https://doi.org/10.1007/978-1-4842-6141-5_5

4. Learn about how to extend RSpec with helper methods in modules.

5. Learn about RSpec metadata.

6. Learn about filtering.

Hooks

You have already learned about the `before` hook that RSpec offers and allows you to *prepare the context*, that is, the *setup* of your test, of your example. However, RSpec offers some extra hooks.

before(:suite)

This is a hook for things you want to execute at the start of the `rspec` runner. Let's see that with an example. Go to the project that you have created in the previous chapter (project: `coffee_shop`) and open the file `spec/sandwich_spec.rb`. At the beginning of the file, write the following piece of code (Listing 5-1).

Listing 5-1. At the Beginning of spec/sandwich_spec.rb

```
RSpec.configure do |config|
  config.before :suite do
    puts 'This is executed only once at the beginning of the
    specifications run'
  end
end
```

Hence, the `spec/sandwich_spec.rb` now looks like the following (Listing 5-2).

Listing 5-2. Full Version of spec/sandwich_spec.rb

```
# File: spec/sandwich_spec.rb
#
RSpec.configure do |config|
  config.before :suite do
```

```
    puts 'This is executed only once at the beginning of the
    specifications run'
  end
end

RSpec.describe 'An ideal sandwich' do
  def sandwich
    @sandwich ||= Sandwich.new('delicious', [])
  end

  it 'is delicious' do
    expect(sandwich.taste).to eq('delicious')
  end

  it 'lets me add toppings' do
    sandwich.toppings << 'cheese'

    expect(sandwich.toppings).not_to be_empty
  end
end
```

The before :suite, since it is not related to any specific example or example group, can only be registered from within an RSpec configuration block. This is what the preceding lines 3–7 do. You start an RSpec.configuration block, and you call config.before :suite do ... end in order to register code that will be executed at the start of the spec runner.

If you run your test suite, you will see this:

```
$ bundle exec rspec

Randomized with seed 1770
This is executed only once at the beginning of the specifications run

An ideal sandwich
  is delicious
  lets me add toppings

A coffee
  costs 1 euro
  with milk
    costs 1.2 euro
```

```
Finished in 0.00873 seconds (files took 0.24097 seconds to load)
4 examples, 0 failures

Randomized with seed 1770

$
```

You can see the message This is executed only once at the beginning of the specifications run that is being printed at the beginning (after the Randomized with seed 1770).

The before :suite hook is usually used to set the correct test execution context for all the tests in your suite, for example, to load your test database with some seed data.

Moreover, because of the fact that it is executed before the instantiation of the examples, you cannot instantiate variables and expect to have them available inside the blocks of code of your examples.

Let's see an example of this error. In Listing 5-3, I enhance the spec/sandwich.rb file to use the instance variable @foo, which is instantiated inside the before :suite hook.

Listing 5-3. Use the Instance Variable @foo

```
# File: spec/sandwich_spec.rb
#
RSpec.configure do |config|
  config.before :suite do
    puts 'This is executed only once at the beginning of the specifications
    run'
    @foo = 5
  end
end

RSpec.describe 'An ideal sandwich' do
  def sandwich
    @sandwich ||= Sandwich.new('delicious', [])
  end

  it 'is delicious' do
    expect(@foo).to eq(5)
    expect(sandwich.taste).to eq('delicious')
  end
```

```
it 'lets me add toppings' do
  sandwich.toppings << 'cheese'

  expect(sandwich.toppings).not_to be_empty
end
end
```

Inside the test is delicious, I have written an expectation to check for the value of @ foo being 5. If you run the specs, you will see that they will fail:

```
$ bundle exec rspec

Randomized with seed 27481
This is executed only once at the beginning of the specifications run

A coffee
  costs 1 euro
  with milk
    costs 1.2 euro

An ideal sandwich
  is delicious (FAILED - 1)
  lets me add toppings

Failures:

  1) An ideal sandwich is delicious
     Failure/Error: expect(@foo).to eq(5)

       expected: 5
            got: nil

       (compared using ==)
     # ./spec/sandwich_spec.rb:16:in `block (2 levels) in <top (required)>'

Finished in 0.0566 seconds (files took 0.20695 seconds to load)
4 examples, 1 failure
```

Failed examples:

rspec ./spec/sandwich_spec.rb:15 # An ideal sandwich is delicious

Randomized with seed 27481

$

Finally, you usually put the before(:suite) hooks inside the spec_helper.rb file. So, before you continue with the rest of this chapter, move that code at the bottom of the existing RSpec.configure block inside the spec/spec_helper.rb file (Listing 5-4).

Listing 5-4. spec/spec_helper.rb File with the before(:suite) Hook

```
# This file was generated by the `rspec --init` command. Conventionally, all
# specs live under a `spec` directory, which RSpec adds to the `$LOAD_PATH`.
# The generated `.rspec` file contains `--require spec_helper` which will
  cause
# this file to always be loaded, without a need to explicitly require it in
  any
# files.
#
# Given that it is always loaded, you are encouraged to keep this file as
# light-weight as possible. Requiring heavyweight dependencies from this
  file
# will add to the boot time of your test suite on EVERY test run, even for an
# individual file that may not need all of that loaded. Instead, consider
  making
# a separate helper file that requires the additional dependencies and
  performs
# the additional setup, and require it from the spec files that actually
  need
# it.
#
# See http://rubydoc.info/gems/rspec-core/RSpec/Core/Configuration
RSpec.configure do |config|
  # rspec-expectations config goes here. You can use an alternate
  # assertion/expectation library such as wrong or the stdlib/minitest
```

```
# assertions if you prefer.
config.expect_with :rspec do |expectations|
  # This option will default to `true` in RSpec 4. It makes the
    `description`
  # and `failure_message` of custom matchers include text for helper
    methods
  # defined using `chain`, e.g.:
  #     be_bigger_than(2).and_smaller_than(4).description
  #     # => "be bigger than 2 and smaller than 4"
  # ...rather than:
  #     # => "be bigger than 2"
  expectations.include_chain_clauses_in_custom_matcher_descriptions =
  true
end

# rspec-mocks config goes here. You can use an alternate test double
# library (such as bogus or mocha) by changing the `mock_with` option here.
config.mock_with :rspec do |mocks|
  # Prevents you from mocking or stubbing a method that does not exist on
  # a real object. This is generally recommended, and will default to
  # `true` in RSpec 4.
  mocks.verify_partial_doubles = true
end

# This option will default to `:apply_to_host_groups` in RSpec 4 (and will
# have no way to turn it off -- the option exists only for backwards
# compatibility in RSpec 3). It causes shared context metadata to be
# inherited by the metadata hash of host groups and examples, rather than
# triggering implicit auto-inclusion in groups with matching metadata.
config.shared_context_metadata_behavior = :apply_to_host_groups

# The settings below are suggested to provide a good initial experience
# with RSpec, but feel free to customize to your heart's content.

# This allows you to limit a spec run to individual examples or groups
# you care about by tagging them with `:focus` metadata. When nothing
# is tagged with `:focus`, all examples get run. RSpec also provides
```

```
# aliases for `it`, `describe`, and `context` that include `:focus`
# metadata: `fit`, `fdescribe` and `fcontext`, respectively.
# config.filter_run_when_matching :focus

# Allows RSpec to persist some state between runs in order to support
# the `--only-failures` and `--next-failure` CLI options. We recommend
# you configure your source control system to ignore this file.
# config.example_status_persistence_file_path = "spec/examples.txt"

# Limits the available syntax to the non-monkey patched syntax that is
# recommended. For more details, see:
#   - http://rspec.info/blog/2012/06/rspecs-new-expectation-syntax/
#   - http://www.teaisaweso.me/blog/2013/05/27/rspecs-new-message-
#     expectation-syntax/
#   - http://rspec.info/blog/2014/05/notable-changes-in-rspec-3/#zero-
#     monkey-patching-mode
config.disable_monkey_patching!

# This setting enables warnings. It's recommended, but in some cases may
# be too noisy due to issues in dependencies.
# config.warnings = true

# Many RSpec users commonly either run the entire suite or an individual
# file, and it's useful to allow more verbose output when running an
# individual spec file.
#if config.files_to_run.one?
#   # Use the documentation formatter for detailed output,
#   # unless a formatter has already been configured
#   # (e.g. via a command-line flag).
#   config.default_formatter = "doc"
#end

# Print the 10 slowest examples and example groups at the
# end of the spec run, to help surface which specs are running
# particularly slow.
# config.profile_examples = 10
```

```
# Run specs in random order to surface order dependencies. If you find an
# order dependency and want to debug it, you can fix the order by
  providing
# the seed, which is printed after each run.
#       --seed 1234
config.order = :random

# Seed global randomization in this process using the `--seed` CLI option.
# Setting this allows you to use `--seed` to deterministically reproduce
# test failures related to randomization by passing the same `--seed` value
# as the one that triggered the failure.
Kernel.srand config.seed

config.before :suite do
  puts 'This is executed only once at the beginning of the
  specifications run'
end
end

require_relative '../all'
```

After you do the preceding change, don't forget to bring spec/spec_helper.rb back to its original state: without the RSpec.configure block and without the expectation for @foo to be 5 inside the is delicious example.

Then, make sure that if you run the whole suite, everything is still green.

before(:all)

This hook attaches code that is executed once for all the examples on a given context/describe. So this should appear inside the do...end block of a describe or context.

In order to see an example of this, you are going to enhance the spec/coffee_spec.rb specifications as follows (Listing 5-5).

Listing 5-5. spec/coffee_spec.rb File with the before :all Hook

```ruby
# File: spec/coffee_spec.rb
#
RSpec.describe 'A coffee' do
  let(:coffee) { Coffee.new }

  it 'costs 1 euro' do
    expect(coffee.price).to eq(1)
  end

  it 'takes 1 minute to prepare' do
    expect(coffee.prepare_duration).to eq(1)
  end

  context 'with milk' do
    before :all do
      puts 'This is a hook that will be executed once for the "with milk"
      context examples'
      @with_milk = 'Milk has been added!'
    end

    before { coffee.add_milk }

    it 'costs 1.2 euro' do
      puts @with_milk
      expect(coffee.price).to eq(1.2)
    end

    it 'takes 2 minutes to prepare' do
      puts @with_milk
      expect(coffee.prepare_duration).to eq(2)
    end
  end
end
```

These are the changes to the code, as in Figure 5-2:

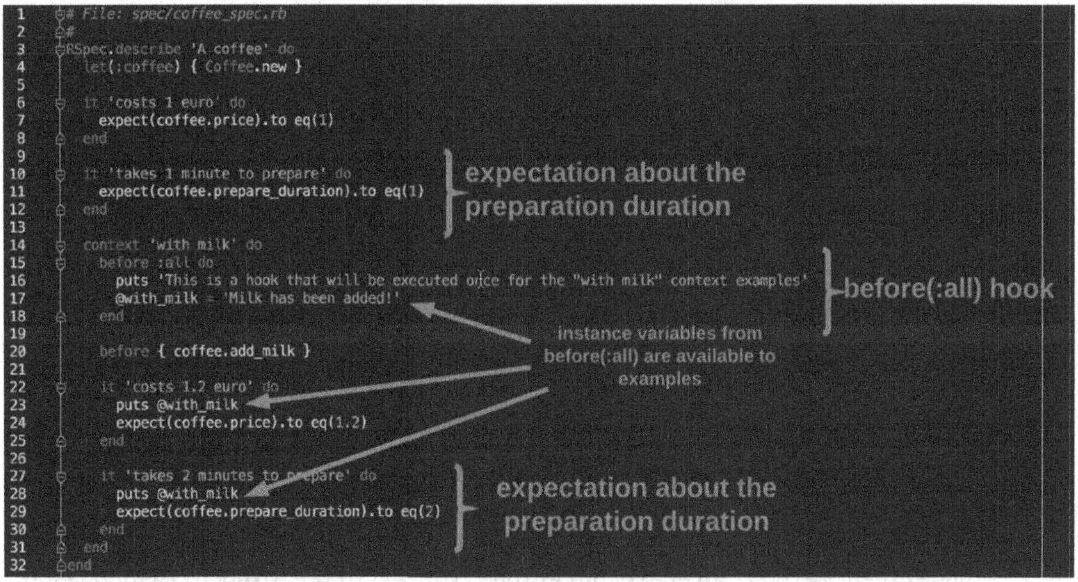

Figure 5-2. *Changes to Code to Demonstrate the before :all Hook*

1. You have added two more expectations that have to do with the duration to prepare a cup of coffee.

2. You have added a before(:all) hook on the context with milk. This code will be executed only once for the two examples in that context.

Let's run the suite:

```
$ bundle exec rspec

Randomized with seed 16834
This is executed only once at the beginning of the specifications run

A coffee
  takes 1 minute to prepare (FAILED - 1)
  costs 1 euro
  with milk
```

This is a hook that will be executed once for the "with milk" context examples
Milk has been added!
    costs 1.2 euro
Milk has been added!
   takes 2 minutes to prepare (FAILED - 2)

An ideal sandwich
  is delicious
  lets me add toppings

Failures:

  1) A coffee takes 1 minute to prepare
    Failure/Error: expect(coffee.prepare_duration).to eq(1)

    NoMethodError:
      undefined method `prepare_duration' for #<Coffee:0x00007f936b09a500
      @ingredients=[]>
    # ./spec/coffee_spec.rb:11:in `block (2 levels) in <top (required)>'

  2) A coffee with milk takes 2 minutes to prepare
    Failure/Error: expect(coffee.prepare_duration).to eq(2)

    NoMethodError:
      undefined method `prepare_duration' for #<Coffee:0x00007f936a8f6010
      @ingredients=["milk"]>
    # ./spec/coffee_spec.rb:29:in `block (3 levels) in <top (required)>'

Finished in 0.00819 seconds (files took 0.26973 seconds to load)
6 examples, 2 failures

Failed examples:

rspec ./spec/coffee_spec.rb:10 # A coffee takes 1 minute to prepare
rspec ./spec/coffee_spec.rb:27 # A coffee with milk takes 2 minutes to prepare

Randomized with seed 16834

$

As expected, the two examples that deal with the preparation duration fail. Before you fix them, see the messages that prove how the before(:all) hook works. It is called once for the whole context, and the instance variables created within its block are available to the code of the examples (Figure 5-3).

```
A coffee
  takes 1 minute to prepare (FAILED - 1)
  costs 1 euro
  with milk
This is a hook that will be executed once for the "with milk" context examples    ◀── executed only once
Milk has been added!
    costs 1.2 euro                        instance variable available in example code
Milk has been added!
    takes 2 minutes to prepare (FAILED - 2)

An ideal sandwich
  is delicious
```

Figure 5-3. *Output of the RSpec Run Proves How the* before(:all) *Hook Works*

Let's quickly fix the code by introducing the #prepare_duration method in the Coffee class (file: coffee.rb – Listing 5-6).

Listing 5-6. Introduce Method prepare_duration

```ruby
# File: coffee.rb
#
class Coffee
  INGREDIENT_PRICES = {
    'milk' => 0.2
  }

  def initialize
    @ingredients = []
  end

  def price
    1 + sum_of_ingredients_price
  end

  def add_milk
    @ingredients << 'milk'
  end
```

```ruby
def prepare_duration
  1 + @ingredients.size
end

private

def sum_of_ingredients_price
  @ingredients.reduce(0) do |result, ingredient|
    result += result + INGREDIENT_PRICES[ingredient]
  end
end
end
```

The new lines added are lines 20–22. Now, if you run the suite, you will get everything green, like this:

```
$ bundle exec rspec

Randomized with seed 8716
This is executed only once at the beginning of the specifications run

An ideal sandwich
  lets me add toppings
  is delicious

A coffee
  costs 1 euro
  takes 1 minute to prepare
  with milk
This is a hook that will be executed once for the "with milk" context examples
Milk has been added!
    takes 2 minutes to prepare
Milk has been added!
    costs 1.2 euro

Finished in 0.01081 seconds (files took 0.24569 seconds to load)
6 examples, 0 failures

Randomized with seed 8716

$
```

Note   `before(:all)` is also available as `before(:context)`.

---

before(:example) or Simply before

You have already seen this hook. It is used to attach code that will be executed before every example in the context/describe it is declared in.

This is what happens on line 20 `before { coffee.add_milk }` inside the file `spec/coffee_spec.rb`.

Note that `before(:example)` is also available as `before(:each)`.

after Hooks

Before I close this part about hooks, I need to tell you that, besides the `before` hooks, RSpec allows you to attach `after` hooks too. Here is the list of `after` hooks:

1. `after :example`, which is executed after every example. Also available as `after :each` or simply `after`

2. `after :all`, which is executed after every context. Also available as `after :context`

3. `after :suite`, which is executed at the end of the execution of the whole suite of examples

Multiple Hooks

Note that you can attach multiple hooks. They will be executed in the order they are declared.

subject

Let's now talk about another technique and best practice that you will frequently encounter. It is about the subject under test.

You will many times see the argument to the outermost `RSpec.describe` being a class, rather than a string:

```
RSpec.describe Foo do
...
end
```

In that case, you can use the method `subject` inside your example code. Then the subject is going to be an instance of that class, instantiated with the default initializer.

Let's see that with the `spec/coffee_spec.rb`. Instead of `RSpec.describe 'A coffee' do...end`, you use the class `Coffee` (Listing 5-7).

Listing 5-7. Use the Coffee class

```ruby
# File: spec/coffee_spec.rb
#
RSpec.describe Coffee do
  let(:coffee) { Coffee.new }

  it 'costs 1 euro' do
    expect(coffee.price).to eq(1)
  end

  it 'takes 1 minute to prepare' do
    expect(coffee.prepare_duration).to eq(1)
  end

  context 'with milk' do
    before :all do
      puts 'This is a hook that will be executed once for the "with milk"
      context examples'
      @with_milk = 'Milk has been added!'
    end

    before { coffee.add_milk }

    it 'costs 1.2 euro' do
      puts @with_milk
      expect(coffee.price).to eq(1.2)
    end
```

```
  it 'takes 2 minutes to prepare' do
    puts @with_milk
    expect(coffee.prepare_duration).to eq(2)
  end
 end
end
```

If you run the specifications for `Coffee`, you will see this:

```
$ bundle exec rspec spec/coffee_spec.rb

Randomized with seed 33151
This is executed only once at the beginning of the specifications run

Coffee
  costs 1 euro
  takes 1 minute to prepare
  with milk
This is a hook that will be executed once for the "with milk" context
examples
Milk has been added!
    costs 1.2 euro
Milk has been added!
    takes 2 minutes to prepare

Finished in 0.00505 seconds (files took 0.25892 seconds to load)
4 examples, 0 failures

Randomized with seed 33151

$
```

Now the `Coffee` string is printed as the outermost `describe` description.

Using the class is helping the reader bind the spec to an implementation, especially when the specs have to do with the unit tests of a class. But as I said earlier, you can use the `subject` to refer to the instance under test. Let's adapt the `spec/coffee_spec.rb` to do that (Listing 5-8).

Listing 5-8. Use subject

```ruby
# File: spec/coffee_spec.rb
#
RSpec.describe Coffee do
  it 'costs 1 euro' do
    expect(subject.price).to eq(1)
  end

  it 'takes 1 minute to prepare' do
    expect(subject.prepare_duration).to eq(1)
  end

  context 'with milk' do
    before :all do
      puts 'This is a hook that will be executed once for the "with milk"
      context examples'
      @with_milk = 'Milk has been added!'
    end

    before { subject.add_milk }

    it 'costs 1.2 euro' do
      puts @with_milk
      expect(subject.price).to eq(1.2)
    end

    it 'takes 2 minutes to prepare' do
      puts @with_milk
      expect(subject.prepare_duration).to eq(2)
    end
  end
end
```

You have removed the let(:coffee)... and all the coffee references. You are now using the subject instead.

If you run your specs for the Coffee, you will see that they will succeed.

So subject saves a little bit of typing, but the problem is that it hides the semantic meaning of the subject under test and the firing phase code is not really easy to understand quickly what it is about. In other words, the coffee.prepare_duration is much more descriptive and friendly to the reader rather than the subject.prepare_duration.

To alleviate that, some developers, including myself, still use the let; but they invoke the subject inside the let block: let(:coffee) { subject }. So here is my preferred version for the spec/coffee_spec.rb (Listing 5-9).

Listing 5-9. Using let and subject

```ruby
# File: spec/coffee_spec.rb
#
RSpec.describe Coffee do
  let(:coffee) { subject }

  it 'costs 1 euro' do
    expect(coffee.price).to eq(1)
  end

  it 'takes 1 minute to prepare' do
    expect(coffee.prepare_duration).to eq(1)
  end

  context 'with milk' do
    before :all do
      puts 'This is a hook that will be executed once for the "with milk"
      context examples'
      @with_milk = 'Milk has been added!'
    end
    before { coffee.add_milk }

    it 'costs 1.2 euro' do
      puts @with_milk
      expect(coffee.price).to eq(1.2)
    end
```

```
    it 'takes 2 minutes to prepare' do
      puts @with_milk
      expect(coffee.prepare_duration).to eq(2)
    end
  end
end
```

This version goes back to be using `coffee` instead of `subject` inside the example code. But the `coffee` is defined in terms of the `subject`.

However, there is always the case in which the `subject` cannot be instantiated by the standard no-arguments initializer. See, for example, the case of the `Sandwich` instances. If you decide to give the `RSpec.describe` the `Sandwich` argument (instead of the `An ideal sandwich`), then `subject` will fail. Let's try the version of `spec/sandwich_spec.rb` that uses `subject` (Listing 5-10).

Listing 5-10. spec/sandwich_spec.rb Using subject

```
# File: spec/sandwich_spec.rb
#
RSpec.describe Sandwich do
  let(:sandwich) do
    subject
  end

  it 'is delicious' do
    expect(sandwich.taste).to eq('delicious')
  end
  it 'lets me add toppings' do
    sandwich.toppings << 'cheese'

    expect(sandwich.toppings).not_to be_empty
  end
end
```

You can see that I have done two changes in order to introduce `subject`:

1. On line 3, I use `RSpec.describe Sandwich do`.

2. On lines 4–6, I define `sandwich` as a `let` of the `subject`.

But, if we run the specs for this file, they will fail:

```
$ bundle exec rspec spec/sandwich_spec.rb

Randomized with seed 30666
This is executed only once at the beginning of the specifications run

Sandwich
  lets me add toppings (FAILED - 1)
  is delicious (FAILED - 2)

Failures:

  1) Sandwich lets me add toppings
     Failure/Error: subject

     ArgumentError:
       wrong number of arguments (given 0, expected 2)
     # ./sandwich.rb:6:in `initialize'
     # ./spec/sandwich_spec.rb:5:in `block (2 levels) in <top (required)>'
     # ./spec/sandwich_spec.rb:13:in `block (2 levels) in <top (required)>'

  2) Sandwich is delicious
     Failure/Error: subject

     ArgumentError:
       wrong number of arguments (given 0, expected 2)
     # ./sandwich.rb:6:in `initialize'
     # ./spec/sandwich_spec.rb:5:in `block (2 levels) in <top (required)>'
     # ./spec/sandwich_spec.rb:9:in `block (2 levels) in <top (required)>'

Finished in 0.00312 seconds (files took 0.26276 seconds to load)
2 examples, 2 failures

Failed examples:

rspec ./spec/sandwich_spec.rb:12 # Sandwich lets me add toppings
rspec ./spec/sandwich_spec.rb:8 # Sandwich is delicious

Randomized with seed 30666

$
```

You can see that the error is the same for all the failing examples:

```
ArgumentError:
      wrong number of arguments (given 0, expected 2)
    # ./sandwich.rb:6:in `initialize'
    # ./spec/sandwich_spec.rb:5:in `block (2 levels) in <top (required)>'
    # ./spec/sandwich_spec.rb:13:in `block (2 levels) in <top (required)>'
```

On line spec/sandwich_spec.rb:5, you are calling subject which internally calls the Sandwich initializer **without** any arguments. That's why you are getting ArgumentError and (0 for 2), that is, the initializer has been called with no arguments when two were expected.

How can you remedy this and still use subject? You need to redefine subject as follows (Listing 5-11).

Listing 5-11. Redefine subject

```
# File: spec/sandwich_spec.rb
#
RSpec.describe Sandwich do
  subject(:sandwich) do
    Sandwich.new('delicious', [])
  end

  it 'is delicious' do
    expect(sandwich.taste).to eq('delicious')
  end

  it 'lets me add toppings' do
    sandwich.toppings << 'cheese'

    expect(sandwich.toppings).not_to be_empty
  end
end
```

You create a named subject, you give it the name sandwich, and then you can use it in your example code.

One might ask, "Why would you want to do that and not just use let?" The answer is that I prefer to use subject to indicate the subject under test. I use let for other helper methods that I might need for my tests.

Note that subject is being memoized and evaluated only once within the execution of an example. So, even if your example calls the named subject multiple times, only the first time is being evaluated, as the let does.

Finally, both subject and let have the alternative subject! and let!, respectively. The subject! and let! evaluate their blocks before the example execution (whereas the subject and let are lazily evaluated at the first occurrence within the example code).

Extending RSpec with Helper Methods in Modules

You have learned how to create helper methods inside an example group. It has been presented in the previous chapter. Those methods were available inside the context in which they were defined, but not outside of it.

RSpec offers you the ability to define helper methods that can be used by any context, since they are attached at the RSpec configuration level.

How do you do that?

First, you need to define a module with the helper methods. Let's see an example. Create the file upcased_and_line_spaced.rb in the root folder of your project (Listing 5-12).

Listing 5-12. Example Module with a Helper Method

```ruby
# File: upcased_and_line_spaced.rb
#
module UpcasedAndLineSpaced
  # Takes "foo" and returns "F O O"
  #
  def upcased_and_line_spaced(value)
    value.upcase.gsub(/./) {|c| "#{c} "}.strip
  end
end
```

This module defines a helper method that takes a string value and returns it with all characters upcased. Also, it adds an extra space after each character (except the last one).

In order for you to be able to use this helper method, you need to attach the module to the RSpec configuration as follows:

The following snippet of code needs to be added to the bottom of the existing RSpec.configure block, inside the spec/spec_helper.rb file:

```
config.include UpcasedAndLineSpaced
```

And in order for the UpcasedAndLineSpaced constant to be found, you will have to require the module file **before** the RSpec.configure block.

Hence, the full content of the spec/spec_helper.rb file should be as shown in Listing 5-13.

Listing 5-13. spec/spec_helper.rb

```
# This file was generated by the `rspec --init` command. Conventionally, all
# specs live under a `spec` directory, which RSpec adds to the `$LOAD_PATH`.
# The generated `.rspec` file contains `--require spec_helper` which will cause
# this file to always be loaded, without a need to explicitly require it
  in any
# files.
#
# Given that it is always loaded, you are encouraged to keep this file as
# light-weight as possible. Requiring heavyweight dependencies from this
  file
# will add to the boot time of your test suite on EVERY test run, even
  for an
# individual file that may not need all of that loaded. Instead, consider
  making
# a separate helper file that requires the additional dependencies and
  performs
# the additional setup, and require it from the spec files that actually need
# it.
#
# See http://rubydoc.info/gems/rspec-core/RSpec/Core/Configuration

require_relative '../upcased_and_line_spaced'

RSpec.configure do |config|
  # rspec-expectations config goes here. You can use an alternate
  # assertion/expectation library such as wrong or the stdlib/minitest
```

```
# assertions if you prefer.
config.expect_with :rspec do |expectations|
  # This option will default to `true` in RSpec 4. It makes the
    `description`
  # and `failure_message` of custom matchers include text for helper
    methods
  # defined using `chain`, e.g.:
  #     be_bigger_than(2).and_smaller_than(4).description
  #     # => "be bigger than 2 and smaller than 4"
  # ...rather than:
  #     # => "be bigger than 2"
  expectations.include_chain_clauses_in_custom_matcher_descriptions = true
end

# rspec-mocks config goes here. You can use an alternate test double
# library (such as bogus or mocha) by changing the `mock_with` option here.
config.mock_with :rspec do |mocks|
  # Prevents you from mocking or stubbing a method that does not exist on
  # a real object. This is generally recommended, and will default to
  # `true` in RSpec 4.
  mocks.verify_partial_doubles = true
end

# This option will default to `:apply_to_host_groups` in RSpec 4 (and will
# have no way to turn it off -- the option exists only for backwards
# compatibility in RSpec 3). It causes shared context metadata to be
# inherited by the metadata hash of host groups and examples, rather than
# triggering implicit auto-inclusion in groups with matching metadata.
config.shared_context_metadata_behavior = :apply_to_host_groups

# The settings below are suggested to provide a good initial experience
# with RSpec, but feel free to customize to your heart's content.

# This allows you to limit a spec run to individual examples or groups
# you care about by tagging them with `:focus` metadata. When nothing
# is tagged with `:focus`, all examples get run. RSpec also provides
# aliases for `it`, `describe`, and `context` that include `:focus`
```

```
# metadata: `fit`, `fdescribe` and `fcontext`, respectively.
# config.filter_run_when_matching :focus

# Allows RSpec to persist some state between runs in order to support
# the `--only-failures` and `--next-failure` CLI options. We recommend
# you configure your source control system to ignore this file.
# config.example_status_persistence_file_path = "spec/examples.txt"

# Limits the available syntax to the non-monkey patched syntax that is
# recommended. For more details, see:
#   - http://rspec.info/blog/2012/06/rspecs-new-expectation-syntax/
#   - http://www.teaisaweso.me/blog/2013/05/27/rspecs-new-message-
#     expectation-syntax/
#   - http://rspec.info/blog/2014/05/notable-changes-in-rspec-3/#zero-
#     monkey-patching-mode
config.disable_monkey_patching!

# This setting enables warnings. It's recommended, but in some cases may
# be too noisy due to issues in dependencies.
# config.warnings = true

# Many RSpec users commonly either run the entire suite or an individual
# file, and it's useful to allow more verbose output when running an
# individual spec file.
#if config.files_to_run.one?
#   # Use the documentation formatter for detailed output,
#   # unless a formatter has already been configured
#   # (e.g. via a command-line flag).
#   config.default_formatter = "doc"
#end

# Print the 10 slowest examples and example groups at the
# end of the spec run, to help surface which specs are running
# particularly slow.
# config.profile_examples = 10

# Run specs in random order to surface order dependencies. If you find an
# order dependency and want to debug it, you can fix the order by providing
```

```
# the seed, which is printed after each run.
#      --seed 1234
config.order = :random

# Seed global randomization in this process using the `--seed` CLI option.
# Setting this allows you to use `--seed` to deterministically reproduce
# test failures related to randomization by passing the same `--seed` value
# as the one that triggered the failure.
Kernel.srand config.seed

config.before :suite do
  puts 'This is executed only once at the beginning of the
  specifications run'
end
```

config.include UpcasedAndLineSpaced
```
end
```

```
require_relative '../all'
```

Now, you can use the helper method inside the example code. Here is the new version of spec/sandwich_spec.rb (Listing 5-14).

Listing 5-14. Using the Helper Method from the Module

```
# File: spec/sandwich_spec.rb
#
RSpec.describe Sandwich do
  subject(:sandwich) do
    Sandwich.new('delicious', [])
  end

  it 'is delicious' do
    expect(sandwich.taste).to eq('delicious')
  end

  it 'is displayed as D E L I C I O U S' do
    expect(upcased_and_line_spaced(sandwich.taste)).to eq('D E L I C I O U S')
  end
```

```
it 'lets me add toppings' do
  sandwich.toppings << 'cheese'

  expect(sandwich.toppings).not_to be_empty
end
end
```

You have added a new specification. See lines 12–14. It is there where you call the upcased_and_line_spaced helper method.

If you run the specs now, you will get this:

```
$ bundle exec rspec spec/sandwich_spec.rb

Randomized with seed 5962
This is executed only once at the beginning of the specifications run

Sandwich
  is delicious
  lets me add toppings
  is displayed as D E L I C I O U S

Finished in 0.00902 seconds (files took 0.23133 seconds to load)
3 examples, 0 failures

Randomized with seed 5962

$
```

This is a very common practice with RSpec. You will encounter it in many projects. Note that when you do config.include <module>, the methods become available inside the example code. However, when you do config.extend <module>, the methods become available inside the do..end blocks of the describes and contexts.

Metadata

RSpec builds a set of metadata around your example groups and examples. Also, it allows you to build your custom metadata.

described_class

The call to described_class returns the class that is described when the outermost
describe is given a class (and not a string description). You usually use it in order to
avoid repeating the class name, hence being easier to change it, if you need to.

Let's change the spec/sandwich_spec.rb to be using the described_class. Here it is
(Listing 5-15).

Listing 5-15. Using described_class

```
# File: spec/sandwich_spec.rb
#
RSpec.describe Sandwich do
  subject(:sandwich) do
    described_class.new('delicious', [])
  end

  it 'is delicious' do
    expect(sandwich.taste).to eq('delicious')
  end

  it 'is displayed as D E L I C I O U S' do
    expect(upcased_and_line_spaced(sandwich.taste)).to eq('D E L I C I O U S')
  end

  it 'lets me add toppings' do
    sandwich.toppings << 'cheese'

    expect(sandwich.toppings).not_to be_empty
  end
end
```

The only change is on line 5. Instead of Sandwich.new, you are using described_
class.new. Again, this allows you to change the class at the top call to described without
having to change its other occurrences inside the spec file.

Custom Metadata

RSpec allows you to attach metadata to example groups or examples. The metadata are given in the form of a Hash as the last argument to describe, context, or it, before the block definition.

Here is an example: You are going to define some metadata in the spec/sandwich_spec.rb file (Listing 5-16).

Listing 5-16. Example of Custom Metadata

```
# File: spec/sandwich_spec.rb
#
RSpec.describe Sandwich, test: :unit do
  subject(:sandwich) do
    described_class.new('delicious', [])
  end

  it 'is delicious' do
    expect(sandwich.taste).to eq('delicious')
  end

  it 'is displayed as D E L I C I O U S' do
    expect(upcased_and_line_spaced(sandwich.taste)).to eq('D E L I C I O U S')
  end

  it 'lets me add toppings' do
    sandwich.toppings << 'cheese'

    expect(sandwich.toppings).not_to be_empty
  end
end
```

The enhancement is on line 3 only (Figure 5-4).

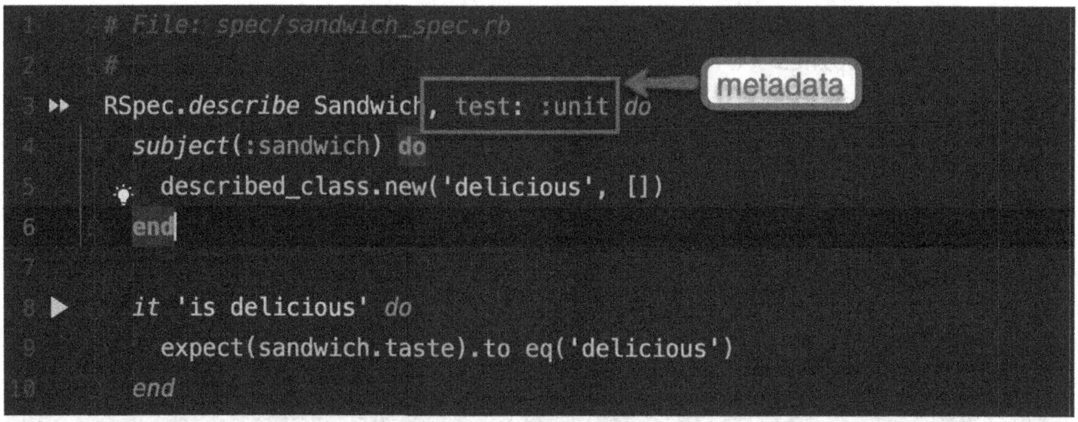

Figure 5-4. Using Metadata

You have attached the metadata `test: :unit`.

Metadata are available inside the example code. They are available via the `example` reference that can optionally be defined as the argument to the example `do..end` block. See how the example is displayed as D E L I C I O U S has access to this variable and to the metadata (Listing 5-17).

Listing 5-17. Access Metadata

```
# File: spec/sandwich_spec.rb
#
RSpec.describe Sandwich, test: :unit do
  subject(:sandwich) do
    described_class.new('delicious', [])
  end

  it 'is delicious' do
    expect(sandwich.taste).to eq('delicious')
  end

  it 'is displayed as D E L I C I O U S' do |example|
    puts "Type of test: #{example.metadata[:test]}"

    expect(upcased_and_line_spaced(sandwich.taste)).to eq('D E L I C I O U S')
  end
```

```
  it 'lets me add toppings' do
    sandwich.toppings << 'cheese'

    expect(sandwich.toppings).not_to be_empty
  end
end
```

In Figure 5-5, I am highlighting the relevant parts of the code.

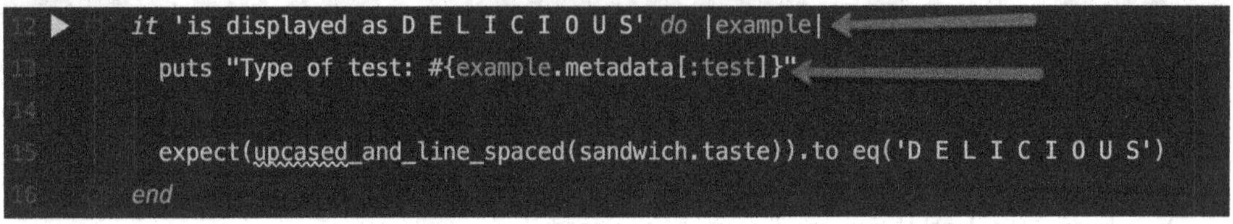

Figure 5-5.   *Metadata Accessed in Example Code*

Note that the metadata are being inherited from the example group to all the enclosed examples and other example groups (`describes` or `contexts`). And each contained example group or example can add more metadata or override the value of metadata inherited.

See how spec on line 18 now overrides the value of the `:test` metadata key (Figure 5-6).

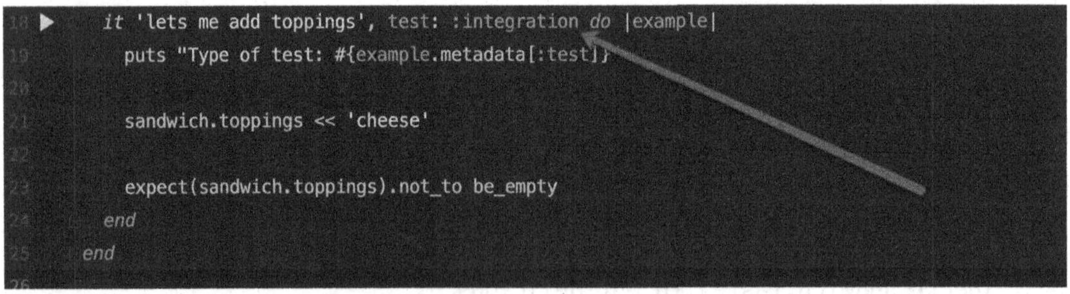

Figure 5-6.   *Override Metadata Values*

The new version of the `spec/sandwich_spec.rb` is as shown in Listing 5-18.

Listing 5-18. Override Metadata Values

```
# File: spec/sandwich_spec.rb
#
RSpec.describe Sandwich, test: :unit do
  subject(:sandwich) do
    described_class.new('delicious', [])
  end

  it 'is delicious' do
    expect(sandwich.taste).to eq('delicious')
  end

  it 'is displayed as D E L I C I O U S' do |example|
    puts "Type of test: #{example.metadata[:test]}"

    expect(upcased_and_line_spaced(sandwich.taste)).to eq('D E L I C I O U S')
  end

  it 'lets me add toppings', test: :integration do |example|
    puts "Type of test: #{example.metadata[:test]}"

    sandwich.toppings << 'cheese'

    expect(sandwich.toppings).not_to be_empty
  end
end
```

Now, let's run the spec/sandwich_spec.rb specs:

```
$ bundle exec rspec spec/sandwich_spec.rb

Randomized with seed 65045
This is executed only once at the beginning of the specifications run

Sandwich
Type of test: integration
  lets me add toppings
Type of test: unit
  is displayed as D E L I C I O U S
  is delicious
```

```
Finished in 0.00841 seconds (files took 0.21139 seconds to load)
3 examples, 0 failures

Randomized with seed 65045

$
```

As you can see in the preceding code, the lets me add toppings has type of test integration, whereas the is displayed as D E L I C I O U S has type of test unit.

Finally, if you want to set a metadata key to the value true, you can always give the key without the value. Here is an example:

```
it 'order contains 5 items`, :wip do
   ...
end
```

In this example, you are attaching the metadata key :wip. This is attached with the value true, even if you have not explicitly set that.

Filtering

Metadata are also useful with regard to what examples you might want to run when invoking rspec. In other words, you can limit the selected examples according to their metadata values.

Here is how you can invoke rspec using metadata:

```
$ bundle exec rspec --tag test:integration
Run options: include {:test=>"integration"}

Randomized with seed 43976
This is executed only once at the beginning of the specifications run

Sandwich
Type of test: integration
  lets me add toppings
Finished in 0.00777 seconds (files took 0.20195 seconds to load)
1 example, 0 failures

Randomized with seed 43976

$
```

As you can see in the preceding code, you have invoked `rspec` with the `--tag test:integration`. This filtered the examples to run only the ones that have the metadata tag `test` with value `integration`.

Tasks and Quizzes

This chapter is coming both with a quiz and a task.

Quiz

The quiz for this chapter can be found here: `www.techcareerbooster.com/quizzes/useful-rspec-tools`.

Task Details

WRITE A RUBY CLASS AND COVER IT WITH RSPEC SPECS

You will need to write a Ruby class that would satisfy the following requirements:

```
NumberEachLine
  prefixes each line with an increasing integer number starting at 1
  when it is configured to start the line count at 8
    prefixes each line with an increasing integer number starting at 8
  when it is configured to pad each number with leading zeros
    prefixes each line with an increasing integer padded with leading zeros
    when it is configured to pad each number with leading blanks
      prefixes each line with an increasing integer padded with leading
      blanks
    when number of lines does not justify padding
      does not pad with leading zeros
  when it is configured to prefix each line with #
    prefixes each line with an increasing integer number starting at 1 and
    prefix each line being #
    and when it is configured to pad each number with leading zeros
      prefixes each line with an increasing integer number starting at 1 and
      pads each number with leading zeros and prefixes the line with #
```

```
    when it is configured to suffix each line number with ". "
      prefixes each line with an increasing integer number starting at 1 and
      suffix on numbers being ". "
    when input is
class Hello
  def initialize(name)
    @name = name
  end

  def greetings
    puts "Hello RSpec::ExampleGroups::NumberEachLine"
  end

  def name
    @name
  end
end
  and we configure pad of numbers with blanks and suffix number with '. '
    generates the following
1. class Hello
2.   def initialize(name)
3.     @name = name
4.   end
5.
6.   def greetings
7.     puts "Hello RSpec::ExampleGroups::NumberEachLine"
8.   end
9.
10.   def name
11.     @name
12.   end
13. end

Finished in 0.00232 seconds (files took 0.07316 seconds to load)
9 examples, 0 failures
```

The preceding code is a sample output of the RSpec dry run for the requirements of the class. And the following screenshot is a colored output that might be more helpful to you (Figure 5-7).

```
NumberEachLine
  prefixes each line with an increasing integer number starting at 1
  when it is configured to start the line count at 8
    prefixes each line with an increasing integer number starting at 8
  when it is configured to pad each number with leading zeros
    prefixes each line with an increasing integer padded with leading zeros
    when it is configured to pad each number with leading blanks
      prefixes each line with an increasing integer padded with leading blanks
    when number of lines does not justify padding
      does not pad with leading zeros
  when it is configured to prefix each line with #
    prefixes each line with an increasing integer number starting at 1 and prefix each line being #
    and when it is configured to pad each number with leading zeros
      prefixes each line with an increasing integer number starting at 1 and pads each number with leading zeros and prefixes the line with #
  when it is configured to suffix each line number with ". "
    prefixes each line with an increasing integer number starting at 1 and suffix on numbers being ". "
  when input is
class Hello
  def initialize(name)
    @name = name
  end

  def greetings
    puts "Hello RSpec::ExampleGroups::NumberEachLine"
  end

  def name
    @name
  end
end
  and we configure pad of numbers with blanks and suffix number with ', '
    generates the following
1. class Hello
2.   def initialize(name)
3.     @name = name
4.   end
5.
6.   def greetings
7.     puts "Hello RSpec::ExampleGroups::NumberEachLine"
8.   end
9.
10.  def name
11.    @name
12.  end
13. end

Finished in 0.00232 seconds (files took 0.07316 seconds to load)
9 examples, 0 failures
```

Figure 5-7. *Requirements of the Task*

But let me give you some more details:

(1) The purpose of this class is to take as input a multiline string and return back each line of the string being suffixed with its corresponding line number. For example, if you have the string

```
This is a multi-line
string. This is second line
And this is third line
```

the class should return back this:

```
1This is a multi-line
2string. This is second line
3And this is third line
```

(2) Besides this main functionality, the class should allow for some kind of
configuration. For example, you want to tell that each number should be
suffixed with the string ". ". If you say that, then the returned string should be
something like this:

```
1. This is a multi-line
2. string. This is second line
3. And this is third line
```

(3) Or you may say that the line numbering should start from 8, not 1. In that case,
the output should be something like this:

```
8This is a multi-line
9string. This is second line
10And this is third line
```

(4) You may also say that you want each number to be padded with 0s or other
character sequence. For example, assuming that you want the numbers to be
padded with blanks, the input is

```
This is a multi-line
string. This is a second line
And this is the third line
And this is the fourth line
And this is the fifth line
And this is the sixth line
And this is the seventh line
And this is the eighth line
And this is the ninth line
And this is the tenth line
And this is the eleventh line
```

And then the output will be

```
1This is a multi-line
2string. This is a second line
3And this is the third line
4And this is the fourth line
5And this is the fifth line
6And this is the sixth line
```

```
 7And this is the seventh line
 8And this is the eighth line
 9And this is the ninth line
10And this is the tenth line
11And this is the eleventh line
```

(5) However, when the number of lines does not justify padding, then padding will
     not be used even if specified. Hence, if you specify that you want padding with
     0s but the input is less than ten lines long, then no padding will take place. In
     other words, the input

```
line 1
line 2
```

is output as

```
1line 1
2line 2
```

(6) You may also ask the class to prefix each line with a prefix string. Assume that
     you have the following input and the prefix you want to attach to each line is '#':

```
line 1
line 2
```

Then the output will be

```
#1line1
#2line2
```

So let's summarize the configuration options:

1. Starting Number: Default value is 1.

2. Pad Numbers With: A string to pad numbers with. Numbers are right justified,
    and the padding string is repeated to the left.

3. Suffix Number With: A string to suffix each number with.

4. Prefix Line With: A string to prefix each line with.

Please note that you don't have to stick to the RSpec specifications that would give the same output as the one presented at the top of this task. You can come up with your own implementation for the RSpec specifications. What I want you to do is to implement the class and make sure that it is well test covered.

Note that this task is inspired by this online text mechanics page: `http://textmechanic.com/text-tools/numeration-tools/number-each-line/`.

Key Takeaways

- How to use RSpec hooks

- How to use subject and named subjects

- How to extend RSpec with helper methods

- How to use RSpec metadata

In the following chapter, you will be introduced to another very popular tool that lives in the BDD (Behavior-Driven Development): Cucumber. Cucumber allows you to write your specifications in plain English.

CHAPTER 6

Introduction to Cucumber

Cucumber (Figure 6-1) is an awesome tool that allows you to develop your software using a Behavior-Driven Approach (BDA). It makes sure that business stakeholders transfer the software requirements to developers in an accurate and rigorous way so that the final software delivered fully satisfies those requirements. Also, the requirements are turned into executable specifications of the application developed, and they are executed on every new commit to make sure that no old features are broken when new ones are introduced. Cucumber is a great tool of collaboration, documentation, and test automation.

Figure 6-1. *Cucumber, Gherkin, and Ruby*

Learning Goals

1. Learn how to install Cucumber.

2. Learn about the `cucumber` executable.

3. Learn how to initialize your project to use Cucumber.

4. Learn how to identify the files that include the feature descriptions.

© Panos Matsinopoulos 2020
P. Matsinopoulos, *Practical Test Automation*, https://doi.org/10.1007/978-1-4842-6141-5_6

5.   Learn how to identify the files that include the step definitions.

6.   Learn about Gherkin.

7.   Learn how to apply the test-first approach to your project development using Cucumber.

8.   Learn how to write feature scenarios.

9.   Learn about pending steps.

10.   Learn how the step invocations can contain runtime arguments that can be used in step definitions.

11.   Learn how to remove duplication in your feature files using Scenario Outlines.

12.   Learn how to integrate RSpec with Cucumber.

Introduction

Cucumber is the tool that allows you to write the requirements of your software in almost plain English. It can then turn them into executable specifications. This means that

1.   Your business and product owners can read the Cucumber artifacts and understand what the application is supposed to be doing.

2.   You are sure that whenever you introduce a change in your application code, the specifications will be executed and any broken feature will be revealed, before it actually reaches the public.

Cucumber bridges the business aspect of the software with the technical aspect of it. I will come back to this later on. First, let's try to use Cucumber so that you can have a better idea of its constituent parts.

The Project and Cucumber Installation

You will learn about Cucumber using a simple project, called calculator (Figure 6-2). So go ahead and create a new RubyMine project with the name calculator. Make sure that you integrate with rbenv (ruby version: 2.x).

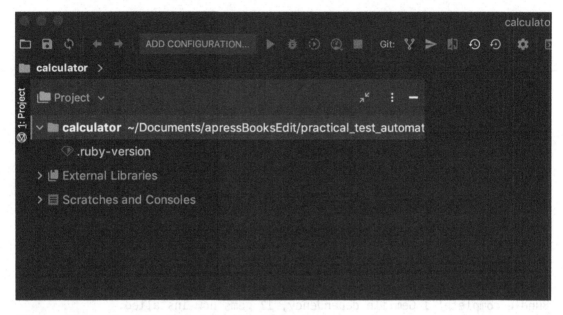

Figure 6-2. *calculator RubyMine Project*

Next, add the Gemfile with reference to the gem cucumber (Listing 6-1).

Listing 6-1. Gemfile

```
# File: Gemfile
#
source 'https://rubygems.org'

gem 'cucumber'
```

Run bundle so that the cucumber gem is installed.

Note   You need to have a bundler installed. If you don't have it, run gem
install bundler when being at the root folder of your project. This will install
the bundle executable that reads the Gemfile and installs the necessary gems
for your project.

This is what happened on my machine when I ran bundle:

```
Using backports 3.17.0
Using builder 3.2.4
Using bundler 2.1.4
Using cucumber-tag_expressions 1.1.1
Using gherkin 5.1.0
Using cucumber-core 3.2.1
Using cucumber-expressions 6.0.1
Using cucumber-wire 0.0.1
Using diff-lcs 1.3
Using multi_json 1.14.1
Using multi_test 0.1.2
Using cucumber 3.1.2
Bundle complete! 1 Gemfile dependency, 12 gems now installed.
Use `bundle info [gemname]` to see where a bundled gem is installed.
```

As you can see, the gem cucumber version 3.1.2 has been installed. But other gems, its dependencies, have been installed too. One very important gem is the gherkin gem, which gives support for the actual language that you will be using when writing Cucumber executable specifications.

cucumber Executable

When you install gem cucumber, you have available the cucumber executable. Try the following command at the terminal prompt (make sure that you are in the root folder of your project):

Note   We invoke project-related commands using bundle exec. This makes sure that the correct project gem dependencies are used when running those commands.

```
$ bundle exec cucumber --version
3.1.2
$
```

You have just invoked the `cucumber` executable giving as runtime argument the option `--version,` and you've got back the version of the `cucumber` installed for your project.

This executable is going to be used to run your executable specifications.

Let's Initialize

Now invoke the `cucumber` executable without any runtime arguments:

```
$ bundle exec cucumber
No such file or directory - features. You can use `cucumber --init` to get
started.
$
```

`cucumber` is looking for the folder `features` in the root folder of your project. This is the folder your project requirements (or executable specifications) should be written into. Since you don't have this folder yet in your project, it is complaining, but it is also suggesting that you run `cucumber --init` to initialize your project for `cucumber`. Let's do that:

```
$ bundle exec cucumber --init
  create    features
  create    features/step_definitions
  create    features/support
  create    features/support/env.rb
$
```

Nice! The preceding invocation created the following folders and files in your project (Figure 6-3):

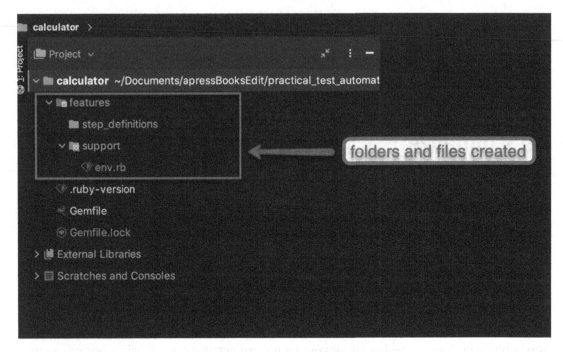

Figure 6-3. *Cucumber – Initialize Folders and Files*

1. The folder features is going to contain files with name extension
   .feature. These files describe the application requirements using
   a language called Gherkin. Gherkin is very easy to write, and all
   the business stakeholders can understand it – very close to plain
   English. This is an example content of such a file:

```
Feature: Sign up
    Sign up should be quick and friendly.

    Scenario: Successful sign up
        New users should get a confirmation email and be greeted
        personally by the site once signed in.

        Given I have chosen to sign up
        When I sign up with valid details
        Then I should receive a confirmation email
        And I should see a personalized greeting message
```

As you can understand by reading it, with Gherkin it becomes very natural for the stakeholders to understand the application requirements given to developers for implementation. Imagine how useful this is going to be when developers will bind actual application code to this and, then, have an automated way to execute this file and make sure that everything that has been required is implemented.

2. The folder features/step_definitions is going to contain files whose name will end with _steps.rb. These are files that contain Ruby code and implement the steps of the Scenarios given in the .feature files. But what are the steps? The steps are the constituent parts of the Scenarios that start with the keywords Given, When, Then, And, and But. In the preceding example, there is, for example, the step Given I have chosen to sign up. The developer is responsible to take this step *declaration* and *define* it inside a Ruby file inside the feature/step_definitions folder. I will talk about steps later on, using a practical example.

3. The folder features/support is used to put any file that will support the automatic execution of the Scenarios. So it is test supporting code. cucumber has already prepared the file env.rb and has put that inside this folder. This will contain Ruby code that will allow cucumber executable to load your core Ruby application before you start executing the Scenarios. In other words, you will use env.rb to tell cucumber where your Ruby application code is (see next chapter for this).

Let's Invoke cucumber

Now that the initialization has been done, let's invoke cucumber once more:

```
$ bundle exec cucumber
0 scenarios
0 steps
0m0.000s
$
```

Perfect! cucumber now ran without any error. But, unfortunately, as it is reported, no scenarios for execution were found. That was expected, of course, since you have not written any scenarios yet.

Write Your First Scenario

Your calculator program is going to help you do, what else, calculations! Having said that, let's write the first feature that this program should offer to the user, the feature of *addition*.

Create the file features/addition.feature with the following content (Listing 6-2).

Listing 6-2. Addition Feature

```
# File: features/addition.feature
#
Feature: Adding

  Scenario: Add two numbers
    Given the input "2+2"
    When the calculator is run
    Then the output should be "4"
```

When you edit the preceding file, make sure that you follow the next rules:

1. Feature: line needs to start at the first column.

2. Scenario: line needs to start with two spaces' right indentation with regard to the Feature: starting column.

3. The step declarations of the Scenario need to start with two spaces' right indentation with regard to the Scenario: starting column.

More details about the Gherkin language will be provided to you later on as you progress with more scenario examples.

Before you go into further work with cucumber, ask yourself whether the scenario text is clear to you. It describes precisely what you want the calculator to come out with, if the input is 2+2. You need the result to be 4. The language used is plain English (with some restrictions that make sure you write something that is Gherkin compatible), so I guess that everybody can understand the logic of the scenario, both the business stakeholders and the developers who will be asked to implement the calculator.

Note that, if you write your Feature and Scenario using RubyMine, you will see that RubyMine underlines the step invocations (Figure 6-4).

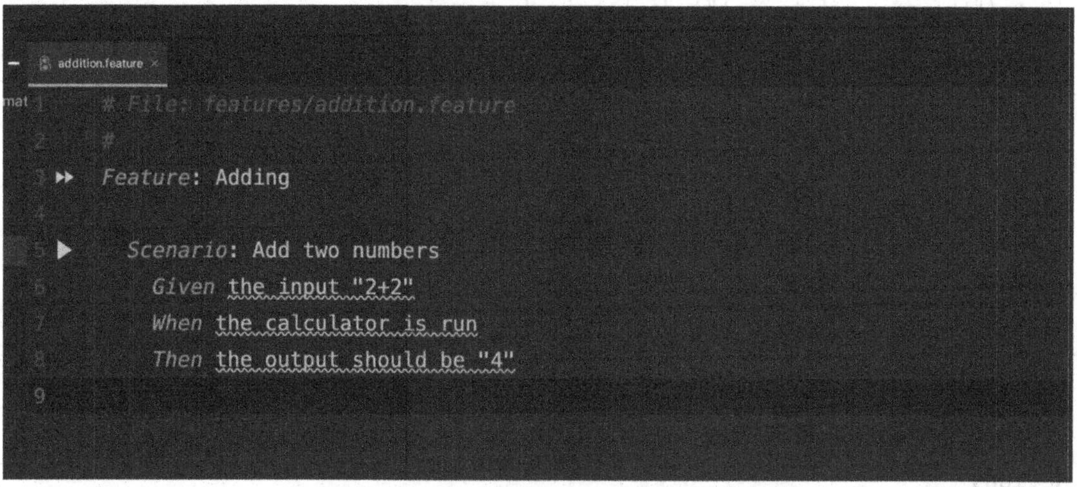

Figure 6-4. *RubyMine Underlines Undefined Step Invocations*

Step invocations (or sometimes called *declarations*) are underlined when the corresponding step definitions are not found by RubyMine. This is because RubyMine cannot find the step definitions of these steps. When you implement them, then RubyMine will remove this text decoration.

Let's invoke cucumber again:

```
$ bundle exec cucumber
# File: features/addition.feature
#
Feature: Adding

  Scenario: Add two numbers        # features/addition.feature:5
    Given the input "2+2"          # features/addition.feature:6
    When the calculator is run     # features/addition.feature:7
    Then the output should be "4"  # features/addition.feature:8
```

```
1 scenario (1 undefined)
3 steps (3 undefined)
0m0.011s

You can implement step definitions for undefined steps with these snippets:

Given("the input {string}") do |string|
  pending # Write code here that turns the phrase above into concrete
actions
end

When("the calculator is run") do
  pending # Write code here that turns the phrase above into concrete
actions
end

Then("the output should be {string}") do |string|
  pending # Write code here that turns the phrase above into concrete
actions
end
$
```

That is a very useful output. Pay attention to the following:

1. Your Cucumber suite has one scenario that is undefined: `1 scenario (1 undefined)`.

2. It also has three steps that are undefined: `3 steps (3 undefined)`.

3. `cucumber` outputs the snippets that you can use to define the steps. This is very useful; you can copy the snippets and put them directly into step definition files.

It is obvious that `cucumber` has found your `.feature` file and has parsed correctly the declaration of your scenario, but it cannot find the step definitions.

Defining Steps (with Pending Implementation)

Let's make cucumber stop complaining for undefined steps by defining the steps it is expecting to find.

Create the file features/step_definitions/calculator_steps.rb with the following content. This is the content of the snippets that have been output earlier by your last run of cucumber. So just copy the content of this output and put it inside the file calculator_steps.rb (Listing 6-3).

Listing 6-3. Calculator Steps – Pending Implementation

```
# File: features/step_definitions/calculator_steps.rb
#
Given("the input {string}") do |string|
  pending # Write code here that turns the phrase above into concrete
actions
end

When("the calculator is run") do
  pending # Write code here that turns the phrase above into concrete
actions
end

Then("the output should be {string}") do |string|
  pending # Write code here that turns the phrase above into concrete
actions
end
```

Save the file and then invoke cucumber again:

```
$ bundle exec cucumber
# File: features/addition.feature
#
Feature: Adding

  Scenario: Add two numbers       # features/addition.feature:5
    Given the input "2+2"         # features/step_definitions/calculator_
                                    steps.rb:3

      TODO (Cucumber::Pending)
```

```
        ./features/step_definitions/calculator_steps.rb:4:in `"the input
        {string}"'
        features/addition.feature:6:in `Given the input "2+2"'
    When the calculator is run    # features/step_definitions/calculator_
                                     steps.rb:7
    Then the output should be "4" # features/step_definitions/calculator_
                                     steps.rb:11

1 scenario (1 pending)
3 steps (2 skipped, 1 pending)
0m0.008s
$
```

Now cucumber is not complaining about undefined steps. It is complaining about pending implementation steps. Do you see that the step Given the input "2+2" has been flagged as pending? Note also that the whole scenario has been reported as pending and the last two steps, after the first pending one, have been skipped.

So cucumber is waiting for you to implement the steps one by one.

Note that the fact that a step definition is *pending* has been identified by cucumber, thanks to the Ruby statement pending which exists as part of the step definition (Figure 6-5).

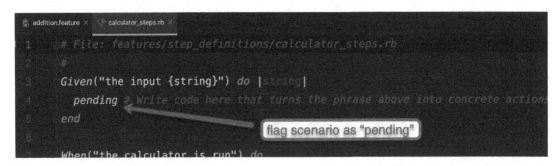

Figure 6-5. *How a Scenario Is Flagged as Pending*

Implement the First Step

cucumber is waiting for you to implement the first step. Let's do it. First, you need to understand how the steps are defined inside the step definition files. Look at this:

```
Given("the input {string}") do |string|
  ...
end
```

The step definition is in such a way that you can get the real runtime argument given at the step invocation as a block-level input argument in the step definition. In other words, the "2+2" that exists as part of the step invocation Given the input "2+2" is stored inside the block-level argument string in the step definition. This is done thanks to the literal string "the input {string}" that is given as argument to the Given(...) method invocation in the step definition. In particular, the part {string} matches to any given runtime argument when you use the step.

This is explained visually in Figure 6-6.

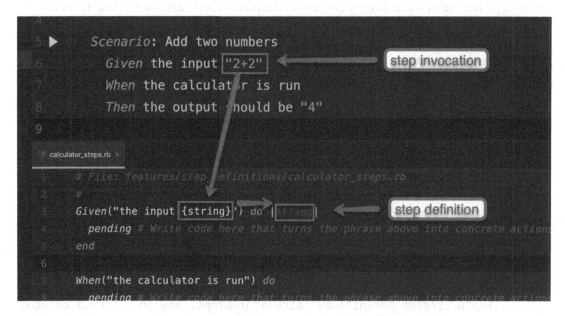

Figure 6-6. *Cucumber Maps Step Invocations to Step Definitions*

Let's enhance the step with a puts command that would print the contents of the string block-level argument. Here is the new version of the file features/step_definitions/calculator_steps.rb (Listing 6-4).

Listing 6-4. Printing the Block-Level Argument Value

```
# File: features/step_definitions/calculator_steps.rb
#
Given("the input {string}") do |string|
  puts "*#{string}*"
end

When("the calculator is run") do
  pending # Write code here that turns the phrase above into concrete actions
end

Then("the output should be {string}") do |string|
  pending # Write code here that turns the phrase above into concrete
actions
end
```

The only change is on line 4. Now, the implementation of the step is not invoking pending, but instead it prints the contents of the block-level variable string. Here is what you will see if you run the cucumber command again:

```
$ bundle exec cucumber
# File: features/addition.feature
#
Feature: Adding

  Scenario: Add two numbers         # features/addition.feature:5
    Given the input "2+2"           # features/step_definitions/calculator_
                                      steps.rb:3

      *2+2*
    When the calculator is run      # features/step_definitions/calculator_
                                      steps.rb:7
      TODO (Cucumber::Pending)
      ./features/step_definitions/calculator_steps.rb:8:in `"the calculator
      is run"'
      features/addition.feature:7:in `When the calculator is run'
    Then the output should be "4" # features/step_definitions/calculator_
    steps.rb:11
```

```
1 scenario (1 pending)
3 steps (1 skipped, 1 pending, 1 passed)
0m0.007s
$
```

Do you see the line *2+2*? This is the result of the puts invocation. Now the step is implemented, that is, no more pending. The pending flag was now raised for the next step (When the calculator is run).

The important thing to note from the preceding code is that the block-level variable string has the actual runtime value "2+2" as given when you use the step inside the Scenario (file .feature).

Let's enhance the first step to have a more meaningful name for the block-level variable and do something useful that will be used in the next steps. Here is the new version of the step definitions file (Listing 6-5).

Listing 6-5. New Version of calculator_steps.rb

```
# File: features/step_definitions/calculator_steps.rb
#
Given("the input {string}") do |input|
  @input = input
end

When("the calculator is run") do
  pending # Write code here that turns the phrase above into concrete
  actions
end

Then("the output should be {string}") do |string|
  pending # Write code here that turns the phrase above into concrete
  actions
end
```

The enhancements are only on lines 3 and 4. You renamed string to input in order to make sure that you have a meaningful variable name, and you saved its value into an instance variable @input that will be used in the next steps to carry out the calculation.

Watch Out   When you create an instance variable (like the @input), this is available for the subsequent steps invoked for the same Scenario. But they don't survive in between Scenarios.

Implement the Second Step

With the first step implemented, let's proceed to the implementation of the next pending step, the second one.

You need to provide an implementation that would take the input and would generate some output. The output would then be evaluated at the next step.

Here is the new version of the step definitions file (Listing 6-6).

Listing 6-6. Implementation of the Second Step

```ruby
# File: features/step_definitions/calculator_steps.rb
#
Given("the input {string}") do |input|
  @input = input
end

When("the calculator is run") do
  @output = `ruby calculator.rb '#{@input}'`
  raise 'Calculator Failed To Run!' unless $?.success?
end

Then("the output should be {string}") do |string|
  pending # Write code here that turns the phrase above into concrete actions
end
```

The changes are for the second step definition, lines 8 and 9. These lines try to invoke the system command ruby with the argument calculator.rb and the value of the @input instance variable. In other words, for the Scenario at hand, it tries to invoke ruby calculator.rb '2+2'. It saves the output into the instance variable @output and then checks whether the exit status of the command, stored inside the global variable $?, is holding a success value. If not success, it raises an exception.

Let's try to run the cucumber command again:

```
$ bundle exec cucumber
# File: features/addition.feature
#
Feature: Adding

  Scenario: Add two numbers        # features/addition.feature:5
    Given the input "2+2"          # features/step_definitions/calculator_
                                     steps.rb:3
Traceback (most recent call last):
ruby: No such file or directory -- calculator.rb (LoadError)
    When the calculator is run     # features/step_definitions/calculator_
                                     steps.rb:7
      Calculator Failed To Run! (RuntimeError)
      ./features/step_definitions/calculator_steps.rb:9:in `"the calculator
      is run"'
      features/addition.feature:7:in `When the calculator is run'
    Then the output should be "4" # features/step_definitions/calculator_
                                     steps.rb:12

Failing Scenarios:
cucumber features/addition.feature:5 # Scenario: Add two numbers

1 scenario (1 failed)
3 steps (1 failed, 1 skipped, 1 passed)
0m0.450s
$
```

As you can see in the preceding code, the Scenario is now considered *failed* because there is a failed step.

The error was raised because the ruby calculator.rb ... command didn't find the calculator.rb file to execute.

How do you fix this? Let's create an empty file calculator.rb inside the root folder of your project. So now you have the following picture of folders and files (Figure 6-7).

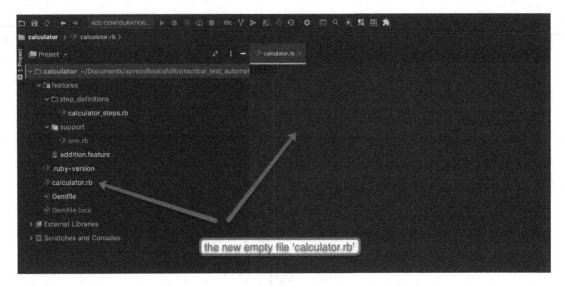

Figure 6-7. *The New Empty File Calculator*

Information   You are following a test-first (or spec-first) approach to development here – TDD. Remember? When you use Cucumber, you are more to BDD (Behavior-Driven Development) rather than to TDD because you start from the functional black-box requirements of the application, its behavior.

Now that you have the file `calculator.rb` in place, let's run the `cucumber` command again:

```
$ bundle exec cucumber
# File: features/addition.feature
#
Feature: Adding

  Scenario: Add two numbers        # features/addition.feature:5
    Given the input "2+2"          # features/step_definitions/calculator_
                                       steps.rb:3
    When the calculator is run     # features/step_definitions/calculator_
                                       steps.rb:7
```

```
Then the output should be "4" # features/step_definitions/calculator_
                            steps.rb:12
    TODO (Cucumber::Pending)
    ./features/step_definitions/calculator_steps.rb:13:in `"the output
    should be {string}"'
    features/addition.feature:8:in `Then the output should be "4"'

1 scenario (1 pending)
3 steps (1 pending, 2 passed)
0m0.890s
$
```

Things have improved. Now both the first and second steps are *passing*. You only have the third step being pending.

Implement the Third Step

In the third step, you need to check that the output has the value that the step defines when called. Here is the proper step definition implementation (Listing 6-7).

Listing 6-7. Third Step Implementation

```
# File: features/step_definitions/calculator_steps.rb
#
Given("the input {string}") do |input|
  @input = input
end

When("the calculator is run") do
  @output = `ruby calculator.rb '#{@input}'`
  raise 'Calculator Failed To Run!' unless $?.success?
end

Then("the output should be {string}") do |expected_output|
  raise 'Expectation Not Met' unless @output == expected_output
end
```

The changes are on lines 12 and 13. You check that the @output instance variable has the value expected, which is stored inside the block-level variable expected_output. For the Scenario that you have written, this step is invoked as Then the output should be "4" which means that the expected_output has the value "4".

If you run the cucumber (try using cucumber --format progress; it does not print verbose output of the Feature and Scenario text), then you will see this:

```
$ bundle exec cucumber --format progress
..F

(::) failed steps (::)

Expectation Not Met (RuntimeError)
./features/step_definitions/calculator_steps.rb:13:in `"the output should
be {string}"'
features/addition.feature:8:in `Then the output should be "4"'

Failing Scenarios:
cucumber features/addition.feature:5 # Scenario: Add two numbers

1 scenario (1 failed)
3 steps (1 failed, 2 passed)
0m0.877s
$
```

The first green dots are for the successful execution of the first two steps. The last red F is for the last step whose execution failed. The execution failed because the RuntimeError exception with message Expectation Not Met was raised. This means that the @output didn't have the value "4".

This was expected, because the calculator.rb file does process its input to generate a proper output. So you need to go to your application code (the calculator.rb file) and introduce the proper piece of code.

Implementing the Feature in Application Code

Now, your objective is to introduce the proper code in the calculator.rb file so that you can make the Scenario pass.

It is true that you need to implement a calculator that knows to carry out additions ("2+2"), but in order to make the Scenario pass, you can also introduce some dummy code like the following (Listing 6-8).

Listing 6-8. Dummy Application Implementation

```
# File: calculator.rb
#
print '4'
```

Save the preceding content into your calculator.rb file and then try to run cucumber again.

```
$ bundle exec cucumber --format progress
...

1 scenario (1 passed)
3 steps (3 passed)
0m0.977s
$
```

Bingo! Your feature is implemented, and your tests run successfully!

But is the calculator finished? Maybe it is. Maybe it is not. Looking at the .feature content that gives you the features of your calculator, you read that it can parse the "2+2" and come up with "4". Is that enough to call it a calculator that can parse any additional expression and produce the correct result?

No. You don't feel confident with the feature content, and you decide to introduce another Scenario.

Introduce One More Scenario

The following is the new version of the .feature file (Listing 6-9).

Listing 6-9. Adding New Scenario

```
# File: features/addition.feature
#
Feature: Adding
```

```
Scenario: Add two numbers
  Given the input "2+2"
  When the calculator is run
  Then the output should be "4"

Scenario: Add two more numbers
  Given the input "2+3"
  When the calculator is run
  Then the output should be "5"
```

The second scenario is not much different from the first. It is trying to prove that the calculator works for another addition expression. Let's run cucumber:

```
$ bundle exec cucumber --format progress
.....F

(::) failed steps (::)

Expectation Not Met (RuntimeError)
./features/step_definitions/calculator_steps.rb:13:in `"the output should
be {string}"'
features/addition.feature:13:in `Then the output should be "5"'

Failing Scenarios:
cucumber features/addition.feature:10 # Scenario: Add two more numbers

2 scenarios (1 failed, 1 passed)
6 steps (1 failed, 5 passed)
0m1.923s
$
```

Now you have one passed and one failed Scenario. And the Scenario that has failed is the Add two more numbers.

It is obvious that your calculator.rb does not work for the "2+3" expression. So let's fix its implementation so that it works for this too. You need to make sure that you don't break the first Scenario though. Here is the new calculator.rb version (Listing 6-10).

Listing 6-10. New Version of calculator.rb

```ruby
# File: calculator.rb
#
expression = ARGV[0]
if expression == '2+2'
  print '4'
elsif expression == '2+3'
  print '5'
end
```

If you save this version and you invoke the cucumber again, you will get this:

```
$ bundle exec cucumber --format progress
......

2 scenarios (2 passed)
6 steps (6 passed)
0m1.703s
$
```

Both of your Scenarios are now passing successfully.

But you know very well that your implementation wouldn't survive a third scenario (Listing 6-11).

Listing 6-11. Adding a Third Scenario

```
# File: features/addition.feature
#
Feature: Adding

  Scenario: Add two numbers
    Given the input "2+2"
    When the calculator is run
    Then the output should be "4"

  Scenario: Add two more numbers
    Given the input "2+3"
    When the calculator is run
    Then the output should be "5"
```

```
Scenario: Add two numbers again
  Given the input "22+50"
  When the calculator is run
  Then the output should be "72"
```

If you run the cucumber for the preceding .feature file, you will get this:

```
$ bundle exec cucumber --format progress
........F

(::) failed steps (::)

Expectation Not Met (RuntimeError)
./features/step_definitions/calculator_steps.rb:13:in `"the output should
be {string}"'
features/addition.feature:18:in `Then the output should be "72"'

Failing Scenarios:
cucumber features/addition.feature:15 # Scenario: Add two numbers again

3 scenarios (1 failed, 2 passed)
9 steps (1 failed, 8 passed)
0m6.462s
$
```

And the story goes on! You can fix this Scenario too by amending the calculator.rb
like this:

```
# File: calculator.rb
#
expression = ARGV[0]
if expression == '2+2'
  print '4'
elsif expression == '2+3'
  print '5'
elsif expression == '22+50'
  print '72'
end
```

But this...does not scale!

It is obvious that such an implementation can only support hard-coded expressions. You need to change it to support any kind of addition expression.

Proper Implementation to Support Any Addition

The following is one version that would survive any addition expression (Listing 6-12).

Listing 6-12. Proper Addition Implementation

```ruby
# File: calculator.rb
#
expression = ARGV[0]
left, right = expression.split('+').map(&:to_i)
print left + right
```

If you save this code and run cucumber again, it will give this:

```
$ bundle exec cucumber --format progress

3 scenarios (3 passed)
9 steps (9 passed)
0m2.895s
$
```

All the three Scenarios pass successfully. Let's try with an extra one (Listing 6-13).

Listing 6-13. Add One More Scenario

```
# File: features/addition.feature
#
Feature: Adding

  Scenario: Add two numbers
    Given the input "2+2"
    When the calculator is run
    Then the output should be "4"
```

```
Scenario: Add two more numbers
  Given the input "2+3"
  When the calculator is run
  Then the output should be "5"

Scenario: Add two numbers again
  Given the input "22+50"
  When the calculator is run
  Then the output should be "72"

Scenario: Add two numbers again and again
  Given the input "125+32"
  When the calculator is run
  Then the output should be "157"
```

If you run cucumber for this new version of .feature, that includes the Scenario for the expression "125+32", then you will get this:

```
$ bundle exec cucumber --format progress

4 scenarios (4 passed)
12 steps (12 passed)
0m3.519s
$
```

It seems that randomly added Scenarios with addition expressions are working ok. Your calculator.rb implementation seems to be ok, at least with regard to the addition expressions.

But hold on! You see a lot of duplication in the .feature file. If you want to write ten different Scenarios with ten different addition expressions, just to expand the scope of testing, do you have to repeat again and again the same Scenario Outline, inventing new names and creating a huge .feature file?

Removing Duplication with Scenario Outlines

You can remove the code duplication in your .feature files if you have Scenarios that are the same, but they only differ in the values they use for their variable parts. In order to do that, you use *Scenario Outlines*.

Here is a version of the file `features/addition.feature` using a Scenario Outline (Listing 6-14).

Listing 6-14. Using Scenario Outlines

```
# File: features/addition.feature
#
Feature: Adding

  Scenario Outline: Add two numbers
    Given the input "<input>"
    When the calculator is run
    Then the output should be "<output>"

    Examples:
      | input  | output |
      |    2+2 |      4 |
      |    2+3 |      5 |
      |  22+50 |     72 |
      | 125+32 |    157 |
```

In the preceding code, you can see how I have turned four different `Scenarios` into one `Scenario Outline` without actually changing any of the step definitions. Only the step invocations have been changed. Instead of taking a specific addition expression, they are invoked by calling the step using a variable enclosed in angle brackets. The variables then are being used inside the `Examples` section in a table having as columns the same names as the variables. The table has values the values that were previously literally encoded inside the distinct `Scenarios` (Figure 6-8).

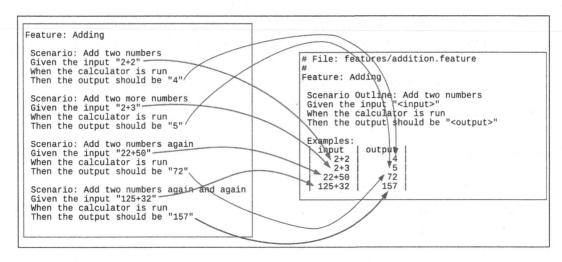

Figure 6-8. *Scenario Outline*

Let's now run the `cucumber` command again:

```
$ bundle exec cucumber --format progress

4 scenarios (4 passed)
12 steps (12 passed)
0m3.514s
$
```

Nothing new! Again, you have four Scenarios. But you have collapsed them behind a `Scenario Outline` definition. Cool! Isn't it?

RSpec Integration

Before you finish the introduction to Cucumber, let's see how this tool is integrated with RSpec. Why would you want to do that? You would like to do that in order to replace check expectation lines like this

```
raise 'Expectation Not Met' unless @output == expected_output
```

with lines like this

```
expect(@output).to eq(expected_output)
```

that is, to use RSpec matchers. If you do that, RSpec will take care of raising the correct exceptions, and also you can make your code read much easier.

Add rspec in Gemfile

First things first. Let's amend the Gemfile to reference the rspec gem (Listing 6-15).

Listing 6-15. Gemfile Referencing RSpec

```
# File: Gemfile
#
source 'https://rubygems.org'

gem 'cucumber'
gem 'rspec'
```

Then run bundle. You will get something like this:

```
$ bundle
Using backports 3.17.0
Using builder 3.2.4
Using bundler 2.1.4
Using cucumber-tag_expressions 1.1.1
Using gherkin 5.1.0
Using cucumber-core 3.2.1
Using cucumber-expressions 6.0.1
Using cucumber-wire 0.0.1
Using diff-lcs 1.3
Using multi_json 1.14.1
Using multi_test 0.1.2
Using cucumber 3.1.2
Using rspec-support 3.9.2
Using rspec-core 3.9.1
Using rspec-expectations 3.9.1
Using rspec-mocks 3.9.1
Using rspec 3.9.0
Bundle complete! 2 Gemfile dependencies, 17 gems now installed.
Use `bundle info [gemname]` to see where a bundled gem is installed.
$
```

Lots of gems are being incorporated. But the main gem is rspec. The others are dependencies of it.

Use RSpec Matchers

Now you are ready to use RSpec matchers. Let's change the step definitions accordingly. The following is the new version of the file features/step_definitions/calculator_steps.rb which uses RSpec matchers (Listing 6-16).

Listing 6-16. Using RSpec Matchers

```ruby
# File: features/step_definitions/calculator_steps.rb
#
Given("the input {string}") do |input|
  @input = input
end

When("the calculator is run") do
  @output = `ruby calculator.rb '#{@input}'`
  expect($?).to be_success, 'Calculator Failed To Run'
end

Then("the output should be {string}") do |expected_output|
  expect(@output).to eq(expected_output)
end
```

You have replaced the code on lines 9 and 13. You are now using RSpec methods and matchers. If you run the cucumber command again, then you will see the four Scenarios succeed as before.

Task Details

> **PLEASE WRITE THE CUCUMBER FEATURES FOR THE FOLLOWING APPLICATION AND IMPLEMENT THE APPLICATION ITSELF**

The application is a Ruby command-line application (let's call the program camelizer) that takes input a string and converts it to a camel-formatted string. Camel-formatted string is the string that capitalizes the first letter of each word and concatenates the words of the string into one big string without blanks. For example, if the input string is "hello world," it returns "HelloWorld."

Other examples are as follows:

- If the input is "Foo bar," it should return "FooBar."

- If the input is "bar," it should return "Bar."

- If the input is "foo_bar," it should return "Foo_bar."

- If the input is "helloWorld," it should return "Helloworld."

- If the input is "this Is gOOd," it should return "ThisIsGood."

Write the features and the program itself. Make sure that you use all the techniques (including RSpec integration) described in this chapter.

Key Takeaways

You had a first encounter with Cucumber and how you can write your requirements using the Gherkin language. Then you turned them to executable specifications. The step definition implementations bound the requirements to our application code (Figure 6-9).

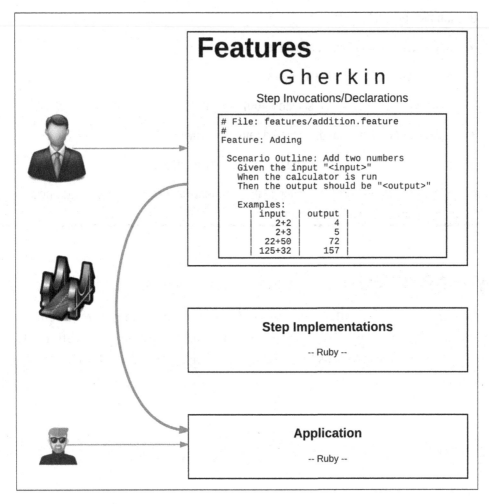

Figure 6-9. *Cucumber Binds to Application*

With Cucumber, business stakeholders and developers can work together. Business stakeholders use a formal language (Gherkin) to express the requirements of the software, and developers implement the step definitions in a way that their implementation binds to the actual application code. When any step fails to be executed, you know that the application has a flaw and needs to be corrected or a new feature needs to be implemented.

In the next, last chapter of this book, you will learn about some of the advanced features of Cucumber, and you will implement a more complex project.

CHAPTER 7

Advanced Cucumber

In the previous chapter, I gave you an introduction to Cucumber. In this chapter, you learn about the more advanced features of Cucumber, and you also go into implementing a more elaborate example case. There is a lot to cover in this chapter, including the extensive test case, making the chapter a little bit longer than the average.

Learning Goals

1. Learn about the Feature keyword.

2. Learn about the Background keyword.

3. Learn about the Scenario keyword.

4. Learn about the different logical phases a scenario needs to be divided into.

5. Learn about the And and But keywords.

6. Learn about the importance of the Scenario name and description.

7. Learn about the state of Scenarios.

8. Learn about data tables.

9. Learn about the internationalization features of Cucumber.

10. Learn how to use a test-first approach by practicing a more complex Cucumber project.

11. Learn how you can use the Cucumber environment files to set up Cucumber using the application code.

© Panos Matsinopoulos 2020
P. Matsinopoulos, *Practical Test Automation*, https://doi.org/10.1007/978-1-4842-6141-5_7

12. Learn how and when to use RSpec alongside Cucumber.

13. Learn about running a dry run.

14. Learn how you can invoke a single Feature file, when you have multiple ones in your project.

15. Learn how to invoke a single Scenario and skip all the others defined in the same or other Feature file.

16. Learn how to invoke a specific Example out of a set of Examples of a Scenario Outline.

17. Learn how to invoke the execution of more than one specific Scenario.

18. Learn how you can use tags to tag specific Scenarios and then invoke or exclude their execution.

19. Learn how you can execute specific Ruby code at specific points in the lifecycle of the execution of a Scenario.

20. Learn about the document strings.

21. Learn how well RubyMine supports Cucumber.

Introduction

In the previous chapter, you had your first encounter with Cucumber and Gherkin. Let's now see some more advanced features. You will now better understand the Gherkin language.

Gherkin Keywords

The language that you use to write your features is called Gherkin. Being a language, it means that you have a specific set of language keywords that you can use. This is the list of them:

- Feature

- Background

- Scenario

- Given

- When

- Then

- And

- But

- *

- Scenario Outline

- Examples

Let's see how these keywords work.

Feature

The Feature is used to give a descriptive name and a longer summary description to your set of Scenarios. Otherwise, it does not affect your test/executable specification.

When you start your Feature, you give a title and a summary description. The title is separated from the keyword Feature with a :. The summary description is a multiline text below the title and needs to be indented by two blanks to the right. Note that the lines in the summary description should not start with any of the words Scenario, Background, or Scenario Outline. This is because these three keywords denote the start of other special blocks in the feature file.

In the following, you can see an example of a feature with name/title Invite a Friend and some summary description:

```
Feature: Invite a Friend

  User is able to invite a friend.
  Inviting friends will bring more users to the platform and will increase
  invitee user reputation.
  Moreover, invited friends will get a discount for signing up

  ...
```

Sometimes a feature is quite simple. But there are times in which a feature is complex. In this case, you need to write some extra documentation to reason for the value the feature will bring. This is the purpose of the summary description. It is optional, but if you believe that it will bear useful business value information, it would be good to be there.

Background

The Background groups together the steps that need to take place before each scenario that is part of the feature at hand. In other words, if many of your Scenarios share a common start that is repeated on all Scenarios, you may want to transfer those steps in the Background area.

Here is a Feature with two Scenarios that share a common start:

```
Feature: Update My Profile Picture

  The user updates their profile picture
  So that their picture appears on all public and private pages next to
  their name.

  Background:
    Given I am signed in as a standard user
    And I visit my profile section

  Scenario: Uploading a new picture
    When I click on my current profile picture
    Then I can see an area on which I can drop my new profile picture

  Scenario: Deleting the current profile picture
    When I click on delete profile picture button
    Then I see that my picture is replaced with a default one
```

The preceding feature content is equivalent to the one here:

```
Feature: Update My Profile Picture

  The user updates their profile picture
  So that their picture appears on all public and private pages next to
  their name.
```

```
Scenario: Uploading a new picture
  Given I am signed in as a standard user
  And I visit my profile section
  When I click on my current profile picture
  Then I can see an area on which I can drop my new profile picture

Scenario: Deleting the current profile picture
  Given I am signed in as a standard user
  And I visit my profile section
  When I click on delete profile picture button
  Then I see that my picture is replaced with a default one
```

But you prefer the first version, with the `Background`, in order to avoid cluttering the main Scenario content with steps that are not really relevant to the actual value of the Scenario.

Scenario

You learned about the `Scenario` keyword using some examples, both in the previous and in the current chapter. What I would like to underline here is the fact that usually, a `Scenario` is decomposed into three logical parts/phases (Figure 7-1).

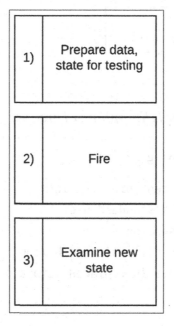

Figure 7-1. *Scenario – Three Phases*

1. You prepare the data in your application so that you have the correct state ready for testing. This is what I also call *context*.

2. You fire the event/action that you want to test.

3. You check that the new state of your application data is as expected.

In Gherkin, you use the keyword Given to identify steps that are part of the first phase, the context preparation. You use the keyword When to identify steps that are part of the second phase, that of firing the action. You use the keyword Then to identify steps that are part of the third phase (Figure 7-2).

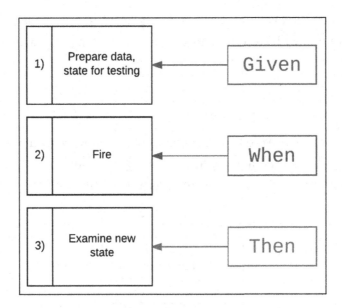

Figure 7-2. *Gherkin Keywords Mapping to Three Scenario Phases*

For example, see the following Scenario:

```
Scenario: Deleting the current profile picture
  Given I am signed in as a standard user
  And I visit my profile section
  When I click on delete profile picture button
  Then I see that my picture is replaced with a default one
```

The first two steps are part of the first phase, the preparation of the context. You could have started both with the Given keyword, but Gherkin allows you to use And and But to avoid repeating Given multiple times, one below the other.

The third step starts with a When, and it is the firing action. This is the action that *changes* the state of the system. Usually, this is one step only, but this is not a hard rule.

The fourth step starts with a Then, and it is the step that checks that the system now has the correct state.

When writing your scenarios, make sure that you clearly identify these three phases in your scenario wording. It helps the reader to understand what the Scenario is trying to specify and test.

And, But, and *

I said that you can use And and But to start your step invocations inside a Scenario. Also, if you find that these keywords add too much of a verbosity to the Scenarios, then you can always use * instead – or a mixture of these. That wouldn't make any difference to cucumber and the way it would be executing your Scenarios.

See the following example:

```
Scenario: Attempt to withdraw with an invalid card
  Given I have $100 in my account
      * my card is invalid
  When I request $50
  Then my card should not be returned
      * and I should be asked to contact the bank
```

It is using a mixture of the Gherkin keywords. It clearly delineates the phases of the Scenario by using the correct keyword at the start of the phase and * for steps in the middle of them.

Scenario Names and Description

As a Feature has a name/title and a description, the same goes for a Scenario. Scenarios should have descriptive names/titles, but they should not be very long. You can always add a multiline summary description to a Scenario as long as the lines of that description do not start with any of the reserved step invocation keywords Given, When, and Then.

Note again that the summary descriptions should not be developer oriented and should not include technical implementation details. They are meant to be read by the business stakeholders and the developers at the same time. So avoid any technical jargon. They need to elaborate on the business aspect of the Scenario they brief about.

Scenario State

Although within the execution of a Scenario you can use instance variables to carry out state from one step to the next, please note that these instance variables do not survive from one Scenario to the next. This is done by design for a good reason. The Scenarios should be independent to each other. Each Scenario should be executable on its own, and its execution should not be dependent on the execution results of the previous Scenarios.

Having said that, make sure that you don't carry over state from one Scenario to the next using any kind of persistent storage. For example, do not persist state into the file system or into a database, expecting to find it ready to be accessed in the next Scenario. This is really a bad design practice.

Data Tables

Sometimes, when you prepare the data of a Scenario, you end up repeating the same step with different runtime arguments multiple times. See the following example:

```
Scenario: Export a CSV file of the customers
  Given the customer "John Woo" with contact phone number "6972669700"
  And the customer "Mary Foo" with contact phone number "6972669701"
  And the customer "Laura Bar" with contact phone number '6972669702"
  When I request to export customers details
  Then I get the file "customers.csv" with the correct data
```

You can see that the first three lines of the preceding Scenario are invocations on the same step with different data. Do you have another way to declare these, so that they would have been less verbose and easier to read?

The answer is Cucumber data tables.

Let's create a project called customers, integrate Cucumber, and write the following content into a .feature file (Listing 7-1).

Listing 7-1. Export to CSV Feature

```
# File: customers/features/export_to_csv.feature
#
Feature: Export to CSV

  Scenario: Export standard CSV file for our customers
    Given the customers
      | name      | phone number |
      | John Woo  | 6972669700   |
      | Mary Foo  | 6972669701   |
      | Laura Bar | 6972669702   |
    When I request to export customer details
    Then I get the file "customers.csv" with the correct data
```

This Scenario bears the same information as the following Scenario:

```
Scenario: Export a CSV file of the customers
  Given the customer "John Woo" with contact phone number "6972669700"
  And the customer "Mary Foo" with contact phone number "6972669701"
  And the customer "Laura Bar" with contact phone number '6972669702'
  When I request to export customers details
  Then I get the file "customers.csv" with the correct data
```

However, it is much easier to read and actually maintain.

Let's run the cucumber executable. This is what you get:

```
$ bundle exec cucumber --format progress
UUU

1 scenario (1 undefined)
3 steps (3 undefined)
0m0.007s
```

You can implement step definitions for undefined steps with these snippets:

```ruby
Given("the customers") do |table|
  # table is a Cucumber::MultilineArgument::DataTable
  pending # Write code here that turns the phrase above into concrete
  actions
end

When("I request to export customer details") do
  pending # Write code here that turns the phrase above into concrete
  actions
end

Then("I get the file {string} with the correct data") do |string|
  pending # Write code here that turns the phrase above into concrete
  actions
end
$
```

All steps are undefined, of course, and Cucumber is suggesting to you which snippets you could start from. Let's create the steps file features/step_definitions/customers_ steps.rb (Listing 7-2).

Listing 7-2. customers_steps.rb File

```ruby
# File: customers/features/step_definitions/customers_steps.rb
#
Given("the customers") do |table|
  # table is a Cucumber::MultilineArgument::DataTable
  pending # Write code here that turns the phrase above into concrete
  actions
end

When("I request to export customer details") do
  pending # Write code here that turns the phrase above into concrete
  actions
end
```

```
Then("I get the file {string} with the correct data") do |string|
  pending # Write code here that turns the phrase above into concrete
  actions
end
```

The interesting thing here is that Cucumber has identified that the step the customers takes its input from a table, rather than interpolated. Having done that, it is proposing you the block local variable table, and also it is telling you that the table is of type Cucumber:: MultilineArgument::DataTable, the documentation of which can be found here: http:// www.rubydoc.info/gems/cucumber/Cucumber/MultilineArgument/DataTable.

How can you use this table variable to have access to the table data specified in the Scenario? One of the most interesting and useful instance methods of this object is the method #hashes which *converts this table into an array of Hash where the keys of each Hash are the headers in the table.*

Let's use this to get access to the customers data, that is, to build the context that the Scenario needs (Listing 7-3).

Listing 7-3. Using the table Variable and hashes Method

```
# File: customers/features/step_definitions/customers_steps.rb
#
Given("the customers") do |table|
  @customers = []
  table.hashes.each do |hash|
    @customers << Customer.new(name: hash['name'], phone_number:
    hash['phone_number'])
  end
end

When("I request to export customer details") do
  pending # Write code here that turns the phrase above into concrete
  actions
end

Then("I get the file {string} with the correct data") do |string|
  pending # Write code here that turns the phrase above into concrete
  actions
end
```

Do you see how I implement the first step? I iterate over the `table.hashes` array. Each item of the array is a `Hash` that has as keys the column headers of the table and values the values of the corresponding row of the table. Hence, the first item has the values of the first row, the second has the values of the third row, and so on. I take advantage of this, and I create the `@customers` instance variable, which I plan to use in the steps that follow.

If you run `cucumber` again, you will get an error for the `Customer` constant, but this is how test-first development works, isn't it?

You will not progress to the implementation of this project. You are working another project in more detail later on in this chapter.

Spoken Languages

You will be surprised to learn that Cucumber allows you to write your Features and Scenarios in more than 40 different spoken languages. That can be a real buy-in when you try to convince your business stakeholders to work together with you on specifying the requirements of the application using Gherkin.

Which Languages?

You can tell which languages your Cucumber installation supports by running the command `cucumber --i18n-languages`. You will get something like this:

```
$ cucumber --i18n-languages
 | af      | Afrikaans      | Afrikaans       |
 | ast     | Asturian       | asturianu       |
 | az      | Azerbaijani    | Azərbaycanca    |
...
 | uz      | Uzbek          | Узбекча         |
...
 | zh-TW   | Chinese traditional |
```

The first two-digit code is important if you want to tell that a Feature file is written in a particular language.

Specify the Language of a Feature File

In order for you to tell Cucumber that the language of the Feature is not English (which is the default language), then you need to use the Ruby comment # `language:` `<language-two-digit-code>` at the first line of your Feature file.

For example, this is a Feature written in Spanish:

```
# language: es

Característica: Retirar dinero

  Escenario: Intentar retirar con una tarjeta no válida
        Dado Tengo $100 en mi cuenta
          * Mi tarjeta no es válida
      Cuando Solicito $50
    Entonces Mi tarjeta no debe ser devuelta
* Y se me pedirá que se ponga en contacto con el banco
```

Localization of Gherkin Keywords

And how do you know which Gherkin keywords should be used for a non-English language? You can get those by invoking the command line cucumber `--i18n-keywords` `<language-code>`. For example, this is how you get back the keywords for the Spanish language:

```
$ cucumber --i18n-keywords es

  | feature          | "Característica"
  | background       | "Antecedentes"
  | scenario         | "Escenario"
  | scenario_outline | "Esquema del escenario"
  | examples         | "Ejemplos"
  | given            | "* ", "Dado ", "Dada ", "Dados ", "Dadas "
  | when             | "* ", "Cuando "
  | then             | "* ", "Entonces "
  | and              | "* ", "Y ", "E "
  | but              | "* ", "Pero "
  | given (code)     | "Dado", "Dada", "Dados", "Dadas"
  | when (code)      | "Cuando"
```

```
| then (code)        | "Entonces"
| and  (code)        | "Y", "E"
| but  (code)        | "Pero"
$
```

A More Extensive Example

Before you finish with Cucumber, let's try a more extensive example.

Here is the high-level description of the application that you want to build:

You own a hotel with rooms for booking. You want to implement a new application that would allow you to offer bookings online. The main feature of the application is going to be the *booking feature.*

Initialize the Project

Initialize the project for the application development. Let's call it booking-with-joy.

Make sure that you

1. Create the .ruby-version file at the root of your project folder. This file should contain the version number of the Ruby that you want to use, for example, 2.6.6. That way, rbenv and RubyMine know which Ruby will be used for your project.

2. Create the RubyMine project.

Gemfile

Create the Gemfile and add references to cucumber and rspec. Then bundle to bring the gems in (Listing 7-4).

Listing 7-4. Gemfile for the booking-with-joy Project

```
# File: Gemfile
#
source 'https://rubygems.org'

gem 'cucumber'
gem 'rspec'
```

Initialize Cucumber

Execute the following command to initialize Cucumber:

```
$ cucumber --init
  create    features
  create    features/step_definitions
  create    features/support
  create    features/support/env.rb
$
```

The Feature File

Let's start with the following feature file. You only have one Scenario, as a start (Listing 7-5).

Listing 7-5. Feature with One Scenario

```
# File: features/booking_a_room.feature
#
Feature: Booking a Room
  Users should be able to book a room.
  The application should ask user the booking details and
  then return back the rooms available.

  Background:
  The table below describes the rooms available. The "number"
  column is the room number. The "accommodates" column is the
  maximum number of people that can stay in the room

    Given there are the following rooms in the hotel
      | number | accommodates |
      |      1 |            2 |
      |      2 |            2 |
      |      3 |            2 |
      |      4 |            2 |
      |      5 |            4 |
      |      6 |            4 |
```

Scenario: All the rooms are free and there are rooms on the capacity
requested
    Given all the rooms are available
    When visitor provides the following booking details
        | check_in | check_out | guests |
        | 23-Mar-2021 | 25-Mar-2021 | 3 |
    Then visitor is provided with the following options for booking
        | number |
        | 5 |
        | 6 |

I will not expand on what this Scenario specifies as a functional requirement of the application. This is the beauty of Gherkin. You can read the Scenario itself and understand what it is about. Maybe you want to take a note that I have decided to put in the Background section, the setup of the context of the particular Scenario. This is because I want to keep in the Scenario the steps that are relevant to the value it brings and not distract the reader with unnecessary noise.

Undefined Steps

Let's run cucumber:

```
$ cucumber --format progress
UUUU

1 scenario (1 undefined)
4 steps (4 undefined)
0m0.136s
```

You can implement step definitions for undefined steps with these snippets:

```
Given("there are the following rooms in the hotel") do |table|
  # table is a Cucumber::MultilineArgument::DataTable
  pending # Write code here that turns the phrase above into concrete
  actions
end
```

```
Given("all the rooms are available") do
  pending # Write code here that turns the phrase above into concrete
  actions
end

When("visitor provides the following booking details") do |table|
  # table is a Cucumber::MultilineArgument::DataTable
  pending # Write code here that turns the phrase above into concrete
  actions
end

Then("visitor is provided with the following options for booking") do
|table|
  # table is a Cucumber::MultilineArgument::DataTable
  pending # Write code here that turns the phrase above into concrete
  actions
end
$
```

All steps are undefined, and you've got back the snippets that you can use to start implementing them. Let's create the step definitions file and put these snippets in (Listing 7-6).

Listing 7-6. Initial Content for the Steps File

```
# File features/step_definitions/booking_with_joy_steps.rb
#
Given("there are the following rooms in the hotel") do |table|
  # table is a Cucumber::MultilineArgument::DataTable
  pending # Write code here that turns the phrase above into concrete
  actions
end

Given("all the rooms are available") do
  pending # Write code here that turns the phrase above into concrete
  actions
end
```

```
When("visitor provides the following booking details") do |table|
  # table is a Cucumber::MultilineArgument::DataTable
  pending # Write code here that turns the phrase above into concrete
  actions
end

Then("visitor is provided with the following options for booking") do
|table|
  # table is a Cucumber::MultilineArgument::DataTable
  pending # Write code here that turns the phrase above into concrete
  actions
end
```

If you run the cucumber command again, you will get this:

```
$ cucumber --format progress
P---

(::) pending steps (::)

features/step_definitions/booking_with_joy_steps.rb:3:in `"there are the
following rooms in the hotel"'

1 scenario (1 pending)
4 steps (3 skipped, 1 pending)
0m0.123s
$
```

This is telling you that the first step is *pending*, whereas the rest of the steps have been skipped.

Implementing the First Step

The first step could have an implementation like the following (Listing 7-7).

Listing 7-7. First Step Implementation

```
Given("there are the following rooms in the hotel") do |table|
  @rooms = []
  table.hashes.each do |hash|
```

248

```
  @rooms << Room.new(number: hash['number'].to_i, accommodates:
  hash['accommodates'].to_i)
  end
end
```

It is building an array of the available rooms, based on the information borne into the table given in the step invocation.

If you run cucumber again, you will get an error about the Room constant being uninitialized:

```
$ cucumber --format progress
F---

(::) failed steps (::)

uninitialized constant Room (NameError)
./features/step_definitions/booking_with_joy_steps.rb:6:in `block (2
levels) in <top (required)>'
./features/step_definitions/booking_with_joy_steps.rb:5:in `each'
./features/step_definitions/booking_with_joy_steps.rb:5:in `"there are the
following rooms in the hotel"'
features/booking_a_room.feature:13:in `Given there are the following rooms
in the hotel'

Failing Scenarios:
cucumber features/booking_a_room.feature:22 # Scenario: All the rooms are
free and there are rooms on the capacity requested

1 scenario (1 failed)
4 steps (1 failed, 3 skipped)
0m0.175s
$
```

Let's start implementing our application by introducing the class Room. You will build this class so that it makes the first step pass successfully. Create the file room.rb, at the root folder of your project, with the following content (Listing 7-8).

Listing 7-8. Room Class Definition

```
# File: room.rb
#
class Room
  def initialize(number:, accommodates:)
    @number = number
    @accommodates = accommodates
  end
end
```

If you run cucumber again, you will get the same error, although you have defined your Room class. I guess this is expected because cucumber does not know anything about this class.

Let's create the file that requires all the application files. Name the file all.rb and create it with the following content in the root folder of your project (Listing 7-9).

Listing 7-9. all.rb Requires All Necessary Files

```
# File: all.rb
#
$LOAD_PATH.unshift('.')

require 'room'
```

Let's make cucumber require this file. Edit the features/support/env.rb so that it requires the all.rb file of your application (Listing 7-10).

Listing 7-10. env.rb File Requires all.rb

```
# File: features/support/env.rb
#
APPLICATION_ROOT_PATH = File.join(File.expand_path('..', __FILE__), '..',
'..')

$LOAD_PATH.unshift(APPLICATION_ROOT_PATH)

require 'all'
```

Now, everything is ready for the first step to pass successfully. Let's run cucumber again:

```
$ cucumber --format progress
.P--

(::) pending steps (::)

features/step_definitions/booking_with_joy_steps.rb:10:in `"all the rooms
are available"'

1 scenario (1 pending)
4 steps (2 skipped, 1 pending, 1 passed)
0m0.126s
$
```

Implementing the Second Step

The second step requires that you set all the rooms in an available state. Let's implement the step like the following (Listing 7-11).

Listing 7-11. Second Step Implementation

```
Given("all the rooms are available") do
  @rooms.each(&:set_available)
end
```

If you run cucumber again, you will get this:

```
$ cucumber --format progress
.F--

(::) failed steps (::)

undefined method `set_available' for #<Room:0x00007f986d8c6970 @number=1,
@accommodates=2> (NoMethodError)
./features/step_definitions/booking_with_joy_steps.rb:11:in `each'
./features/step_definitions/booking_with_joy_steps.rb:11:in `"all the rooms
are available"'
features/booking_a_room.feature:23:in `Given all the rooms are available'
```

Failing Scenarios:
cucumber features/booking_a_room.feature:22 # Scenario: All the rooms are free and there are rooms on the capacity requested

1 scenario (1 failed)
4 steps (1 failed, 2 skipped, 1 passed)
0m0.169s
$

The second step fails because the method set_available is not part of the Room class interface. Let's implement this (Listing 7-12).

Listing 7-12. Implementing the Method set_available

```ruby
# File: room.rb
#
class Room
  def initialize(number:, accommodates:)
    @number = number
    @accommodates = accommodates
  end

  def set_available
    @state = :available
  end
end
```

The method set_available flags the room as available. Now, let's run the cucumber command again:

```
$ cucumber --format progress
..P-

(::) pending steps (::)

features/step_definitions/booking_with_joy_steps.rb:14:in `"visitor
provides the following booking details"'
```

```
1 scenario (1 pending)
4 steps (1 skipped, 1 pending, 2 passed)
0m0.164s
$
```

Perfect! The second step has now passed.

Implementing the Third Step

The third step is about the visitor providing their booking request details. As you did with room details, you are going to create the step to hold the booking request details. Here is the content of the features/step_definitions/booking_with_joy_steps.rb with the implementation of the step (Listing 7-13).

Listing 7-13. Implementation of the Third Step

```ruby
# File features/step_definitions/booking_with_joy_steps.rb
#
require 'date'

Given("there are the following rooms in the hotel") do |table|
  @rooms = []
  table.hashes.each do |hash|
    @rooms << Room.new(number: hash['number'].to_i, accommodates:
    hash['accommodates'].to_i)
  end
end

Given("all the rooms are available") do
  @rooms.each(&:set_available)
end
When("visitor provides the following booking details") do |table|
  # Note that "table" will only hold 1 line/row. The whole table
  # refers to 1 instance of a booking request

  hash = table.hashes.first
```

```
  @booking_request = BookingRequest.new(
    check_in: Date.strptime(hash['check_in'], '%d-%b-%Y'),
    check_out: Date.strptime(hash['check_out'], '%d-%b-%Y'),
    guests: hash['guests'].to_i
  )
  @available_rooms = @hotel.check_availability(@booking_request)
end

Then("visitor is provided with the following options for booking") do
|table|
  # table is a Cucumber::MultilineArgument::DataTable
  pending # Write code here that turns the phrase above into concrete
  actions
end
```

Caution   You have added the statement `require 'date'` at the beginning of the file. This is necessary because the implementation is using the Ruby standard library class Date (read about it here: `https://ruby-doc.org/stdlib-2.6.6/libdoc/date/rdoc/Date.html`).

As you can read from the comment in the step implementation, the `table` variable will always have one row, referring to just one instance of the BookingRequest class.

Obviously, if you run the `cucumber` executable now, you will get an error about the missing constant BookingRequest:

```
$ cucumber --format progress
..F-

(::) failed steps (::)

uninitialized constant BookingRequest (NameError)
./features/step_definitions/booking_with_joy_steps.rb:20:in `"visitor
provides the following booking details"'
features/booking_a_room.feature:24:in `When visitor provides the following
booking details'
```

```
Failing Scenarios:
cucumber features/booking_a_room.feature:22 # Scenario: All the rooms are
free and there are rooms on the capacity requested

1 scenario (1 failed)
4 steps (1 failed, 1 skipped, 2 passed)
0m0.107s
$
```

Let's introduce this class (Listing 7-14).

Listing 7-14. Introducing Class BookingRequest

```ruby
# File booking_request.rb
#
class BookingRequest
  def initialize(check_in:, check_out:, guests:)
    @check_in = check_in
    @check_out = check_out
    @guests = guests
  end
end
```

You need to make sure this file is required. So let's amend the file all.rb (Listing 7-15).

Listing 7-15. all.rb Requires booking_request.rb

```ruby
# File: all.rb
#
$LOAD_PATH.unshift('.')

require 'room'
require 'booking_request'
```

Let's run cucumber again:

```
$ cucumber --format progress
..F-
```

```
(::) failed steps (::)
```

undefined method `check_availability' for nil:NilClass (NoMethodError)
./features/step_definitions/booking_with_joy_steps.rb:27:in `"visitor
provides the following booking details"'
features/booking_a_room.feature:24:in `When visitor provides the following
booking details'

Failing Scenarios:
cucumber features/booking_a_room.feature:22 # Scenario: All the rooms are
free and there are rooms on the capacity requested

```
1 scenario (1 failed)
4 steps (1 failed, 1 skipped, 2 passed)
0m0.066s
$
```

The third step is still failing. Now, it is because of calling the check_availability method on something that is nil. It is this line of step implementation that is failing:

```
@available_rooms = @hotel.check_availability(@booking_request)
```

The instance variable @hotel is representing your booking management object, the *hotel*, and needs to be instantiated somehow.

Where do you instantiate this? There are quite some good points in the testing code where you can do this. Let's take a simple approach to instantiate it here, in this step that you need it. So you enhance the step implementation to be as follows (Listing 7-16).

Listing 7-16. Instantiating @hotel

```
When("visitor provides the following booking details") do |table|
  # Note that "table" will only hold 1 line/row. The whole table
  # refers to 1 instance of a booking request

  hash = table.hashes.first
```

```
@booking_request = BookingRequest.new(
  check_in: Date.strptime(hash['check_in'], '%d-%b-%Y'),
  check_out: Date.strptime(hash['check_out'], '%d-%b-%Y'),
  guests: hash['guests'].to_i
)
@hotel = Hotel.new
@available_rooms = @hotel.check_availability(@booking_request)
end
```

Obviously, now, if you run the cucumber executable, you will get an error that the Hotel constant is not initialized:

```
$ cucumber --format progress
..F-

(::) failed steps (::)

uninitialized constant Hotel (NameError)
./features/step_definitions/booking_with_joy_steps.rb:27:in `"visitor
provides the following booking details"'
features/booking_a_room.feature:24:in `When visitor provides the following
booking details'

Failing Scenarios:
cucumber features/booking_a_room.feature:22 # Scenario: All the rooms are
free and there are rooms on the capacity requested

1 scenario (1 failed)
4 steps (1 failed, 1 skipped, 2 passed)
0m0.043s
$
```

Let's define this constant in the file hotel.rb (Listing 7-17).

Listing 7-17. Defining Constant Hotel in the hotel.rb File

```
# File: hotel.rb
#
class Hotel
end
```

Require the file inside all.rb (Listing 7-18).

Listing 7-18. all.rb Requires hotel.rb

```
# File: all.rb
#
$LOAD_PATH.unshift('.')

require 'room'
require 'booking_request'
require 'hotel'
```

And let's run cucumber again. I am reminding you that you are following a BDD approach to developing your application:

```
$ cucumber --format progress
..F-

(::) failed steps (::)

undefined method `check_availability' for #<Hotel:0x00007f87f38a1ad8>
(NoMethodError)
./features/step_definitions/booking_with_joy_steps.rb:28:in `"visitor
provides the following booking details"'
features/booking_a_room.feature:24:in `When visitor provides the following
booking details'

Failing Scenarios:
cucumber features/booking_a_room.feature:22 # Scenario: All the rooms are
free and there are rooms on the capacity requested

1 scenario (1 failed)
4 steps (1 failed, 1 skipped, 2 passed)
0m0.043s
$
```

Now the error has to do with the undefined method check_availability for the Hotel instance. Let's implement this method too (Listing 7-19).

Listing 7-19. Implementing the check_availability Method

```
# File: hotel.rb
#
class Hotel
  def check_availability(booking_request)
  end
end
```

Let's run cucumber again:

```
$ cucumber --format progress
...P

(::) pending steps (::)

features/step_definitions/booking_with_joy_steps.rb:31:in `"visitor is
provided with the following options for booking"'

1 scenario (1 pending)
4 steps (1 pending, 3 passed)
0m0.049s
$
```

Nice! It looks like the third step is now implemented. Let's proceed to the next step.

Implementing the Fourth Step

In the final step, you need to test that the available rooms presented to the visitor are the ones expected and given by the step invocation inside the feature file. The Scenario says that the available rooms should be the rooms 5 and 6.

The following is the implementation of this step (Listing 7-20).

Listing 7-20. Implementation of the Fourth Step

```
Then("visitor is provided with the following options for booking") do
|table|
  expect(@available_rooms.size).to eq(table.hashes.size)
  @available_rooms.each_with_index do |available_room, index|
    expect(available_room.number).to eq(table.hashes[index]['number'].to_i)
  end
end
```

You make sure that the @available_rooms variable holds the correct information, both in terms of number of rooms and in terms of specific rooms.

Let's run cucumber now:

```
$ cucumber --format progress
...F

(::) failed steps (::)

undefined method `size' for nil:NilClass (NoMethodError)
./features/step_definitions/booking_with_joy_steps.rb:32:in `"visitor is
provided with the following options for booking"'
features/booking_a_room.feature:27:in `Then visitor is provided with the
following options for booking'

Failing Scenarios:
cucumber features/booking_a_room.feature:22 # Scenario: All the rooms are
free and there are rooms on the capacity requested

1 scenario (1 failed)
4 steps (1 failed, 3 passed)
0m0.048s
$
```

The step is failing because you are calling size on something that is nil. It is the @available_rooms.size that is raising the error. @available_rooms is nil because the method #check_availability does not return anything.

You need to work more on the implementation of the #check_availability method. Let's see a better implementation that would make more sense for the step to succeed (Listing 7-21).

Listing 7-21. Correct Hotel Class Implementation

```ruby
# File: hotel.rb
#
class Hotel
  def initialize(rooms:)
    @rooms = rooms
  end

  def check_availability(booking_request)
    existing_available_rooms.select do |existing_available_room|
      existing_available_room.accommodates >= booking_request.guests
    end
  end

  private

  attr_reader :rooms

  def existing_available_rooms
    rooms.select { |room| room.available? }
  end
end
```

The preceding implementation requires the hotel rooms to be given when constructing the Hotel instance. So let's enhance the previous step too, the one that instantiates the Hotel class. Instead of @hotel = Hotel.new, it needs to be @hotel = Hotel.new(rooms: @rooms) since @rooms holds the rooms of the hotel, as instantiated in the first step. Do this change in the file features/step_definitions/booking_with_joy_steps.rb before proceeding.

Also, the new Hotel class implementation will require that the Room instance responds to the method #available? (see the preceding line 19). You will also need the public readers for @accommodates and @number instance variables. Let's implement these changes too, inside the room.rb file (Listing 7-22).

Listing 7-22. New Room Implementation

```ruby
# File: room.rb
#
class Room
  attr_reader :accommodates, :number

  def initialize(number:, accommodates:)
    @number = number
    @accommodates = accommodates
  end

  def set_available
    @state = :available
  end

  def available?
    @state == :available
  end
end
```

Finally, for the BookingRequest instances, you need the public reader for the @guests instance variable. Add the line attr_reader :guests, inside the class BookingRequest (file booking_request.rb).

You are all set. Let's run the cucumber executable again:

```
$ cucumber --format progress

1 scenario (1 passed)
4 steps (4 passed)
0m0.049s
$
```

Perfect! All the steps run successfully, and the Scenario is green.

Scenario Outline

Let's introduce some more examples in the same Scenario logic but with different data. In this scenario, it seems that the check-in and checkout dates are not relevant, since all the rooms are initially free. So you will write a Scenario Outline so that you can check the availability depending on the number of guests requested only.

Here is how you turn the current Scenario to a Scenario Outline that would allow you to try different numbers of guests (Listing 7-23).

Listing 7-23. Using Scenario Outline

```
# File: features/booking_a_room.feature
#
Feature: Booking a Room
  Users should be able to book a room.
  The application should ask user the booking details and
  then return back the rooms available.

  Background:
  The table below describes the rooms available. The "number"
  column is the room number. The "accommodates" column is the
  maximum number of people that can stay in the room

    Given there are the following rooms in the hotel
      | number | accommodates |
      |      1 |            2 |
      |      2 |            2 |
      |      3 |            2 |
      |      4 |            2 |
      |      5 |            4 |
      |      6 |            4 |

  Scenario Outline: All the rooms are free and there are rooms on the
  capacity requested
    Given all the rooms are available
    When visitor provides the following booking details
      | check_in    | check_out   | guests   |
      | 23-Mar-2017 | 25-Mar-2017 | <guests> |
```

```
Then visitor is provided with rooms "<rooms>"
```

```
Examples:
  | guests | rooms |
  |      3 | 5, 6  |
```

The preceding code changes the Scenario to Scenario Outline and introduces a new step visitor is provided with rooms "<rooms>". Then you provide the examples list, with a single example for the time being, the example that corresponds to three guests and the expected rooms 5 and 6 given in a comma-separated list. Hence, this single example corresponds to the original Scenario that you had.

Let's run cucumber:

```
$ cucumber --format progress
...U

1 scenario (1 undefined)
4 steps (1 undefined, 3 passed)
0m0.071s
```

You can implement step definitions for undefined steps with these snippets:

```
Then("visitor is provided with rooms {string}") do |string|
  pending # Write code here that turns the phrase above into concrete
  actions
end
$
```

The new step is undefined, of course. It is easy to implement like the following (Listing 7-24).

Listing 7-24. Undefined Step Definition

```
Then("visitor is provided with rooms {string}") do |rooms_list|
  expected_room_numbers = rooms_list.split(',').map {|room_number| room_
  number.to_i}

  expect(@available_rooms.size).to eq(expected_room_numbers.size)
  @available_rooms.each_with_index do |available_room, index|
    expect(available_room.number).to eq(expected_room_numbers[index])
  end
end
```

264

You take the room_list, and you build the array with the expected room numbers (expected_room_numbers). Then comparing this array to the @available_rooms is easy and similar to what you did earlier (in the previous step definition).

Now, let's run cucumber again:

```
$ cucumber --format progress

1 scenario (1 passed)
4 steps (4 passed)
0m0.055s
$
```

Great! The feature is green, and one scenario is defined and passed.

But now, the Scenario Outline allows you to test other guests' cases. See this new version of the Examples section (Listing 7-25).

Listing 7-25. Examples Section with More Examples

```
Examples:
  | guests | rooms            |
  |      1 | 1, 2, 3, 4, 5, 6 |
  |      2 | 1, 2, 3, 4, 5, 6 |
  |      3 |             5, 6 |
  |      4 |             5, 6 |
  |      5 |                  |
  |      6 |                  |
  |      7 |                  |
```

If you run cucumber again, you will get this:

```
$ cucumber --format progress

7 scenarios (7 passed)
28 steps (28 passed)
0m0.063s
$
```

Nice!

Some Rooms Are Not Available

The preceding scenarios assume that all rooms are available. Let's expand to assume that some of the rooms are not available (Listing 7-26).

Listing 7-26. Assuming Some Rooms Are Not Available

```
# File: features/booking_a_room.feature
#
Feature: Booking a Room
  Users should be able to book a room.
  The application should ask user the booking details and
  then return back the rooms available.

  Background:
  The table below describes the rooms available. The "number"
  column is the room number. The "accommodates" column is the
  maximum number of people that can stay in the room

    Given there are the following rooms in the hotel
      | number | accommodates |
      |      1 |            2 |
      |      2 |            2 |
      |      3 |            2 |
      |      4 |            2 |
      |      5 |            4 |
      |      6 |            4 |

  Scenario Outline: All the rooms are free and there are rooms on the
  capacity requested
    Given all the rooms are available
    When visitor provides the following booking details
      | check_in    | check_out   | guests   |
      | 23-Mar-2017 | 25-Mar-2017 | <guests> |
    Then visitor is provided with rooms "<rooms>"
```

Examples:

```
| guests | rooms             |
|      1 | 1, 2, 3, 4, 5, 6 |
|      2 | 1, 2, 3, 4, 5, 6 |
|      3 |             5, 6 |
|      4 |             5, 6 |
|      5 |                   |
|      6 |                   |
|      7 |                   |
```

Scenario Outline: Some rooms are not available
   Given the rooms "<reserved_rooms>" are reserved
   When visitor provides the following booking details
      | check_in | check_out | guests |
      | 23-Mar-2017 | 25-Mar-2017 | <guests> |
   Then visitor is provided with rooms "<rooms>"

Examples:

```
| reserved_rooms    | guests | rooms          |
| 1                 | 1      | 2, 3, 4, 5, 6 |
| 1, 2              | 1      | 3, 4, 5, 6    |
| 1, 2, 3           | 1      | 4, 5, 6       |
| 1, 2, 3, 4        | 1      | 5, 6          |
| 1, 2, 3, 4, 5     | 1      | 6             |
| 1, 2, 3, 4, 5, 6 | 1      |               |
```

As you can see in the preceding code, you have compiled a new Scenario Outline that has some scenarios that include reserved rooms. If you run cucumber, you will get six new scenarios being undefined:

```
$ cucumber --format progress
.............................U--.U--.U--.U--.U--.U--

13 scenarios (6 undefined, 7 passed)
52 steps (12 skipped, 6 undefined, 34 passed)
0m0.070s
```

You can implement step definitions for undefined steps with these snippets:

```
Given("the rooms {string} are reserved") do |string|
  pending # Write code here that turns the phrase above into concrete
  actions
end
$
```

Let's implement the new step (Listing 7-27).

Listing 7-27. Implementation of the Undefined Step

```
Given("the rooms {string} are reserved") do |rooms_list|
  reserved_rooms = rooms_list.split(',').map(&:to_i)
  reserved_rooms.each { |room_number| @hotel.reserve_room(room_number) }
end
```

The step calls #reserve_room on the @hotel instance to render the particular room unavailable. However, the @hotel instance is not instantiated, and if you run cucumber, you get undefined method 'reserve_room' for nil:NilClass (NoMethodError). Why? You thought you had it instantiated, but the instantiation was done inside a step that is no longer called in this new Scenario Outline. It's better if you move the line @hotel = Hotel.new(rooms: @rooms) to be in the Background step, which is called for all scenarios. Let's do that (Listing 7-28).

Listing 7-28. New Content of the Step Implementation File

```
# File features/step_definitions/booking_with_joy_steps.rb
#
require 'date'

Given("there are the following rooms in the hotel") do |table|
  @rooms = []
  table.hashes.each do |hash|
    @rooms << Room.new(number: hash['number'].to_i, accommodates:
    hash['accommodates'].to_i)
  end
  @hotel = Hotel.new(rooms: @rooms)
end
```

```ruby
Given("all the rooms are available") do
  @rooms.each(&:set_available)
end

When("visitor provides the following booking details") do |table|
  # Note that "table" will only hold 1 line/row. The whole table
  # refers to 1 instance of a booking request

  hash = table.hashes.first

  @booking_request = BookingRequest.new(
    check_in: Date.strptime(hash['check_in'], '%d-%b-%Y'),
    check_out: Date.strptime(hash['check_out'], '%d-%b-%Y'),
    guests: hash['guests'].to_i
  )
  @available_rooms = @hotel.check_availability(@booking_request)
end

Then("visitor is provided with the following options for booking") do |table|
  expect(@available_rooms.size).to eq(table.hashes.size)
  @available_rooms.each_with_index do |available_room, index|
    expect(available_room.number).to eq(table.hashes[index]['number'].to_i)
  end
end

Then("visitor is provided with rooms {string}") do |rooms_list|
  expected_room_numbers = rooms_list.split(',').map {|room_number| room_
  number.to_i}

  expect(@available_rooms.size).to eq(expected_room_numbers.size)
  @available_rooms.each_with_index do |available_room, index|
    expect(available_room.number).to eq(expected_room_numbers[index])
  end
end

Given("the rooms {string} are reserved") do |rooms_list|
  reserved_rooms = rooms_list.split(',').map(&:to_i)
  reserved_rooms.each { |room_number| @hotel.reserve_room(room_number) }
end
```

As you can see in the preceding code, you have added line 10

```
@hotel = Hotel.new(rooms: @rooms)
```

and you have removed the instantiation of the @hotel variable from the When(/^visitor provides the following booking details$/) implementation.

Nevertheless, now, if you run cucumber, you get the error undefined method 'reserve_room' for #<Hotel:0x007fd34d84c240> (NoMethodError), which is expected, since the method #reserve_room has not been defined for instances of the Hotel class.

Let's fix this. Here is the new content of the hotel.rb file (Listing 7-29).

Listing 7-29. New Content of the hotel.rb File

```ruby
# File: hotel.rb
#
class Hotel
  def initialize(rooms:)
    @rooms = rooms
  end

  def check_availability(booking_request)
    existing_available_rooms.select do |existing_available_room|
      existing_available_room.accommodates >= booking_request.guests
    end
  end

  def reserve_room(room_number)
    @rooms.select {|r| r.number == room_number}.first.reserve
  end

  private

  attr_reader :rooms

  def existing_available_rooms
    rooms.select { |room| room.available? }
  end
end
```

See the new lines, 14–16. This is where you define the method #reserve_room for the instances of the Hotel class. If you run cucumber again, you will get errors like undefined method 'reserve' for #<Room:0x007fcd2389dfd0 @number=1, @accommodates=2> (NoMethodError). This is because you are calling #reserve on Room instances. But this class does not expose such method.

Let's implement this method. The following is the new content of the room.rb file (Listing 7-30).

Listing 7-30. New Content of the room.rb File

```ruby
# File: room.rb
#
class Room
  attr_reader :accommodates, :number

  def initialize(number:, accommodates:)
    @number = number
    @accommodates = accommodates
  end

  def set_available
    @state = :available
  end

  def available?
    @state == :available
  end

  def reserve
    @state = :reserved
  end
end
```

See the implementation of the method #reserve in between lines 19 and 21. Now, let's run cucumber:

```
$ cucumber --format progress
...............................F...F...F...F...F....

(::) failed steps (::)

expected: 5
     got: 0

(compared using ==)
 (RSpec::Expectations::ExpectationNotMetError)
./features/step_definitions/booking_with_joy_steps.rb:41:in `"visitor is
provided with rooms {string}"'
features/booking_a_room.feature:48:in `Then visitor is provided with rooms
"2, 3, 4, 5, 6"'
features/booking_a_room.feature:44:in `Then visitor is provided with rooms
"<rooms>"'

expected: 4
     got: 0

(compared using ==)
 (RSpec::Expectations::ExpectationNotMetError)
./features/step_definitions/booking_with_joy_steps.rb:41:in `"visitor is
provided with rooms {string}"'
features/booking_a_room.feature:49:in `Then visitor is provided with rooms
"3, 4, 5, 6"'
features/booking_a_room.feature:44:in `Then visitor is provided with rooms
"<rooms>"'

expected: 3
     got: 0

(compared using ==)
 (RSpec::Expectations::ExpectationNotMetError)
./features/step_definitions/booking_with_joy_steps.rb:41:in `"visitor is
provided with rooms {string}"'
```

features/booking_a_room.feature:50:in `Then visitor is provided with rooms "4, 5, 6"'
features/booking_a_room.feature:44:in `Then visitor is provided with rooms "<rooms>"'

expected: 2
     got: 0

(compared using ==)
 (RSpec::Expectations::ExpectationNotMetError)
./features/step_definitions/booking_with_joy_steps.rb:41:in `"visitor is provided with rooms {string}"'
features/booking_a_room.feature:51:in `Then visitor is provided with rooms "5, 6"'
features/booking_a_room.feature:44:in `Then visitor is provided with rooms "<rooms>"'

expected: 1
     got: 0

(compared using ==)
 (RSpec::Expectations::ExpectationNotMetError)
./features/step_definitions/booking_with_joy_steps.rb:41:in `"visitor is provided with rooms {string}"'
features/booking_a_room.feature:52:in `Then visitor is provided with rooms "6"'
features/booking_a_room.feature:44:in `Then visitor is provided with rooms "<rooms>"'

Failing Scenarios:
cucumber features/booking_a_room.feature:48 # Scenario Outline: Some rooms are not available, Examples (#1)
cucumber features/booking_a_room.feature:49 # Scenario Outline: Some rooms are not available, Examples (#2)
cucumber features/booking_a_room.feature:50 # Scenario Outline: Some rooms are not available, Examples (#3)
cucumber features/booking_a_room.feature:51 # Scenario Outline: Some rooms are not available, Examples (#4)

```
cucumber features/booking_a_room.feature:52 # Scenario Outline: Some rooms
are not available, Examples (#5)
```

```
13 scenarios (5 failed, 8 passed)
52 steps (5 failed, 47 passed)
0m0.107s
$
```

You can see the same error for all the scenarios:

```
./features/step_definitions/booking_with_joy_steps.rb:41:in `"visitor is
provided with rooms {string}"'
```

This is pointing here:

```
expect(@available_rooms.size).to eq(expected_room_numbers.size)
```

So the @available_rooms which is instantiated as the result of @hotel.check_availability(@booking_request) returns an empty array.

Looking at the implementation of this method, you don't see any error. But with little debugging, you can see that the problem is that, although some rooms are flagged as reserved, the rest of the rooms were not flagged as available. You now know that you should change the design of your Hotel class to render the rooms as available at the beginning. Let's do it. The following is the new version of the hotel.rb file (Listing 7-31).

Listing 7-31. New Version of the hotel.rb File That Flags Rooms as Available

```ruby
# File: hotel.rb
#
class Hotel
  def initialize(rooms:)
    @rooms = rooms
    @rooms.each { |room| room.set_available }
  end

  def check_availability(booking_request)
    existing_available_rooms.select do |existing_available_room|
      existing_available_room.accommodates >= booking_request.guests
    end
  end
```

```
def reserve_room(room_number)
  @rooms.select {|r| r.number == room_number}.first.reserve
end

private

attr_reader :rooms

def existing_available_rooms
  rooms.select { |room| room.available? }
end
end
```

You have only added line 6, which renders all the rooms the hotel is initialized with to be available.

If you run cucumber again, you will get this:

```
$ cucumber --format progress

13 scenarios (13 passed)
52 steps (52 passed)
0m0.067s
$
```

Excellent! All the Scenarios are now passing successfully!

Increase Your Confidence with Some Extra Examples

The second Scenario Outline has examples only for guests being 1. Let's add some more examples for other guests numbers (Listing 7-32).

Listing 7-32. Second Scenario Outline Examples, New Version

```
Examples:
  | reserved_rooms | guests | rooms         |
  | 1              | 1      | 2, 3, 4, 5, 6 |
  | 1, 2           | 1      | 3, 4, 5, 6    |
  | 1, 2, 3        | 1      | 4, 5, 6       |
  | 1, 2, 3, 4     | 1      | 5, 6          |
  | 1, 2, 3, 4, 5  | 1      | 6             |
```

```
| 1, 2, 3, 4, 5, 6 | 1       |                   |                  |
| 1                | 2       | 2, 3, 4, 5, 6 |                  |
| 1, 2             | 2       | 3, 4, 5, 6    |                  |
| 1, 2, 3          | 2       | 4, 5, 6       |                  |
| 1, 2, 3, 4       | 2       | 5, 6          |                  |
| 1, 2, 3, 4, 5    | 2       | 6             |                  |
| 1, 2, 3, 4, 5, 6 | 2       |               |                  |
| 1                | 3       | 5, 6          |                  |
| 1, 2             | 3       | 5, 6          |                  |
| 1, 2, 3          | 3       | 5, 6          |                  |
| 1, 2, 3, 4       | 3       | 5, 6          |                  |
| 1, 2, 3, 4, 5    | 3       | 6             |                  |
| 1, 2, 3, 4, 5, 6 | 3       |               |                  |
| 1                | 4       | 5, 6          |                  |
| 1, 2             | 4       | 5, 6          |                  |
| 1, 2, 3          | 4       | 5, 6          |                  |
| 1, 2, 3, 4       | 4       | 5, 6          |                  |
| 1, 2, 3, 4, 5    | 4       | 6             |                  |
| 1, 2, 3, 4, 5, 6 | 4       |               |                  |
| 1                | 5       |               |                  |
| 1, 2             | 5       |               |                  |
| 1, 2, 3          | 5       |               |                  |
| 1, 2, 3, 4       | 5       |               |                  |
| 1, 2, 3, 4, 5    | 5       |               |                  |
| 1, 2, 3, 4, 5, 6 | 5       |               |                  |
| 1                | 6       |               |                  |
| 1, 2             | 6       |               |                  |
| 1, 2, 3          | 6       |               |                  |
| 1, 2, 3, 4       | 6       |               |                  |
| 1, 2, 3, 4, 5    | 6       |               |                  |
| 1, 2, 3, 4, 5, 6 | 6       |               |                  |
```

Try running cucumber again, and you will see that all examples are passing successfully:

```
$ cucumber --format progress

43 scenarios (43 passed)
172 steps (172 passed)
0m0.113s
$
```

RSpec and Unit Tests

You will continue writing more Scenarios to cover for the various business cases. These will change/enhance your classes' public interfaces and their implementation. But relying only on the Cucumber Features and Scenarios to build robust classes is not always/usually enough. You will need to write some *unit tests* that would demonstrate and cover for the classes being used under edge/unexpected cases.

For example, calling Hotel#reserve_room(1000) would raise an exception. Try to execute the following commands in the irb console like I have done in the following:

```
$ bundle exec irb
irb(main):001:0> require_relative 'all'
=> true
irb(main):002:0> @hotel = Hotel.new(rooms: [Room.new(number: 1,
accommodates: 5)])
=> #<Hotel:0x00007fb2c41d9f10 @rooms=[#<Room:0x00007fb2c41d9fb0 @number=1,
@accommodates=5, @state=:available>]>
irb(main):003:0> @hotel.reserve_room(1)
=> :reserved
irb(main):004:0> @hotel.reserve_room(1000)
Traceback (most recent call last):
....<traceback here>....
NoMethodError (undefined method `reserve' for nil:NilClass)
irb(main):005:0>
```

As you can see, the NoMethodError exception is raised when you call @hotel. reserve_room(1000).

It may not be good for your class to behave like this. Instead of raising the NoMethodError exception, you might want to raise a more meaningful error, like ArgumentError with a descriptive message.

How would you go for the development of this, if you were to do TDD? You would have to go with a unit test.

You will write your unit test using RSpec, and before you do, you have to initialize RSpec with the following command. Run it at the root folder of your project:

```
$ bundle exec rspec -init
  create .rspec
  create spec/spec_helper.rb
$
```

Then, make sure that the line require_relative '../all' exists at the bottom of the spec/spec_helper.rb file.

Now, you are ready to write your Hotel class unit tests. Create the file spec/hotel_spec.rb like the following (Listing 7-33).

Listing 7-33. Content of the New File spèc/hotel_spec.rb

```ruby
# File spec/hotel_spec.rb
#
describe Hotel do
  describe '#reserve_room' do
    context 'when room number does not exist' do
      let(:maximum_room_number) { rooms.map(&:number).max }
      let(:room_number) { maximum_room_number + 1 }
      let(:rooms) do
        [
          Room.new(number: 1, accommodates: 2),
          Room.new(number: 2, accommodates: 2),
        ]
      end
      subject(:hotel) { Hotel.new(rooms: rooms) }
```

```
  it 'raises a meaningful exception' do
    expect do
      hotel.reserve_room room_number
    end.to raise_error(ArgumentError, /room_number: #{room_number}
    given is not part of the numbers of the rooms of the hotel./)
  end
 end
end
end
```

This file contains a unit test for the #reserve_room method that will fail as follows the first time you run it:

```
$ bundle exec rspec
F

Failures:

  1) Hotel#reserve_room when room number does not exist raises a meaningful
     exception
     Failure/Error:
       expect do
         hotel.reserve_room room_number
       end.to raise_error(ArgumentError, /room_number: #{room_number} given
       is not part of the numbers of the rooms of the hotel./)

       expected ArgumentError with message matching /room_number: 3
       given is not part of the numbers of the rooms of the hotel./, got
       #<NoMethodError: undefined method `reserve' for nil:NilClass> with
       backtrace:
         # ./hotel.rb:16:in `reserve_room'
         # ./spec/hotel_spec.rb:18:in `block (5 levels) in <top
           (required)>'
         # ./spec/hotel_spec.rb:17:in `block (4 levels) in <top
           (required)>'
       # ./spec/hotel_spec.rb:17:in `block (4 levels) in <top (required)>'
```

```
Finished in 0.03986 seconds (files took 0.16413 seconds to load)
1 example, 1 failure

Failed examples:

rspec ./spec/hotel_spec.rb:16 # Hotel#reserve_room when room number does
not exist raises a meaningful exception
$
```

In order to fix this specification, you need to change the implementation of the Hotel#reserve_room to do what the specification requires. The following is the new content of the file hotel.rb that deals with this (Listing 7-34).

Listing 7-34. Raise ArgumentError to Cover for the Requirement

```ruby
# File: hotel.rb
#
class Hotel
  def initialize(rooms:)
    @rooms = rooms
    @rooms.each { |room| room.set_available }
  end

  def check_availability(booking_request)
    existing_available_rooms.select do |existing_available_room|
      existing_available_room.accommodates >= booking_request.guests
    end
  end

  def reserve_room(room_number)
    room_found = @rooms.select {|r| r.number == room_number}.first
    raise ArgumentError, "room_number: #{room_number} given is not part of
    the numbers of the rooms of the hotel." if room_found.nil?
    room_found.reserve
  end

  private

  attr_reader :rooms
```

```
def existing_available_rooms
  rooms.select { |room| room.available? }
end
end
```

See lines 15–19. The new implementation of the Hotel#reserve_room makes sure it raises the correct exception with the correct message, according to the requirement.

Let's run rspec again:

```
$ bundle exec rspec
.

Finished in 0.00742 seconds (files took 0.22031 seconds to load)
1 example, 0 failures
$
```

Excellent!

What have you seen? You have seen how parts of your tests are covered with business-facing scenarios using Cucumber and Gherkin and how other parts of your code are tests covered with unit tests using RSpec. With Rspec, you specify implementation details that have a technical focus that would make your class design more robust.

Rest of the Feature

The Feature for booking is missing scenarios that would cover the cases to take into account the dates rooms are available. I leave this as an exercise to you.

Cucumber Command Line

Before I close the chapter on Cucumber, I am going to present to you some aspects of the cucumber tool itself. Then I will show you how RubyMine integrates with Cucumber.

Dry Run

cucumber allows you to execute a *dry run*. The *dry run* parses your .feature files and makes sure that they are ok with regard to their syntax. Basically, the dry run skips all the steps. Also, it reports any step definitions that are not defined.

Try, for example, the *dry run* for the booking-with-joy project:

```
$ cucumber --dry-run
# File: features/booking_a_room.feature
#
Feature: Booking a Room
  Users should be able to book a room.
  The application should ask user the booking details and
  then return back the rooms available.

  Background:                        # features/booking_a_room.feature:8
  The table below describes the rooms available. The "number"
  column is the room number. The "accommodates" column is the
  maximum number of people that can stay in the room
    Given there are the following rooms in the hotel # features/step_
    definitions/booking_with_joy_steps.rb:5
      | number | accommodates |
      | 1      | 2            |
      | 2      | 2            |
      | 3      | 2            |
      | 4      | 2            |
      | 5      | 4            |
      | 6      | 4            |

  Scenario Outline: All the rooms are free and there are rooms on the
  capacity requested # features/booking_a_room.feature:22
    Given all the rooms are available      # features/booking_a_room.
    feature:23
    When visitor provides the following booking details
    # features/booking_a_room.feature:24
      | check_in     | check_out    | guests   |
      | 23-Mar-2017  | 25-Mar-2017  | <guests> |
    Then visitor is provided with rooms "<rooms>"
    # features/booking_a_room.feature:27
```

Examples:

guests	rooms
1	1, 2, 3, 4, 5, 6
2	1, 2, 3, 4, 5, 6
3	5, 6
4	5, 6
5	
6	
7	

Scenario Outline: Some rooms are not available
features/booking_a_room.feature:39
  Given the rooms "<reserved_rooms>" are reserved
  # features/booking_a_room.feature:40
  When visitor provides the following booking details
  # features/booking_a_room.feature:41

check_in	check_out	guests
23-Mar-2017	25-Mar-2017	<guests>

  Then visitor is provided with rooms "<rooms>"
  # features/booking_a_room.feature:44

Examples:

reserved_rooms	guests	rooms
1	1	2, 3, 4, 5, 6
1, 2	1	3, 4, 5, 6
1, 2, 3	1	4, 5, 6
1, 2, 3, 4	1	5, 6
1, 2, 3, 4, 5	1	6
1, 2, 3, 4, 5, 6	1	
1	2	2, 3, 4, 5, 6
1, 2	2	3, 4, 5, 6
1, 2, 3	2	4, 5, 6
1, 2, 3, 4	2	5, 6
1, 2, 3, 4, 5	2	6
1, 2, 3, 4, 5, 6	2	
1	3	5, 6

```
| 1, 2            | 3   | 5, 6   |
| 1, 2, 3         | 3   | 5, 6   |
| 1, 2, 3, 4      | 3   | 5, 6   |
| 1, 2, 3, 4, 5   | 3   | 6      |
| 1, 2, 3, 4, 5, 6 | 3  |        |
| 1               | 4   | 5, 6   |
| 1, 2            | 4   | 5, 6   |
| 1, 2, 3         | 4   | 5, 6   |
| 1, 2, 3, 4      | 4   | 5, 6   |
| 1, 2, 3, 4, 5   | 4   | 6      |
| 1, 2, 3, 4, 5, 6 | 4  |        |
| 1               | 5   |        |
| 1, 2            | 5   |        |
| 1, 2, 3         | 5   |        |
| 1, 2, 3, 4      | 5   |        |
| 1, 2, 3, 4, 5   | 5   |        |
| 1, 2, 3, 4, 5, 6 | 5  |        |
| 1               | 6   |        |
| 1, 2            | 6   |        |
| 1, 2, 3         | 6   |        |
| 1, 2, 3, 4      | 6   |        |
| 1, 2, 3, 4, 5   | 6   |        |
| 1, 2, 3, 4, 5, 6 | 6  |        |
```

```
43 scenarios (43 skipped)
172 steps (172 skipped)
```

Invoking a Single Feature

Usually, your project is going to have multiple .feature files. Calling cucumber will execute all the Scenarios defined in all these files. How can you invoke cucumber for the Scenarios of a particular .feature file only?

This is how you should do it: In the following example, I invoke the Scenarios inside the file features/booking_online.feature. Other .feature files are ignored:

```
$ cucumber features/booking_online.feature
```

Invoking a Single Scenario

Besides being able to specify a specific `.feature` file, you are able to specify a specific
Scenario within a specific `.feature` file.

Let's consider again the booking-with-joy project and the `.feature` file:

```
# File: features/booking_a_room.feature
#
Feature: Booking a Room
  Users should be able to book a room.
  The application should ask user the booking details and
  then return back the rooms available.

  Background:
    The table below describes the rooms available. The "number"
    column is the room number. The "accommodates" column is the
    maximum number of people that can stay in the room

    Given there are the following rooms in the hotel
      | number | accommodates |
      |      1 |            2 |
      |      2 |            2 |
      |      3 |            2 |
      |      4 |            2 |
      |      5 |            4 |
      |      6 |            4 |

  Scenario Outline: All the rooms are free and there are rooms on the
  capacity requested
    Given all the rooms are available
    When visitor provides the following booking details
      | check_in     | check_out    | guests    |
      | 23-Mar-2017  | 25-Mar-2017  | <guests>  |
    Then visitor is provided with rooms "<rooms>"
```

Examples:

guests	rooms
1	1, 2, 3, 4, 5, 6
2	1, 2, 3, 4, 5, 6
3	5, 6
4	5, 6
5	
6	
7	

Scenario Outline: Some rooms are not available
  Given the rooms "<reserved_rooms>" are reserved
  When visitor provides the following booking details

check_in	check_out	guests
23-Mar-2017	25-Mar-2017	<guests>

  Then visitor is provided with rooms "<rooms>"

Examples:

reserved_rooms	guests	rooms
1	1	2, 3, 4, 5, 6
1, 2	1	3, 4, 5, 6
1, 2, 3	1	4, 5, 6
1, 2, 3, 4	1	5, 6
1, 2, 3, 4, 5	1	6
1, 2, 3, 4, 5, 6	1	
1	2	2, 3, 4, 5, 6
1, 2	2	3, 4, 5, 6
1, 2, 3	2	4, 5, 6
1, 2, 3, 4	2	5, 6
1, 2, 3, 4, 5	2	6
1, 2, 3, 4, 5, 6	2	
1	3	5, 6
1, 2	3	5, 6
1, 2, 3	3	5, 6
1, 2, 3, 4	3	5, 6
1, 2, 3, 4, 5	3	6

1, 2, 3, 4, 5, 6	3		
1	4	5, 6	
1, 2	4	5, 6	
1, 2, 3	4	5, 6	
1, 2, 3, 4	4	5, 6	
1, 2, 3, 4, 5	4	6	
1, 2, 3, 4, 5, 6	4		
1	5		
1, 2	5		
1, 2, 3	5		
1, 2, 3, 4	5		
1, 2, 3, 4, 5	5		
1, 2, 3, 4, 5, 6	5		
1	6		
1, 2	6		
1, 2, 3	6		
1, 2, 3, 4	6		
1, 2, 3, 4, 5	6		
1, 2, 3, 4, 5, 6	6		

You can execute the Scenarios corresponding to the Scenario Outline defined on line 22 as follows:

```
$ cucumber features/booking_a_room.feature:22
# File: features/booking_a_room.feature
#
Feature: Booking a Room
  Users should be able to book a room.
  The application should ask user the booking details and
  then return back the rooms available.

  Background:                           # features/booking_a_room.feature:8
  The table below describes the rooms available. The "number"
  column is the room number. The "accommodates" column is the
```

maximum number of people that can stay in the room
    Given there are the following rooms in the hotel
    # features/step_definitions/booking_with_joy_steps.rb:5

number	accommodates
1	2
2	2
3	2
4	2
5	4
6	4

    Scenario Outline: All the rooms are free and there are rooms on the
capacity requested # features/booking_a_room.feature:22
    Given all the rooms are available
    # features/booking_a_room.feature:23
    When visitor provides the following booking details
    # features/booking_a_room.feature:24

check_in	check_out	guests
23-Mar-2017	25-Mar-2017	\<guests\>

    Then visitor is provided with rooms "\<rooms\>"
    # features/booking_a_room.feature:27

    Examples:

guests	rooms
1	1, 2, 3, 4, 5, 6
2	1, 2, 3, 4, 5, 6
3	5, 6
4	5, 6
5	
6	
7	

7 scenarios (7 passed)
28 steps (28 passed)
0m0.208s
$

As you can see, I have managed to call the Scenarios that correspond to the Scenario Outline on line 22, by specifying the line number next to the filename of the feature: `cucumber features/booking_a_room.feature:22`.

But you can take it even further. You can ask `cucumber` to execute the Scenario that corresponds to a specific example. Here is how you can execute the Scenario that corresponds to the example on line 34:

```
$ cucumber features/booking_a_room.feature:34
# File: features/booking_a_room.feature
#
Feature: Booking a Room
  Users should be able to book a room.
  The application should ask user the booking details and
  then return back the rooms available.

  Background:                             # features/booking_a_room.feature:8
  The table below describes the rooms available. The "number"
  column is the room number. The "accommodates" column is the
  maximum number of people that can stay in the room
    Given there are the following rooms in the hotel
    # features/step_definitions/booking_with_joy_steps.rb:5
      | number | accommodates |
      | 1      | 2            |
      | 2      | 2            |
      | 3      | 2            |
      | 4      | 2            |
      | 5      | 4            |
      | 6      | 4            |

  Scenario Outline: All the rooms are free and there are rooms on the
capacity requested # features/booking_a_room.feature:22
    Given all the rooms are available
    # features/booking_a_room.feature:23
    When visitor provides the following booking details
    # features/booking_a_room.feature:24
      | check_in    | check_out   | guests    |
      | 23-Mar-2017 | 25-Mar-2017 | <guests>  |
```

289

```
    Then visitor is provided with rooms "<rooms>"
    # features/booking_a_room.feature:27

    Examples:
      | guests | rooms          |
      | 4      | 5, 6           |
1 scenario (1 passed)
4 steps (4 passed)
0m0.075s
$
```

So, instead of specifying the line of the Scenario Outline, you specified the line of the Example.

Note that you can ask cucumber to execute more than one scenario at the same time. For example, in the following, I execute the scenarios that correspond to the examples for lines 34 and 35. See how I give the list of line numbers in a : -separated list:

```
$ cucumber features/booking_a_room.feature:34:35
# File: features/booking_a_room.feature
#
Feature: Booking a Room
  Users should be able to book a room.
  The application should ask user the booking details and
  then return back the rooms available.

  Background:                       # features/booking_a_room.feature:8
  The table below describes the rooms available. The "number"
  column is the room number. The "accommodates" column is the
  maximum number of people that can stay in the room
    Given there are the following rooms in the hotel
    # features/step_definitions/booking_with_joy_steps.rb:5
      | number | accommodates |
      | 1      | 2            |
      | 2      | 2            |
      | 3      | 2            |
      | 4      | 2            |
      | 5      | 4            |
      | 6      | 4            |
```

```
Scenario Outline: All the rooms are free and there are rooms on the
capacity requested # features/booking_a_room.feature:22
    Given all the rooms are available           # features/booking_a_room.
                                                    feature:23

  When visitor provides the following booking details
  # features/booking_a_room.feature:24
    | check_in     | check_out    | guests   |
    | 23-Mar-2017  | 25-Mar-2017  | <guests> |
  Then visitor is provided with rooms "<rooms>"
  # features/booking_a_room.feature:27

  Examples:
    | guests | rooms     |
    | 4      | 5, 6      |
    | 5      |           |

2 scenarios (2 passed)
8 steps (8 passed)
0m0.070s
$
```

Tags

Cucumber allows you to tag your Features and your Scenarios (including Scenario Outlines) with tags. Then, you can tell cucumber which tags you are interested in, and cucumber will only execute the Scenarios tagged with these tags.

For example, let's tag one of the two Scenario Outlines with the tag @foo (Listing 7-35).

Listing 7-35. Using Tags

```
# File: features/booking_a_room.feature
#
Feature: Booking a Room
  Users should be able to book a room.
  The application should ask user the booking details and
  then return back the rooms available.
```

Background:
The table below describes the rooms available. The "number"
column is the room number. The "accommodates" column is the
maximum number of people that can stay in the room

    Given there are the following rooms in the hotel

number	accommodates
1	2
2	2
3	2
4	2
5	4
6	4

Scenario Outline: All the rooms are free and there are rooms on the
capacity requested
    Given all the rooms are available
    When visitor provides the following booking details

check_in	check_out	guests
23-Mar-2017	25-Mar-2017	\<guests\>

    Then visitor is provided with rooms "\<rooms\>"

    Examples:

guests	rooms
1	1, 2, 3, 4, 5, 6
2	1, 2, 3, 4, 5, 6
3	5, 6
4	5, 6
5	
6	
7	

@foo
Scenario Outline: Some rooms are not available
    Given the rooms "\<reserved_rooms\>" are reserved
    When visitor provides the following booking details

check_in	check_out	guests
23-Mar-2017	25-Mar-2017	\<guests\>

Then visitor is provided with rooms "<rooms>"

Examples:

reserved_rooms	guests	rooms
1	1	2, 3, 4, 5, 6
1, 2	1	3, 4, 5, 6
1, 2, 3	1	4, 5, 6
1, 2, 3, 4	1	5, 6
1, 2, 3, 4, 5	1	6
1, 2, 3, 4, 5, 6	1	
1	2	2, 3, 4, 5, 6
1, 2	2	3, 4, 5, 6
1, 2, 3	2	4, 5, 6
1, 2, 3, 4	2	5, 6
1, 2, 3, 4, 5	2	6
1, 2, 3, 4, 5, 6	2	
1	3	5, 6
1, 2	3	5, 6
1, 2, 3	3	5, 6
1, 2, 3, 4	3	5, 6
1, 2, 3, 4, 5	3	6
1, 2, 3, 4, 5, 6	3	
1	4	5, 6
1, 2	4	5, 6
1, 2, 3	4	5, 6
1, 2, 3, 4	4	5, 6
1, 2, 3, 4, 5	4	6
1, 2, 3, 4, 5, 6	4	
1	5	
1, 2	5	
1, 2, 3	5	
1, 2, 3, 4	5	
1, 2, 3, 4, 5	5	
1, 2, 3, 4, 5, 6	5	
1	6	
1, 2	6	

```
| 1, 2, 3          | 6    |          |              |
| 1, 2, 3, 4       | 6    |          |              |
| 1, 2, 3, 4, 5    | 6    |          |              |
| 1, 2, 3, 4, 5, 6 | 6    |          |              |
```

Do you see line 39? This is the only change. I have tagged the Scenario Outline with the tag @foo. Now, let's invoke cucumber and tell it to execute the Scenarios that are tagged with this tag only:

```
$ cucumber --tags @foo
# File: features/booking_a_room.feature
#
Feature: Booking a Room
  Users should be able to book a room.
  The application should ask user the booking details and
  then return back the rooms available.

  Background:                     # features/booking_a_room.feature:8
  The table below describes the rooms available. The "number"
  column is the room number. The "accommodates" column is the
  maximum number of people that can stay in the room
    Given there are the following rooms in the hotel
    # features/step_definitions/booking_with_joy_steps.rb:5
      | number | accommodates |
      | 1      | 2            |
      | 2      | 2            |
      | 3      | 2            |
      | 4      | 2            |
      | 5      | 4            |
      | 6      | 4            |

  @foo
  Scenario Outline: Some rooms are not available
  # features/booking_a_room.feature:40
    Given the rooms "<reserved_rooms>" are reserved
    # features/booking_a_room.feature:41
```

When visitor provides the following booking details
features/booking_a_room.feature:42
    | check_in | check_out | guests |
    | 23-Mar-2017 | 25-Mar-2017 | <guests> |
Then visitor is provided with rooms "<rooms>"
features/booking_a_room.feature:45

Examples:
    | reserved_rooms | guests | rooms |
    | 1 | 1 | 2, 3, 4, 5, 6 |
    | 1, 2 | 1 | 3, 4, 5, 6 |
    | 1, 2, 3 | 1 | 4, 5, 6 |
    | 1, 2, 3, 4 | 1 | 5, 6 |
    | 1, 2, 3, 4, 5 | 1 | 6 |
    | 1, 2, 3, 4, 5, 6 | 1 | |
    | 1 | 2 | 2, 3, 4, 5, 6 |
    | 1, 2 | 2 | 3, 4, 5, 6 |
    | 1, 2, 3 | 2 | 4, 5, 6 |
    | 1, 2, 3, 4 | 2 | 5, 6 |
    | 1, 2, 3, 4, 5 | 2 | 6 |
    | 1, 2, 3, 4, 5, 6 | 2 | |
    | 1 | 3 | 5, 6 |
    | 1, 2 | 3 | 5, 6 |
    | 1, 2, 3 | 3 | 5, 6 |
    | 1, 2, 3, 4 | 3 | 5, 6 |
    | 1, 2, 3, 4, 5 | 3 | 6 |
    | 1, 2, 3, 4, 5, 6 | 3 | |
    | 1 | 4 | 5, 6 |
    | 1, 2 | 4 | 5, 6 |
    | 1, 2, 3 | 4 | 5, 6 |
    | 1, 2, 3, 4 | 4 | 5, 6 |
    | 1, 2, 3, 4, 5 | 4 | 6 |
    | 1, 2, 3, 4, 5, 6 | 4 | |
    | 1 | 5 | |
    | 1, 2 | 5 | |
    | 1, 2, 3 | 5 | |

```
| 1, 2, 3, 4         | 5  |        |          |
| 1, 2, 3, 4, 5      | 5  |        |          |
| 1, 2, 3, 4, 5, 6   | 5  |        |          |
| 1                  | 6  |        |          |
| 1, 2               | 6  |        |          |
| 1, 2, 3            | 6  |        |          |
| 1, 2, 3, 4         | 6  |        |          |
| 1, 2, 3, 4, 5      | 6  |        |          |
| 1, 2, 3, 4, 5, 6   | 6  |        |          |
```

```
36 scenarios (36 passed)
144 steps (144 passed)
0m0.246s
$
```

I invoked cucumber as cucumber --tags @foo, and this executed only the Scenarios that were tagged with the @foo tag. You can ask for more than one tag to be executed – cucumber --tags @tag1,@tag2,@tag3 – in a comma-separated list after the --tags switch.

But tags can also be useful when you want to exclude some Scenarios from being executed. For example, you may not want some Scenarios to be executed in your continuous integration server.

How can you tell that Scenarios of a specific tag should be excluded? This is done by pre-pending the name of the tag with the ~ symbol.

The following invokes cucumber on the booking-with-joy project, without executing the @foo-tagged Scenarios:

```
$ cucumber --tags ~@foo
Deprecated: Found tags option '~@foo'. Support for '~@tag' will be removed
from the next release of Cucumber. Please use 'not @tag' instead.
# File: features/booking_a_room.feature
#
Feature: Booking a Room
  Users should be able to book a room.
  The application should ask user the booking details and
  then return back the rooms available.

  Background:                              # features/booking_a_room.feature:8
  The table below describes the rooms available. The "number"
```

column is the room number. The "accommodates" column is the
maximum number of people that can stay in the room
   Given there are the following rooms in the hotel
   # features/step_definitions/booking_with_joy_steps.rb:5

number	accommodates
1	2
2	2
3	2
4	2
5	4
6	4

Scenario Outline: All the rooms are free and there are rooms on the
capacity requested # features/booking_a_room.feature:22
   Given all the rooms are available   # features/booking_a_room.
                                             feature:23
   When visitor provides the following booking details
   # features/booking_a_room.feature:24

check_in	check_out	guests
23-Mar-2017	25-Mar-2017	<guests>

Then visitor is provided with rooms "<rooms>"
   # features/booking_a_room.feature:27

   Examples:

guests	rooms
1	1, 2, 3, 4, 5, 6
2	1, 2, 3, 4, 5, 6
3	5, 6
4	5, 6
5	
6	
7	

7 scenarios (7 passed)
28 steps (28 passed)
0m0.107s
$

Hooks

Cucumber allows you to hook a piece of Ruby code that will be executed at specific points in the lifecycle of the execution of your Scenarios, in particular

1. Before every Scenario

2. After every Scenario

3. Around every Scenario

4. After every Step

The hooks are usually defined inside the file features/support/hooks.rb. Let's put some dummy implementation for our booking-with-joy project inside this file (Listing 7-36).

Listing 7-36. Dummy Hooks Implementation

```
# File: features/support/hooks.rb
#
Before do |scenario|
  print "Before starting scenario #{scenario.name}"
end

After do |scenario|
  puts "> after scenario #{scenario.name}"
end
```

In the preceding features/support/hooks.rb file, you hook some Ruby code that would be executed both before and after each Scenario. Note that you do have access to the metadata of the Scenario that is executed via the block-level variable (scenario).

If you run the cucumber command, you will get this:

```
$ cucumber --format progress
Before starting scenario All the rooms are free and there are rooms on the
capacity requested, Examples (#1)....
> after scenario All the rooms are free and there are rooms on the capacity
requested, Examples (#1)
Before starting scenario All the rooms are free and there are rooms on the
capacity requested, Examples (#2)....
```

> after scenario All the rooms are free and there are rooms on the capacity requested, Examples (#2)
Before starting scenario All the rooms are free and there are rooms on the capacity requested, Examples (#3)....
> after scenario All the rooms are free and there are rooms on the capacity requested, Examples (#3)
Before starting scenario All the rooms are free and there are rooms on the capacity requested, Examples (#4)....
> after scenario All the rooms are free and there are rooms on the capacity requested, Examples (#4)
Before starting scenario All the rooms are free and there are rooms on the capacity requested, Examples (#5)....
> after scenario All the rooms are free and there are rooms on the capacity requested, Examples (#5)
Before starting scenario All the rooms are free and there are rooms on the capacity requested, Examples (#6)....
> after scenario All the rooms are free and there are rooms on the capacity requested, Examples (#6)
Before starting scenario All the rooms are free and there are rooms on the capacity requested, Examples (#7)....
> after scenario All the rooms are free and there are rooms on the capacity requested, Examples (#7)
Before starting scenario Some rooms are not available, Examples (#1)....
> after scenario Some rooms are not available, Examples (#1)
Before starting scenario Some rooms are not available, Examples (#2)....
> after scenario Some rooms are not available, Examples (#2)
Before starting scenario Some rooms are not available, Examples (#3)....
> after scenario Some rooms are not available, Examples (#3)
Before starting scenario Some rooms are not available, Examples (#4)....
> after scenario Some rooms are not available, Examples (#4)
Before starting scenario Some rooms are not available, Examples (#5)....
> after scenario Some rooms are not available, Examples (#5)
Before starting scenario Some rooms are not available, Examples (#6)....
> after scenario Some rooms are not available, Examples (#6)
Before starting scenario Some rooms are not available, Examples (#7)....
> after scenario Some rooms are not available, Examples (#7)

```
Before starting scenario Some rooms are not available, Examples (#8)....
> after scenario Some rooms are not available, Examples (#8)
Before starting scenario Some rooms are not available, Examples (#9)....
> after scenario Some rooms are not available, Examples (#9)
Before starting scenario Some rooms are not available, Examples (#10)....
> after scenario Some rooms are not available, Examples (#10)
Before starting scenario Some rooms are not available, Examples (#11)....
> after scenario Some rooms are not available, Examples (#11)
Before starting scenario Some rooms are not available, Examples (#12)....
> after scenario Some rooms are not available, Examples (#12)
Before starting scenario Some rooms are not available, Examples (#13)....
> after scenario Some rooms are not available, Examples (#13)
Before starting scenario Some rooms are not available, Examples (#14)....
> after scenario Some rooms are not available, Examples (#14)
Before starting scenario Some rooms are not available, Examples (#15)....
> after scenario Some rooms are not available, Examples (#15)
Before starting scenario Some rooms are not available, Examples (#16)....
> after scenario Some rooms are not available, Examples (#16)
Before starting scenario Some rooms are not available, Examples (#17)....
> after scenario Some rooms are not available, Examples (#17)
Before starting scenario Some rooms are not available, Examples (#18)....
> after scenario Some rooms are not available, Examples (#18)
Before starting scenario Some rooms are not available, Examples (#19)....
> after scenario Some rooms are not available, Examples (#19)
Before starting scenario Some rooms are not available, Examples (#20)....
> after scenario Some rooms are not available, Examples (#20)
Before starting scenario Some rooms are not available, Examples (#21)....
> after scenario Some rooms are not available, Examples (#21)
Before starting scenario Some rooms are not available, Examples (#22)....
> after scenario Some rooms are not available, Examples (#22)
Before starting scenario Some rooms are not available, Examples (#23)....
> after scenario Some rooms are not available, Examples (#23)
Before starting scenario Some rooms are not available, Examples (#24)....
> after scenario Some rooms are not available, Examples (#24)
```

```
Before starting scenario Some rooms are not available, Examples (#25)....
> after scenario Some rooms are not available, Examples (#25)
Before starting scenario Some rooms are not available, Examples (#26)....
> after scenario Some rooms are not available, Examples (#26)
Before starting scenario Some rooms are not available, Examples (#27)....
> after scenario Some rooms are not available, Examples (#27)
Before starting scenario Some rooms are not available, Examples (#28)....
> after scenario Some rooms are not available, Examples (#28)
Before starting scenario Some rooms are not available, Examples (#29)....
> after scenario Some rooms are not available, Examples (#29)
Before starting scenario Some rooms are not available, Examples (#30)....
> after scenario Some rooms are not available, Examples (#30)
Before starting scenario Some rooms are not available, Examples (#31)....
> after scenario Some rooms are not available, Examples (#31)
Before starting scenario Some rooms are not available, Examples (#32)....
> after scenario Some rooms are not available, Examples (#32)
Before starting scenario Some rooms are not available, Examples (#33)....
> after scenario Some rooms are not available, Examples (#33)
Before starting scenario Some rooms are not available, Examples (#34)....
> after scenario Some rooms are not available, Examples (#34)
Before starting scenario Some rooms are not available, Examples (#35)....
> after scenario Some rooms are not available, Examples (#35)
Before starting scenario Some rooms are not available, Examples (#36)....
> after scenario Some rooms are not available, Examples (#36)

43 scenarios (43 passed)
172 steps (172 passed)
0m0.154s
$
```

You can see how the Ruby code hooked to Before and After hooks is being invoked and its output is being printed in between the standard cucumber output.

The hooks may be scoped for specific tags. Let's change the features/support/ hooks.rb file to hook to the @foo-tagged Scenarios only (Listing 7-37).

Listing 7-37. Hooks for Specific Tags

```
# File: features/support/hooks.rb
#
Before('@foo') do |scenario|
  print "Before starting scenario #{scenario.name}"
end

After('@foo') do |scenario|
  puts "> after scenario #{scenario.name}"
end
```

You can see how I scope the hooks, by giving the tag I want to scope for as argument to the hook methods. If you run cucumber again, you will see that the Ruby code output is only printed for the Scenarios that are tagged with the @foo tag:

```
$ cucumber --format progress
...........................Before starting scenario Some rooms are not
available, Examples (#1)....
> after scenario Some rooms are not available, Examples (#1)
Before starting scenario Some rooms are not available, Examples (#2)....
> after scenario Some rooms are not available, Examples (#2)
Before starting scenario Some rooms are not available, Examples (#3)....
> after scenario Some rooms are not available, Examples (#3)
Before starting scenario Some rooms are not available, Examples (#4)....
> after scenario Some rooms are not available, Examples (#4)
Before starting scenario Some rooms are not available, Examples (#5)....
> after scenario Some rooms are not available, Examples (#5)
Before starting scenario Some rooms are not available, Examples (#6)....
> after scenario Some rooms are not available, Examples (#6)
Before starting scenario Some rooms are not available, Examples (#7)....
> after scenario Some rooms are not available, Examples (#7)
Before starting scenario Some rooms are not available, Examples (#8)....
> after scenario Some rooms are not available, Examples (#8)
Before starting scenario Some rooms are not available, Examples (#9)....
> after scenario Some rooms are not available, Examples (#9)
```

Before starting scenario Some rooms are not available, Examples (#10)....
> after scenario Some rooms are not available, Examples (#10)
Before starting scenario Some rooms are not available, Examples (#11)....
> after scenario Some rooms are not available, Examples (#11)
Before starting scenario Some rooms are not available, Examples (#12)....
> after scenario Some rooms are not available, Examples (#12)
Before starting scenario Some rooms are not available, Examples (#13)....
> after scenario Some rooms are not available, Examples (#13)
Before starting scenario Some rooms are not available, Examples (#14)....
> after scenario Some rooms are not available, Examples (#14)
Before starting scenario Some rooms are not available, Examples (#15)....
> after scenario Some rooms are not available, Examples (#15)
Before starting scenario Some rooms are not available, Examples (#16)....
> after scenario Some rooms are not available, Examples (#16)
Before starting scenario Some rooms are not available, Examples (#17)....
> after scenario Some rooms are not available, Examples (#17)
Before starting scenario Some rooms are not available, Examples (#18)....
> after scenario Some rooms are not available, Examples (#18)
Before starting scenario Some rooms are not available, Examples (#19)....
> after scenario Some rooms are not available, Examples (#19)
Before starting scenario Some rooms are not available, Examples (#20)....
> after scenario Some rooms are not available, Examples (#20)
Before starting scenario Some rooms are not available, Examples (#21)....
> after scenario Some rooms are not available, Examples (#21)
Before starting scenario Some rooms are not available, Examples (#22)....
> after scenario Some rooms are not available, Examples (#22)
Before starting scenario Some rooms are not available, Examples (#23)....
> after scenario Some rooms are not available, Examples (#23)
Before starting scenario Some rooms are not available, Examples (#24)....
> after scenario Some rooms are not available, Examples (#24)
Before starting scenario Some rooms are not available, Examples (#25)....
> after scenario Some rooms are not available, Examples (#25)
Before starting scenario Some rooms are not available, Examples (#26)....
> after scenario Some rooms are not available, Examples (#26)
Before starting scenario Some rooms are not available, Examples (#27)....
> after scenario Some rooms are not available, Examples (#27)

```
Before starting scenario Some rooms are not available, Examples (#28)....
> after scenario Some rooms are not available, Examples (#28)
Before starting scenario Some rooms are not available, Examples (#29)....
> after scenario Some rooms are not available, Examples (#29)
Before starting scenario Some rooms are not available, Examples (#30)....
> after scenario Some rooms are not available, Examples (#30)
Before starting scenario Some rooms are not available, Examples (#31)....
> after scenario Some rooms are not available, Examples (#31)
Before starting scenario Some rooms are not available, Examples (#32)....
> after scenario Some rooms are not available, Examples (#32)
Before starting scenario Some rooms are not available, Examples (#33)....
> after scenario Some rooms are not available, Examples (#33)
Before starting scenario Some rooms are not available, Examples (#34)....
> after scenario Some rooms are not available, Examples (#34)
Before starting scenario Some rooms are not available, Examples (#35)....
> after scenario Some rooms are not available, Examples (#35)
Before starting scenario Some rooms are not available, Examples (#36)....
> after scenario Some rooms are not available, Examples (#36)

43 scenarios (43 passed)
172 steps (172 passed)
0m0.109s
$
```

The Around hook is a useful hook too. For example, you can replace the two Before and After hooks with the following Around hook (Listing 7-38).

Listing 7-38. Using the Around Hook

```ruby
# File: features/support/hooks.rb
#
Around('@foo') do |scenario, block|
  print "Before starting scenario #{scenario.name}"
  block.call
  puts "> after scenario #{scenario.name}"
end
```

The point with the Around hook is that its block takes two arguments: the scenario and the block that you can #call on and execute the Scenario itself. If you don't call block.call, the Scenario is never actually called, and you get an error. Otherwise, whatever code you put before the block.call statement is executed *before* the Scenario, and whatever you put *after* the block.call statement is executed *after* the Scenario at hand.

Besides the Scenario-level hooks, sometimes you might want to take advantage of the hook that is called after a step has finished. This is the AfterStep hook.

Let's add the AfterStep hook for the @foo Scenarios (Listing 7-39).

Listing 7-39. Using the AfterStep Hook

```
# File: features/support/hooks.rb
#
Around('@foo') do |scenario, block|
  print "Before starting scenario #{scenario.name}"
  block.call
  puts "> after scenario #{scenario.name}"
end

AfterStep do |result, step_info|
  puts "Result OK?: #{result.ok?} - Step: #{step_info.text}"
end
```

As you can see, the AfterStep hook yields two arguments to the called block. The result holds information about the result of the execution. The step_info is about which step has just finished execution.

Let's run cucumber for the Scenario at line 22:

```
$ cucumber features/booking_a_room.feature:22 --format progress
.
Result OK?: true - Step: there are the following rooms in the hotel
.
Result OK?: true - Step: all the rooms are available
.
Result OK?: true - Step: visitor provides the following booking details
.
```

Result OK?: true - Step: visitor is provided with rooms "1, 2, 3, 4, 5, 6"

.

Result OK?: true - Step: there are the following rooms in the hotel

.

Result OK?: true - Step: all the rooms are available

.

Result OK?: true - Step: visitor provides the following booking details

.

Result OK?: true - Step: visitor is provided with rooms "1, 2, 3, 4, 5, 6"

.

Result OK?: true - Step: there are the following rooms in the hotel

.

Result OK?: true - Step: all the rooms are available

.

Result OK?: true - Step: visitor provides the following booking details

.

Result OK?: true - Step: visitor is provided with rooms "5, 6"

.

Result OK?: true - Step: there are the following rooms in the hotel

.

Result OK?: true - Step: all the rooms are available

.

Result OK?: true - Step: visitor provides the following booking details

.

Result OK?: true - Step: visitor is provided with rooms "5, 6"

.

Result OK?: true - Step: there are the following rooms in the hotel

.

Result OK?: true - Step: all the rooms are available

.

Result OK?: true - Step: visitor provides the following booking details

.

Result OK?: true - Step: visitor is provided with rooms ""

.

```
Result OK?: true - Step: there are the following rooms in the hotel
.
Result OK?: true - Step: all the rooms are available
.
Result OK?: true - Step: visitor provides the following booking details
.
Result OK?: true - Step: visitor is provided with rooms ""
.
Result OK?: true - Step: there are the following rooms in the hotel
.
Result OK?: true - Step: all the rooms are available
.
Result OK?: true - Step: visitor provides the following booking details
.
Result OK?: true - Step: visitor is provided with rooms ""

7 scenarios (7 passed)
28 steps (28 passed)
0m0.070s
$
```

Do you see the lines that are printed after the execution of each step?

Doc Strings

Doc strings or *document strings* are long strings that you want to use in step invocations. These strings are usually multiline strings that cannot fit in one line. Let's see, for example, the following Scenario:

```
Scenario: Multiline input example
  Given the user provides a string such as
    """

    This is a two line string. First Line.
    Second Line.
    """
```

```
When we invoke the encryption of this string
Then we get a result such as this
  """

  Uijt!jt!b!uxp!mjof!tusjoh/!Gjstu!Mjof/
  Tfdpoe!Mjof/
  """
```

The *doc string* is provided in between two lines, each of which has triple quotes """. You usually write the triple quotes indented by two spaces to the right relative to the beginning column of the step the doc string belongs to. Then each line of the doc string needs to start at that column too.

Cucumber and RubyMine Integration

RubyMine has seamless integration for Cucumber:

1. When you invoke a new step that is not defined, it underlines the step (Figure 7-3).

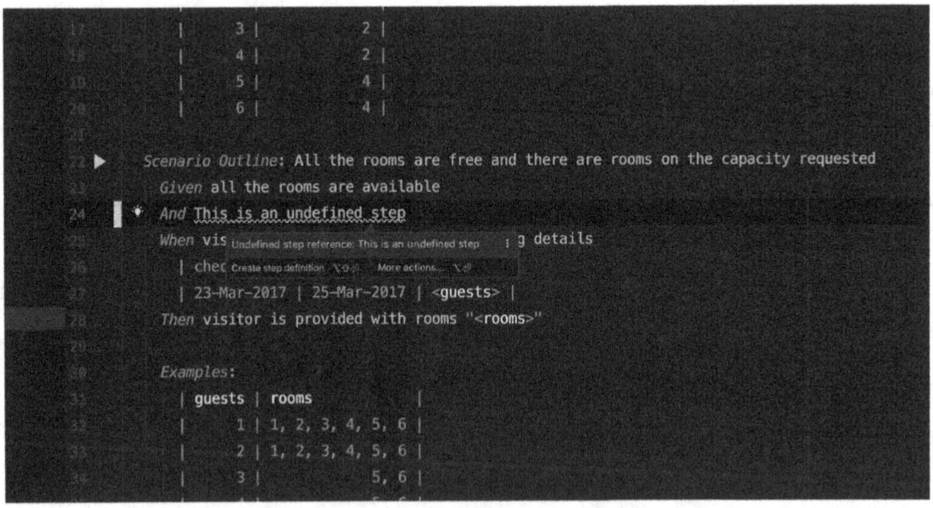

Figure 7-3. *How RubyMine Underlines Undefined Steps*

2. When you Cmd+Click a step invocation, it takes you directly to the step definition.

3. You can right-click a Scenario, and you can invoke the execution of the specific Scenario.

4. You can right-click a Feature file, and you can invoke the execution of the particular Feature file.

Task Details

RUBY APPLICATION WITH CUCUMBER AND RSPEC

You need to implement the following Ruby application covered with both Cucumber Scenarios and RSpec unit tests:

You are selling products, and you would like your application to cover for the following scenarios in the context of generating an invoice:

1. If the total price of the products sold in an order is above 50, then a discount of 10% should be applied.

2. When a product is tagged with the tag PROMO25, then a 25% discount should be applied to the product price.

3. All the products have a VAT of 20%. Note that the VAT is applied after any product or order discount is applied.

You will need to write a Feature file containing various Scenarios that would document the proper order total amount. You will also have to implement the order total calculating logic.

Key Takeaways

Cucumber is a fantastic tool to minimize the impedance mismatch between business stakeholders and developers. And it is available for many programming languages, not only for Ruby. It is used by many companies that want to have living documentation of the features of their applications.

The more you read and practice, the better you become on how to apply Cucumber.

Here is the list of the most important things you learned in this chapter:

- Important Gherkin keywords, like Feature, Scenario, Scenario Outline, and Examples

- Three different scenario phases

- Scenarios states

- Data tables

- Feature and Scenario internationalization

- Using tags

- Using hooks

This is the last chapter of this book, your journey to practical test automation. I hope that you have learned something from it, namely, practical tips that I use on a daily basis when I develop a project. Hopefully, they will be useful to you too. They will help you become a better developer with increased quality of your software deliverables.

Index

A

ageRange method, 49–51
ArgumentError method, 27
assert_equal command, 104
assert_nil command, 84, 104

B

before (:all) hooks
    code changing, 169–170
    do...end block, 167
    output window, 171
    #prepare_duration method, 171–173
    spec/coffee_spec.rb file, 167–168
before(:example)/before(:each), 173
before (:suite) hooks
    instance variable @foo, 162–164
    RSpec.configuration block, 161–162
    spec_helper.rb file, 164–167
    spec/sandwich_spec.rb, 160–161
Behavior-Driven Approach (BDA),
    see Cucumber tool

C

Cucumber tool
    addition/feature, 206–208
    BDA software, 199
    code extensive, 244
    command execution, 202, 245

data tables, 238–242
defining step (pending
    implementation)
    block-level argument value, 212
    calculator_steps.rb, 213–214
    empty file calculator, 216
    files, 211
    format progress, 218
    implementation, 217
    maps step invocations, 211
    pending implementation,
      209–210, 217
    running option, 215
    RuntimeError exception, 218
doc strings (document strings), 307
dry run parses, 281–284
dummy application code, 219
feature file scenario, 219–226
folders/files initialization, 204–206
Gemfile project, 244
Gherkin (*see* Gherkin keywords)
hooks
    AfterStep hook, 305–308
    dummy implementation, 298–301
    around hook, 304
    scenarios, 298
    specific tags, 301–304
i18n-languages, 242
installation, 200–202
invoke, 205

© Panos Matsinopoulos 2020
P. Matsinopoulos, *Practical Test Automation*, https://doi.org/10.1007/978-1-4842-6141-5

T, U, V, W, X, Y, Z

Printed in the United States
By Bookmasters